FIRST COMES SUCCESS, THEN COMES LOVE . . .

At the elaborate party after the premiere, Gregory Peck introduced Audrey to a great friend of his — and a partner in the La Jolla Playhouse — the director, actor, and writer Mel Ferrer. Audrey had seen Ferrer twice in what had become one of her favorite movies, *Lili*, in which he played a puppet master in love with a plain but sweet-natured young girl played by Leslie Caron. Audrey adored Ferrer's performance, and she told him so. She also was, to his surprise, fully familiar with his work at La Jolla and with his impressive performances as the celebrated torero in *The Brave Bulls* and the black-clad villain of the costume drama *Scaramouche*. On the rebound from Holden, Audrey felt an immediate attraction to this charismatic leading man.

AUDREY

The Life of Audrey Hepburn

ALSO BY CHARLES HIGHAM

AUDREY
The Life of Audrey Hepburn

Charles Higham

PaperJacks LTD.

TORONTO   NEW YORK

PaperJacks

AUDREY
THE LIFE OF AUDREY HEPBURN

PaperJacks LTD.

330 Steelcase Rd. E., Markham, Ont. L3R 2M1
210 Fifth Ave., New York, N.Y. 10010

Published by arrangement with Macmillan Publishing Company
Macmillan edition published 1984

PaperJacks edition published January 1986

Cover design: Brant Cowie/Artplus Ltd.

ISBN 0-7701-0354-5
Printed in Canada

862396

This book is dedicated to Henry Gris

Acknowledgments

I am grateful to Anthony Slide, Ann Hoffmann, and Howard Davis for their assistance in conducting the many interviews and exhaustive research for this book, and Robert Gitt for generously screening the films. Among those who contributed their memories to these pages are the following, listed in the order of their appearance: L. DeJong; Simon Koster; Geoff Donaldson; Huguenot van der Linden; H. M. Josephson, now known as Henry M. Martin; Agnes de Mille; Moira Lister; Alec Guinness; Thorold Dickinson; Lindsay Anderson, whose book about the making of *The Secret People,* entitled *Making a Film,* was an indispensable source; Felix Man (who in England described to me much about Audrey at the time of her working there); the late Anita Loos; Mary Loos, her niece; the late William Wyler, whom I interviewed and knew personally, and who gave me many insights long before I intended writing this book; Henri Alekan; Mme. Raymond Rouleau, whose moving letters, inspired by love of her late husband, were an inspiration to me; the late Cathleen Nesbitt, who, at a dinner party at the home of the author Robert Nathan, kept a group of us enthralled with her memories of Audrey, and whose memories gave a touching further portrait to flesh out those reminiscences; Billy and Audrey Wilder; the late Edith Head, whom I often interviewed over the years, again before this book was contemplated; the late William Holden; Lady Barlow; Maurice Zolotow; the late King Vidor, a close personal friend of mine; Michael Powell; Thomas Shaw; Jack Cardiff; Hal Wallis; Leonard Gershe; Fred Astaire; Mme. Jean Renoir; the late Roger Edens, whom I interviewed in the 1960s; Lee Minnelli and her husband Vincente; I. A. L. Diamond; Charles Lang; Herb Sterne; Walter Chiari; the late Henry King; the late Joseph Ruttenberg; the late Henry Blanke; Henry Silva; Dame Peggy Ashcroft; Clarence Brown; Lillian Gish; the late Alfred Hitchcock; the late John Williams; Zsa Zsa Gabor; Richard Quine; Claude Renoir; the late George Cukor; Rex Harrison; the late Cecil Beaton; Limey Plews; Miles Krueger; Marni Nixon; Lady Claire Rendlesham; Christopher Challis; William Daniels; Terence Young; Walter MacEwan; the late Jack L. Warner; Ross Hunter; Henry Gris, whose superb devotion to Audrey and unique knowledge of her rendered this book possible; the Rijkinstituut Voor Oorlogsdokumentaire and Genbentearchieven in Holland; and Dr. Robert Knutson of the University of Southern California. And my most grateful thanks to the splendid editorial team of Arlene Friedman, Andrea Raab, Jane Low, and Pauline Piekarz.

Chapter One

In 1929, Belgium's capital city of Brussels, where Audrey Hepburn was to spend her early childhood, was one of the most attractive cities in Europe. A city of comfort, charm, graciousness, and good manners, Brussels was not so large as to be exhausting, nor so small that it was provincial. It was a city of torchlight parades, masked balls, and elaborate festivals — resembling versions of the Mardi Gras or the Rio Carnival — that filled the public squares with excitement for many nights during the year.

Yet against the gaiety of the city's events could be set its tone of gray, rational sobriety, cleanliness, and Belgian bourgeois orderliness. In the raffish twenties, Brussels was an oasis of good sense, and although it was not Paris, it offered a distinguished range of musical and theatrical entertainment.

The Grand' Place, or public square at the heart of the city, and the Ville Basse, or shopping district, were spacious, elegant, and beautifully maintained. Every tree in Brussels and every blade of grass was groomed to a fault. It was a city of restaurants, with a proliferation of taverns, bars, tearooms, dairy shops, bakeries, lunchrooms, and even newfangled automats known as Vite Fini, which served sizzling hot dogs and double espressos. Brussels was, however, above all, a musical city. Its recently completed Palais, with a grand auditorium for 2,200 people, was the home in various seasons for such luminaries as Toscanini, Kleiber, and Mengelberg.

The people of Brussels were characterized by solidity, reliability, and stolid virtues. Yet there was a powerful artistic group that encouraged avant-garde theater, ballet, and music and even risked exhibitions of Dadaist art. The newspapers, always a reflection of a community, were beautifully written, designed, and composed, and in those far-off days a typographical error would have been almost unthinkable. Brussels kept its seams straight, minded its manners, and kept its nose clean, but it was always capable of breaking into a jig and letting its hair down when the occasion called for it.

The residential districts, outside which lived the people on the fringe of the country, were those best known to Audrey as a child. They had a secure, spacious, and elevated dignity, with tall gray walls, cool shaded streets alive with the cries of ice cream vendors and filled with the scent of pine needles, rhododendrons, and freshly baked bread. The houses provided odd juxtapositions: some had arrowhead chinks in the walls from medieval times; others, right next door, had modern sliding glass windows. A contemporary observer wrote: "[In Brussels] one moves from the Grand' Place to the most outlying sections without a break, from the Fourteenth Century to the present day in an unbroken flow of time, neatly channeled in stonespace. The diverse periods are fused into one period — that of the bourgeois Empire from the Middle Ages to the early Twentieth Century."

It is said that cities are reflected forever in the minds of those to whom they have given birth. Audrey Hepburn became living proof of this idea. She combined an intense gravity, delicacy, firmness, and strictness of temperament with a surprising capacity to dissolve into laughter and to embrace life with a totally unpredictable excitement and enthusiasm. She was extremely disciplined, orderly, and precise, yet she possessed a strong romantic streak. Like Brussels itself, she combined a sense of the very ancient, of mysterious times gone past, with a striking modernity. She had a classical love of balance and symmetry that was reflected in her clothing, her acting, her dancing, and her mode of living. Simplicity was everything; no impurities could be allowed in her existence. Yet, like most people of Brussels, she could open her heart unreservedly to music and dancing.

Audrey Hepburn was born on May 4, 1929, in a house of ideal proportions, with a handsome garden, a small fruit orchard, and high excluding walls of pale gray Belgian stone. The windows were tall and admitted the maximum amount of light, even in winter. The house was built in the nineteenth century; it was gracious, with carefully polished parquet floors and distinguished-looking mirrors, paintings, and curtains.

Audrey's parents constituted a slightly indelicate pairing of the aristocracy and the bourgeoisie, of the Dutch and the British. Her father, the handsome and beautifully tailored Joseph Anthony Hepburn-Ruston, was the managing director of the Brussels branch of the Bank of England. In every way, Hepburn-Ruston reflected the attitudes of his superior, Montagu Norman, governor of the bank in London. Like Norman, he was extremely right wing, violent in his opposition to Communism, and already attracted to the rising figure of Adolf Hitler. His sentiments were so fascistic that, in due course, he would back the activities of Oswald Mosley, who would enlist him as an officer in his Black Shirt Brigade. Mosley was the foremost supporter of Hitler in Great Britain and an advocate of negotiated peace with Nazi Germany in 1940.

Hepburn-Ruston was also involved in the financial dealings of the Bank of England with the Bank for International Settlements in Basel, Switzerland, since, following its formation in 1929, the bank had both Montagu Norman and his associate — Sir Otto Niemeyer — on its board. During the thirties, Hepburn-Ruston and other Bank of England officials would be involved in securing, through the Bank for International Settlements, a fascist cordon sanitaire against the Soviet Union.

Audrey's maternal background was equally interesting. Her mother was the Baroness Ella van Heemstra, and was descended from a long line of aristocrats connected directly to the royal court of Holland. Their traditional and ancestral residence had been the Castle of Doorn, which became the residence of the exiled German kaiser Wilhelm II in the final years of his life. Ella van Heemstra's father, the Baron Aernoud, was governor of Dutch Guiana (later known as Surinam) from 1921 to 1928, spending his time in that exotic colony trying to interest private Dutch investors in plunging capital into the country. He was a striking, dignified, and much-admired gentleman, lording it over the tiny capital city of Paramaribo, with its dusty streets, shabby palms, ill-painted wooden houses, and stores painted pink and blue, and its jalousies rattling constantly in the restless trade winds. The baron had little recreation save trips by dugout canoe or primitive ferry down-river into the dense and noisy jungle, crocodiles slithering out into the gray-green waters to greet him. Perhaps some echo of his experience vibrated in Audrey's mind, because she loved Kipling's *Just So Stories* in her childhood.

The baron had to tolerate the dangerous activities of a Communistic popular front, which constantly threatened him with acts of violence despite his efforts to bring prosperity to the colony. Finally, after seven years of struggle, he gave up and returned to Holland, leaving the post of governor to his successor, Abraham Rutgers, who faced a full-scale revolution in 1932.

Baron Aernoud settled down and became comfortably installed in the royal circle. Meanwhile, his family had become most accomplished. His sons, elder to Ella, were distinguished in law and politics. Ella herself was a remarkable woman. Audrey's mother was very beautiful and energetic, with a dashing personality and a fondness for good living. Men found her irresistible, but her chief weakness was an incapacity to see beyond appearances in a man. She was easily flattered, and could not prevent herself from entering into disastrous marriages. Although only in her twenties, during her father's and mother's absence in the tropics, she went through two marriages very rapidly — quite uncommon among those stolid aristocrats, whose normal practice was to marry for life within their own circle and then take lovers on the side. Romantic by nature, and essentially moral, she could not entertain any such arrangements, and committed herself wholeheartedly to her husbands. Both marriages collapsed, however, and she was left high and dry by her second husband to raise their two sons without a father.

The boys, Alexander and Jan (also known as Ian), were typically muscular, stocky, robust Dutch children fond of play but still raised strictly, and made to appreciate and earn every pleasure. Ella may have been restless and guilty of bad judgment in her choice of husbands, but she adored her sons and wanted them to grow up handsome, athletic, and vigorous in the tradition of the van Heemstra men. A career in the diplomatic service in the colonies of Surinam, Curaçao, or the Dutch East Indies must clearly be envisaged and solid marriages, robust children, and a continuing sensible use of the family fortune looked forward to.

Audrey, born Edda, was a changeling in a family of sturdy charmers. Whereas a bluff, outgoing Dutchness symbolized her breed, she herself was from the beginning exceedingly quiet and reserved — the sort of baby that visiting old ladies tend to dub "an old soul." She was shy and nervous, and to everyone's confusion flatly refused to have anything to do with dolls. She preferred the company of singing birds, small dogs, and kittens. She daydreamed all the time, and would create in her fantasy world a fairy castle from a bush, a tree, or a corner of her nursery.

She was musical from the beginning, and would be seen with her tiny, elfin face screwed up in rapture, listening to the rapidly turning 78-rpm disks of that era, as from the mahogany phonograph emerged the strains of the great orchestras of the time. She loved rich, romantic music, as well as Beethoven and Bach.

She and her mother liked to attend concerts given by the famous Concertgebouw Orchestra of The Hague, which frequently performed in Amsterdam but also made seasonal visits to Brussels. Going to the ballet was a magical experience for Audrey, as it was for most young girls in their preteens. She was typical of her group and period in dreaming of being an actress or a ballet dancer, but she had little faith that she would achieve her ambition. As she grew more physically aware of herself, she became dissatisfied with her appearance. She disliked her face intensely, and dreaded mirrors. She thought that her eyes were too large and that her teeth grew irregularly, and for some reason the baroness did not insist on braces for them. Indeed, Audrey's irregular teeth plagued her for most of her life, and were to present a peculiar problem to cameramen and still photographers.

She also despaired of her figure. She was roly-poly, and it seemed that even a cookie or a small cake would make her blow up in the wrong places. She danced whenever she could, but even this activity, and occasional surprising bursts of tomboy-ish tree-climbing or racing across fields with her brothers, didn't seem to work off the baby fat. Dancers of childhood age were supposed to be skinny — all legs — with slender arms that looked well in a port-de-bras position. Her dimpled knees and plump, fatty elbows greatly depressed her.

She withdrew into herself, and became more and more peculiar, formal, and distant with everyone. She was the absolute despair of her teachers at infant school. Her unhap-piness was enhanced by her parents' quarrels.

By 1935, the marriage ended. Unlike her half brothers, who were better able to cope, Audrey suffered from the rift. Like many young girls, she favored her father, and it was agreed that she would spend much of the custody periods allowed by the divorce court with him in London. Eventually, however, it became difficult for her to commute from household to household across the North Sea. She had to adjust to an English girls' day school with her very poor knowledge of English and a heavy, not very attractive Dutch accent. She looked lost among the gamy, buxom, strapping English girls with their love of hockey and lacrosse, and her delicate shyness made her the victim of endless ragging that reduced her to silence and tears.

Her father was busy in Threadneedle Street and she saw little of him; governesses and nannies came and went in the traditional British manner, and she was often lonely. By the age of ten, she had begun to grow taller, but she still was too plump and, in a classical syndrome, found paradoxical comfort in an excessive love of chocolate.

London, of course, offered a child wonders: the National Gallery, with its many Dutch paintings, the Tower of London, with its echoes of medieval tortures, its haunting mementoes of Anne Boleyn and other ill-fated British queens, and of course the changing of the guard and the occasional public appearances by royalty. There was the London Zoo in Regent's Park, with its display of rare and wonderful creatures, and Madame Tussaud's Wax Museum, with its creepy frozen charm and dreaded Chamber of Horrors.

London in the 1930s offered a galaxy of fine entertainment, and the West End glowed with superb musicals produced by C. B. Cochran or Prince and Emile Littler or Firth Shepherd. Plays by Noël Coward, Somerset Maugham, the young Terence Rattigan, and Frederick Lonsdale were all the rage, and performances by stars like Coward himself, Evelyn Laye, Gertrude Lawrence, Nora Swinburne, Ivor Novello, John Gielgud, Laurence Olivier, and Ralph Richardson were richly rewarding. But Audrey most enjoyed that unusual form of British entertainment, the Christmas pantomime. Unknown in the United States, it was a bizarre compendium of legend, in which men dressed as women and women as men in a peculiarly British sexual potpourri for some reason considered suitable for children. The leading man, or Principal Boy, was always played by a woman in male attire and tights, while the comic old lady as, for example, the Widow Twankey in *Aladdin*, was played by a famous comedian. The shows were notable for their lavishness and their extravagant and wonderful transformation scenes. Against the knockabout humor of the banana-skin variety, calculated to enchant children, there were the fairy tale caves, the mysterious treasures, and the sudden evocations of Faerie Seas forlorn. And of course there was *Peter Pan*, which Audrey later dreamed of filming, with its unforgettable plea from Tinkerbell.

Audrey began studying ballet in 1938, at the age of nine,

with a fierce dedication beyond that of the other pupils. She mastered the five basic positions with great self-discipline, and learned to perform arabesques, assemblés, attitudes, and a whole alphabet of steps and movements which were to lead to her first clumsy attempts at a tour en l'air. She was uncoordinated and awkward, lumpy in the wrong places, as usual, but determined to make something of herself. While Audrey was devoted to dance, she was only vaguely aware of the declining political situation around her.

During the Abdication crisis and the imminent onset of World War II, Audrey's father became more and more committed to fascism. He marched with the Black Shirts in parades that were stoned by angry crowds and broken up by police. His singleminded devotion to Oswald and Diana Mosley and the dangerous Cliveden set was frowned upon by such patriotic figures as Winston Churchill, then first lord of the admiralty, and Sir Leslie Hore-Belisha, minister of war. Indeed, Churchill made up his mind that if he became prime minister he would lock up Mosley and his men for the duration.

When war broke out on September 1, 1939, Audrey's mother in Holland panicked. She feared that Hitler would invade England and that Audrey would be a prisoner of war. She never envisaged any danger for Holland. Moreover, she was afraid that her ex-husband's pro-Nazi activities would affect her daughter. In a state of great tension, she arranged with the court for custody of Audrey. The baroness brought her over to the small city of Arnhem, which, by an unpleasant irony, was very close to the German border. But nobody in Holland seemed to understand Hitler's plans. Indeed, Queen Wilhelmina was rather foolishly trying to appease the German government with letters and telegrams right up until the spring of 1940.

Arnhem, where Audrey arrived after flying to Amsterdam in September, was to be the focus of her life for the next six years. It was a town alive with bells from a dozen towers, chiming the quarters and the hours or ringing with festive carillons on Sundays and holidays. There were strong British elements in the town, and the baroness was president of the local branch of the British-Netherlands Society, which encouraged that association. In 1638, the first of many English families had settled there, and indeed their descendants, who were bilingual, played an important part in the municipality. The famous English poet and war hero Sir Philip Sidney died in Arnhem, and it was an obligation for all schoolchildren to visit the place of his death.

The city, spacious and ancient in its appeal, boasted the famous Groote Kerk, with the grand tomb of Charles van Egmont, duke of Gelderland, and the Devil's House, the sinister name of the harmless but beautiful dwelling of the well-known warrior Martin Van Rossum. Near Arnhem were hills of great beauty relieving the monotonous flatness of the Dutch landscape, the delicious woodlands of the Klarenbeeksche, the Falls of Sonbek, tumbling delectably over rocks, and the richly scenic districts of Renkum and Heelsum. The sumptuous colors of the traditional tulips were a blaze of pleasure in the parks, and there were wonderful walks through the Rhine Valley, through beech and lime trees, woodland copses, and rolling heaths. There was a fine art gallery, and a number of museums, including the Arnhem Open Air Museum, the Museum of East Indian Curiosities, and the Castles of Zypendaal and Doorweth, with their great armory collections. There was a local symphony orchestra, second-rate but game, that at least strove to give good concerts for the children on weekend afternoons.

Audrey enlisted with the junior class of the Arnhem Conservatory of Music and Dance and also joined the Arnhem Day School. The family home outside the town was large and comfortable. Unfortunately, the Arnhem Conservatory was not very efficient and the teaching staff was undistinguished. But Audrey, at ten, was beginning to improve as a dancer. She gradually learned better posture, and her tendency to slump and be round-shouldered was improved when her teachers forced her to stand straight, with head well back, shoulders trim, and spine drawn up in a single line with the legs. One of her problems was that she chronically lacked flexibility and tended to be as stiff as a board in stretching routines. She was still a little awkward at the barre, and it was some time before her weak feet and ankles could take the strain of wearing toe shoes and standing en pointe. When she did go en pointe, the shoes, of course, became the center of her existence. The baroness made sure she had the finest shoes possible, and they were meticulously maintained, with expensive wax applied to the boxes in the toes. Actually, the baroness never attended class nor even watched Audrey in class performances. One might interpret this as indifference to her daughter's achievements, but this seems unlikely in view of her devotion to Audrey's perfect appearance — ensuring her not only the best shoes money could buy but the best leotards and tutus. Her refusal to watch her daughter may have been prompted by a desire not to render her self-conscious and embarrassed, and to remove any sense of pressure from her. Certainly, there is no evidence that Audrey asked her mother to be present, nor that she was unhappy when she was not.

Audrey was a very serious pupil, grave, restrained, determined, seldom enjoying the giggling, gossip, and fun-poking at teachers typical of a ballet class of young girls. Painfully aware of her physical short-comings even then, she had made up her mind that she would one day be a soloist and ultimately a star. Whereas the other girls were simply satisfying a normal adolescent love of dancing, Audrey had stronger ambitions. The others sensed this and, by all accounts, it made them uncomfortable.

Dancing became Audrey's whole life. Kipling, the idol of her earlier years, in the famous dark red, gilt-tooled, limp leather edition, was replaced by lives of Pavlova and Nijinsky on her bookshelf. She became obsessed with Pavlova, the legendary and glorious Russian danseuse and prima ballerina assoluta who had conquered the world before Audrey was born. Films held no interest for her whatsoever. Children did not go to movies in those days nearly as often as they do today. A visit to a movie was a special treat on birthdays, or at Christmas. And then, only Disney or adventure stories or period romances were considered suitable. If anyone had mentioned Garbo or Katharine Hepburn to her, she would not have had the slightest idea who they were. Whereas most young girls of her generation had movie star idols and cut pictures of them out of movie magazines to paste in their private albums, Audrey said later that she never had any such interests. Arnhem, straitlaced and bourgeois, offered very few American or British movies, and fan magazines were virtually unknown in her household. The baroness did not encourage them, and she herself had little interest in motion pictures.

Audrey had a problem enrolling in the Arnhem Day School because she had a poor command of Dutch. She had spent so much of her childhood in England and her mother had been more familiar with French and Walloon dialect and had for some reason not taught Audrey extensively in her native tongue.

For six months, while Audrey attended school, the baroness fretted. She had many friends in England, and the phony war threatened every day to end in an explosion of brutal violence, bombing, and invasion. Holland hung on the edge of a precipice. Yet the family roots were deep: the baroness clearly couldn't contemplate leaving Europe along with everything that was near and dear to her.

It seems that even at that stage, according to Audrey, the baroness laid the groundwork for a Dutch Underground in Arnhem. She encouraged a group of people who would be dedicated to resistance if the Germans walked in. At the many meals of fattening Dutch food, the herring, the spicy sausages, the hot pots, the Dutch East Indian nasi gorengs and rijsttafels in the many solid restaurants at Arnhem, there would be discussions of who could be relied upon and who would be the Quislings when the time came.

In the spring of 1940, Hitler was poised to strike against the Netherlands. The country was armed to the teeth. Barbed-wire fences were set up across the flat countryside near the van Heemstra family estate. Soldiers tramped the streets of

Arnhem or crossed the famous bridge. Trains carried more soldiers up and down the front line. Searchlights swept the sky at night, and already by late April there was the occasional explosion and burst of gunfire as frontier guards panicked that the invasion was taking place.

As a child of eleven, Audrey was painfully aware of the grave danger that threatened. But she was buoyed up by a remarkable piece of news. The Sadler's Wells Ballet, arguably the finest in England, was courageously visiting Holland in the middle of the war to bring a morale booster to the beleaguered nation. The brilliant company, led by the great Irish choreographer and producer Ninette de Valois and musical director Constant Lambert, featured as its stars Robert Helpmann, Margot Fonteyn, and Frederick Ashton in a repertoire that included *The Rake's Progress, Checkmate, Dante Sonata, Horoscope, Façade,* and *Les Patineurs.*

After a triumphant appearance at the Theatre Royal in The Hague, the Sadler's Wells Ballet proceeded by autobus to Hengelo, passing across bridges heavily armed by soldiers, and past fields of barbed wire to Eindhoven, where they danced at the Philips Electronics Factory, and thence to Arnhem.

Audrey was especially fortunate because, since her mother was president of the British-Netherlands Society, she received the company as their personal hostess. Thus, the starstruck child was able to meet her idols personally.

Audrey's pleasure, and her mother's, in meeting these dazzling visitors was undermined, however, by the dancers' nervousness at having to perform on the very edge of Germany, and on the very brink of invasion. The performance on the night of May 17, 1940, featured *Façade,* which was danced to records of Edith Sitwell reciting the lines and William Walton's music. It was a captivating presentation, despite the cast's extreme nervous tension that at any minute it might fall into German hands and be sent to concentration camps. Audrey watched enchanted as the curtain rose on the façade of a large gray-white Victorian mansion; two girls and a boy walked slowly onto the stage in tartans and danced a Scottish rhapsody, followed by a mimicry of yodeling. A milkmaid, admired by three handsome boys in Alpine costume, danced with a milk stool; a solo polka was followed by a foxtrot, waltz, and country dance; a witty tango in parody of a thé dansant — with a gigolo fascinating a dizzy debutante and at the end an extravagant tarantella — brought the audience to its feet.

After the performance, the explosions and gunfire had the cast looking nervously about them through their heavy makeup. They were seized by an overwhelming impulse to rush, costumes and all, onto the autobus and get out of there as fast as wheels could carry them. Instead, they had to suffer patiently while the baroness, seemingly oblivious to approaching disaster, thanked them in what was arguably the longest speech ever delivered in the history of Arnhem. She droned on with a complete history of the Sadler's Wells Ballet until desperation began to set in among the company.

At the very end of the speech, the cast was poised for flight when the baroness introduced Audrey at a splendid dinner of ham and salad. After her mother described Audrey's desire to be a dancer, the child walked forward in her ankle-length party dress with a large bouquet of red tulips for Margot Fonteyn and another for Ninette de Valois. Despite their tension, both Ninette and Margot were very impressed by Audrey's remarkable personality and poise, which overcame her shyness and embarrassment.

After nibbling at the ham and salad, the performers, choreographer, and music director disappeared, leaving their scenery, costumes, and even their music behind in their flight. It may well be asked why the baroness created such an excruciating situation for them. It was not until years later that Robert Helpmann had an opportunity to find out. He asked Audrey at a Hollywood party why her mother had so drawn out that evening. Audrey said that there were a number of Nazi collaborators in the audience and at the reception. If the baroness had rushed things through she would have been suspected of being unreliable and pro-British when the Germans walked in. It was already part of her plan to pose as a pro-German aristocrat whose family castle had given shelter to the kaiser. If she appeared to be delaying the company to the point where they might be seized, she would provide a perfect cover for herself as future head of the Resistance in Arnhem. However, she seems to have overdone this a little, since only ten minutes after the company left, the Germans crossed the Rhine and bitter street fighting filled Arnhem with gunshots and cries.

Parachutes mushroomed in the night sky. Sirens screamed. Air-raid alarms filled the air, and at the same time the Sadler's Wells Ballet was fleeing to the coast. The company almost did not make it across a mine-strewn channel to England. Some of the music and scenery was never recovered.

As morning broke, with Audrey and her mother hiding in the cellar of their house, German tanks, trucks, armored cars, motorcycles, and artillery caissons filled the streets of Arnhem. Public address systems on streetcorners blared out guttural announcements that Arnhem was now part of the Third Reich. All newspapers, radios, and other means of communication were under German control, and the slightest disobedience on the part of the citizenry was instantly punishable. At the same time, with the baroness's knowledge, Dutch Resistance forces instigated a railway strike to hamper the invasion and blew up trains, bridges, and ammunition dumps. The next day, the German general in charge of the onslaught compelled the Dutch general Winkelman to announce that the Dutch troops were in a state of surrender. That afternoon, it was announced that Queen Wilhelmina had gone to London to set up a government-in-exile.

After a brief hiatus, Audrey was able to resume her education. By posing as, at least, not overtly hostile to the Germans, her mother managed to save her from punishment. However, the baroness's brother, an attorney, and one of her cousins were executed as enemies of the Third Reich. The shocking incidents increased the baroness's desire to lead the Underground in Arnhem.

Audrey continued her studies, riding into town on the tramcar every day. Her position was difficult and dangerous.

If discovered to be pro-Jewish, she could have been refused tuition or worse. Jewish teachers were eliminated from the faculty. Moreover, the public prosecutor of The Hague insisted that anyone who taught school at the Conservatory or elsewhere must be pro-German. The League of Netherlands Teachers was made to serve the Third Reich, and at Audrey's day school she was compelled to learn German and German history.

But the Roman Catholic and other Christian teachers at the school and the Conservatory managed to find times at which they could teach the children decent principles without being overruled. Moreover, music was a world beyond politics, and although all composers who were not German or Austrian were forbidden, the glories of Bach, Mozart, Beethoven, and Haydn could be intensely enjoyed without any feeling of guilt. Audrey said later: "People don't realize that, during a war of this kind, nothing basically changes inside you. Conditions can change, but the human doesn't. If you wanted to be a dancer before the war you wanted to be one just as much despite the war. Nobody believed the war would last five years. It was always, 'Next year it will be over.'"

As the Occupation intensified, life became more difficult. The children were forbidden to wear any Dutch patriotic insignia, nor could they wear school uniforms. Eighteen months after the Occupation, the last of the noncollaborative teachers were removed, and the girls had to accept schoolmistresses appointed by the Nazi Secretary-General for Education. Any political discussion was absolutely forbidden. All schoolbooks were confiscated and, when returned, were heavily censored. German schoolbooks filled with propaganda were introduced.

In 1942, the baroness's home was commandeered, and all her rights and deeds to it were canceled. Her properties were confiscated and her bank account attached. Because she was not suspected of treason, however, she was allowed to go free and subsist on a tiny income — a token allowance from the occupying government. There was just enough money to pay for Audrey's schooling. Mother and daughter had very little to eat, and any sums that come from the Dutch government in London went to support Underground guerrilla fighters.

Audrey's elder brothers, Alexander and Ian, refused to join the Nazi Jugend or NIVO, also known as the Netherlands Institute for Folkish Education, near Arnhem. At this head-quarters, athletic boys between ten and sixteen were trained rigorously in calisthenics and sports in order to achieve the high physical standards required by the Third Reich. They then became part of the Nazi movement. As a result of this refusal, Alexander, who was of age, was sent to work in a labor camp in Germany for the duration. Ian was too young to be useful in a camp and stayed behind.

The anguish caused by this separation was even more intolerable to the baroness and to Audrey than the deaths of their kinfolk. It was impossible to get word back through the Red Cross.

Studying for Audrey became increasingly difficult. There was no coal to heat the classrooms, which were icy and damp in winter. The ceaseless instruction of the German teachers was oppressive and hateful. Behind their schoolbooks, the girls whispered of news, transmitted on the Freedom Radio — listened to late at night behind locked doors — of every Allied success in the war. Any girl known to be the child of a colla-borator was subtly ostracized.

To eke out some kind of a living, Audrey taught dancing and piano to younger girls at the Conservatory. According to an interview given by Audrey in the British magazine *Dance* in 1951, she also danced in fragments of classical ballets in shuttered homes, closing off all noise, to try and raise money for the Underground. There was no applause, not a sound that could draw attention, sometimes not even a piano, as the child pirouetted and performed arabesques or fouettés in her cheap costume, whirling around drawing rooms on sleepy summer afternoons.

According to Audrey, from the beginning she worked day and night against the Nazi leaders. There was always great danger that she might be caught. She was never able to forget that when seventy Dutch school-children were caught planning to destroy Nazi cables and gas supply centers, they were sent to prison. She exemplified the words of the Dutch author, L. De Jong, in his book *Lion Rampant: The Story of Holland's Resistance to the Nazis:* "As general obstructionism, both passive and active, grew throughout the entire country, youth followed the example of their elders. The adolescents were fully aware of what had happened to their Fatherland; the younger and youngest sensed the true and tragic state of affairs . . . They were told that the Queen and the princely family had been forced to leave the Netherlands and were staying in foreign countries. They wondered at the strange men in outlandish uniforms, speaking an incomprehensible language. And with all the spontaneity of a child's mind that does not think of ultimate results, that lives for the moment only, these youthful patriots threw themselves into the battle against the occupying power and against the traitors." It was the kind of courage epitomized by Audrey's compatriot, the unforgettable Anne Frank.

Chapter Two

By 1943, the Arnhem Conservatory of Music was the most important front for the so-called Operation Diver, also known as the LO, an organization which specialized in concealing the whereabouts of Dutch patriots, helping them with printing presses which supplied false ration cards and travel documents, and supplying them with scraps of food and places of shelter. The children were considered too young to be suspect but, in fact, were acting as secret couriers and agents, carrying messages in every direction. Bicycle tire frames, coat linings, or horse saddles were used. Audrey, with great trepidation, concealed messages in the soles of her shoes. Furthermore, she has said in magazines over the years (starting with *Dance* in 1951) that she was actually sent on special missions to aid British troops when they landed by parachute in the neighboring forests because she spoke such good English. In the spring of 1942, she was given word via another courier that an English paratrooper had landed in the forest. The Germans were constantly exploring the woods, and the soldier was in grave danger of being discovered.

In interviews in *Dance* magazine, and later in *The American Weekly* (May 1958), Audrey recalled that she was to bring the soldier a message. The thirteen-year-old girl skipped through the woods, hearing German voices not far off. Somebody saw her but shrugged and turned away. She reached the rock where she had been told the soldier was hiding. She said just enough to establish in English that she was a friend, then slipped the message through the rocks and skipped off, picking more flowers.

As she was walking down a forest path, a German soldier loomed up ahead of her. She smiled sweetly at him and gave him her wildflowers. Delighted at this sign of friendliness, he touched his cap and patted her shoulder, and she strolled off towards Arnhem. When she alighted from the streetcar, she signaled the street cleaner that the British soldier would be coming that night to stay with him.

Although she risked her life every day, Audrey still lived for music and for dancing. Her life became more and more secretive. She told her friend Henry Gris: "To all intents and purposes I had been cut off from the world of youngsters of my own age because the war had made me a prisoner not only physically but mentally, never allowing me to peep out to see what was really outside. Obviously, there were youngsters there my age or close to my age, but somehow they didn't fit into the frame of my personal longings. And in the oppression of Occupation I, for one, had been left to my own devices. These devices drew me into the enchanted world of music, where one didn't have to talk, only listen."

Audrey's most pressing problem, as she danced to support the Underground and as she taught dancing to keep her and her mother alive, was the very basic matter of suitable clothes and shoes. There was so little wool that the baroness had to pull sweaters apart to patch tears in the tights. Felt for slippers was virtually impossible to find: all the animals had been slaughtered to provide food, and felt and leather were commandeered by the army. Audrey's toe shoes wore out constantly, and it was impossible to obtain substitutes without spending long hours waiting on lines, and sometimes paying black market prices. Audrey kept rubbing the wornout boxes of the shoes with furniture varnish until at last they were ruined, and she had to suffer the pain of wearing wooden shoes to dance in.

The privations grew worse and worse, yet somehow the family struggled on. In 1943, the Germans confiscated all radios and amplifiers. It was virtually impossible to get news of the outside world. The only movies were Nazi propaganda films. The rabidly anti-Semitic *The Eternal Jew* and *With Germany for a Free Europe* were compulsory viewing for children. At the same time, Audrey and her fellow pupils at the Conservatory daringly helped Jewish musicians disguise their origins and appear with the Arnhem Symphony Orchestra. When a well-known first violinist fell ill, he was replaced by a Jewish student nominee.

There was no way to suppress the spirit of these young people. But shortage of food reduced many, including Audrey, to a condition of severe malnutrition. She shot up to a skinny five feet, six-and-three-quarters inches on a meager, five-hundred-calorie-a-day diet. She had to eat a depressing watery soup every day, followed by a kind of bread loaf made out of peas.

Every day, she and her mother prayed for a miracle to happen. Then, at last, came the longed-for British onslaught on Arnhem. The battle of Arnhem was destined to become famous as one of the bloodiest and most horrifying in the history of World War II; eight thousand men of the Red Devils (or First British Airborne Division), under Major General Robert Urquhart, were parachuted in to seize the bridge. Audrey and her fellow pupils saw the parachutes mushrooming in the gray sky overhead. In icy, drizzling rain, the men swooped down on the bridge, but the onslaught was unfortunately too rash and undermanned and rapidly became a shambles.

Arnhem had become like a slaughterhouse. While Audrey, her mother and brother and their friends hid in a cellar, the noise of men being maimed, burned, and shot echoed down the stairs. In an area of not much more than three square miles, German tanks and fighter planes decimated the Red Devils. Hundreds of shells an hour shattered the town, and the hotels and hospitals were jammed with the wounded. The stench of death hung like a cloud over the once beautiful city.

At last, General Urquhart was captured (although he later

escaped), and the Red Devils were driven back into the blood-streaked river. Remnants of the Devils in groups of ten, using passwords and marking their way with parachute tape, managed to escape downstream with the aid of the Underground in a scattered small-craft flotilla.

"There can be no episode so glorious," said Field Marshal Sir Bernard Montgomery of the defeat, which had resulted in a victory: the attempt on the Arnhem bridgehead had successfully distracted the German troops and had enabled the Allies to seize the bridge at Nijmegen immediately afterward in one of the decisive battles of the war.

The evacuation of Arnhem was an episode of great terror and violence. No sooner were the Red Devils beaten into retreat than the Germans decided that they dared not risk allowing any citizen to remain in the city, so great had been the internal cooperation with the British troops. The commandant met with representatives of the International Red Cross and gave instructions that every man, woman, and child was to leave within twenty-four hours. Anyone found after 8 P.M. on the day after the attack would be shot on sight.

The exodus began at dawn. Audrey, her mother, and all those close to them had to leave virtually everything behind as they fitted whatever they could carry into hand cases, bicycle pouches, backpacks, and handbags. Some pushed baby carriages full of precious belongings. It was cold and damp as the long procession of refugees walked, bicycled, or took horsecarts out of town. Since all gasoline was commandeered, no cars could be used.

Under a gray drizzle from the sky, women and children sobbed helplessly as they walked. Planes were dogfighting overhead. Bombs and shells exploded in the air and on the ground. The injured, sick, and dying were dragged from the hospitals and forced to crawl on the ground. Allard Martens described the scene in his book *The Silent War*: "Prams were piled so high with personal belongings that you couldn't see over them; wheels broke off; overloaded bicycles with wooden tires (for rubber tires had long since vanished from the scene) clattered to the ground. Sick people fell unconscious from luggage carriers; women gave birth on the ground. Of the hundred thousand who set out from Arnhem, nearly three thousand died . . ."

In the wake of destruction, Arnhem was ransacked by scavengers and German troops from one end to the other. The house where Audrey had been living was stripped down to the shelves in the larder and the fixtures in the walls. Furniture, paintings, photographs, crockery, knives, forks, carpets — all were seized, taken as souvenirs, or burned.

At least, the baroness was able to find refuge with her daughter in a country house. However, soon, over four hundred people (according to Audrey) crowded in, covering every inch of the floors. The house was extremely damp, dark, and cold, and there was very little food. There were no books or radios — even candles were virtually unobtainable — and when the grim darkness of the European winter closed in, there was nothing to do except huddle in heaps and try to sleep.

Audrey and her brother Ian made their way into the fields to grub for endives, and subsisted on these and a gruely soup; later, Audrey was reduced to eating grass and tulip bulbs to survive. Although very weak, she tried to sustain morale by struggling to give ballet classes for people of various ages in the large dining room, where a carpenter managed to supply a barre. But eventually even these brave efforts, conducted to the scratchy sounds of an ancient windup phonograph, had to be discontinued. All except the youngest and sturdiest had become too hungry and exhausted even to stand. Besides, Audrey had developed a painful edema, a swelling from fluid in her ankles and knees that might have killed her had it spread to her brain.

The Germans became more and more desperate for manpower as the Allied troops penetrated the Netherlands. Finally, German soldiers invaded Audrey's refuge and, at gunpoint, dragged every man capable of moving off to work on barricades. Young Ian was taken with them. Audrey and her mother were in acute anguish, wondering what would become of him and their other friends. They watched the men tottering out of the house, most of them reduced almost to skeletons. It was a night that Audrey would never forget.

The Germans had even begun rounding up the younger womenfolk. When she got wind of this, Audrey escaped and somehow found the strength to hide in the cellar of a deserted building. She hid for almost a month in near total darkness, with the barest means of subsistence, and contracted hepatitis in the process. Then, one day, she finally heard the sounds of advancing troops. A friend told her an Underground radio was announcing that the Allied forces were pushing into Arnhem. It was late April 1945.

In a magnificent act of courage and defiance the population, almost dead from exhaustion and starvation, emerged from their refuges and made their way up the roads toward Arnhem to greet the Allied parachutists as they fell from the sky. They embraced them with their sticklike arms and wept in gratitude. Audrey was among the first to greet the rescuers. And at last, on May 5, almost five years after the invasion had begun, Freedom Radio and a series of public address announcements gave the blessed news that Arnhem was free.

Gradually, Audrey and her mother and brother Ian, who had returned safely to them, regained their strength. They were pathetically grateful for corned beef, Spam, and even whale meat brought to them as provender. At last it was possible to obtain milk, bread, and even eggs, all of which had been available only to the Germans. But it would be years before the baroness would receive reparations for war damages and reclaim her seized properties, and the Arnhem Conservatory of Music was a total shambles. Obviously, she and Audrey had to leave Arnhem and find some other home.

Rotterdam was devastated almost down to the last brick. That left Amsterdam, where the family at least had friends and room and lodging. Mother, daughter, and son packed whatever meager possessions they had and took the overcrowded diesel train to the famous city. They were quite penniless on arrival, but the baroness was a good cook and was able to obtain a job through contacts as cook-general to a middle-class family. She found a tiny flat for herself and her children, and it was a wondrous day when her eldest son, Alexander, was restored to her from the German labor camp in which he had been held captive.

Alexander and Ian had naturally robust constitutions, and bit by bit they gained decent weight and muscle, but Audrey never completely recovered from the war. The edema and hepatitis caused low red corpuscle count, thinness, and lack of muscular strength. In order to rebuild Audrey's frail body and her morale, the baroness somehow scraped together enough guilders to send Audrey to the most gifted dancing teacher in Holland, the remarkable Sonia Gaskell. A White Russian, Madame Gaskell was an extremely gifted woman with a rare and independent nature. She had trained with the greatest, and believed in innovation as a principle. She was forty-two when Audrey began to train with her, but her body was as firm and limber as it had been in her teens. She used modern music extensively — including jazz and *musique concrète* — and formed a select group of five to which all her pupils aspired. It was known as the Ballet Recital, and quickly obtained critical attention on both sides of the Atlantic.

Sonia Gaskell was concerned about Audrey's extreme delicacy and physical weakness. She could put her small hand around Audrey's upper arm. But she admired her, and saw the iron will, the unshakable resolution that had carried Audrey through the Occupation. Audrey responded to her gifted tutor. She danced a wide range of roles in class, from the lush romanticism of *The Sleeping Beauty* through the joyous classicism of Bach's Italian Concerto to the Latin rhythms of *Les Amours de Perlimplinet de Belisa* of Villa-Lobos, and the angular tonalities of Stravinsky's *Ragtime*. Audrey began to feel ambition burning in her heart once more. She looked like a dancer: she had the poise, posture, steeliness, centeredness, concentration, and elevation. But she was too tall, at almost five-foot-seven. Her slightly slanting gazelle's eyes, high checkbones, delicate nose, square shoulders, small hips, tiny breasts, and flat, hard stomach betokened a ballerina.

She was intense, driven, and dedicated. While the other Gaskell pupils took things in their stride, more or less fulfilling parental ambitions or simply wanting to correct posture, improve their bodies, and become more attractive, she was one of the tiny handful consumed by dreams of joining the Ballet Recital's charmed quintet. She showed little interest in the handsome boys who practiced with the girls at the barre. As a result of her training, Audrey for years would point with fingers snapping out like jackknives, and would stand with legs straddled and pointed toes. Whenever she picked something up, she would not bend her knees, and she never kept her feet together as most women did.

Her life once again focused on music. She must, she felt, go to concerts, and the baroness struggled to make that possible.

The Concertgebouw Orchestra was stripped of its Nazi collaborator members, who had performed for the Germans all through the war, and Mengelberg, its traitorous conductor, was exiled to Switzerland. His former assistant, the inspired Eduard van Beinum, whose performances of Bruckner and Shostakovich and of Bach's *St. Matthew Passion* were events of the 1946 season, took over as conductor. Van Beinum had been loyal to Holland and had refused to work for the Nazis.

The tickets to the concerts were expensive, and Audrey and her mother could barely pay their rent on a cook's wages. The baroness scraped together a few guilders and, at last, on Audrey's seventeenth birthday, May 4, 1946, the young, lonely, shy, and deeply reserved girl woke up to find the glory of all glories: a season ticket for six months on the night table beside her bed! She almost cried with happiness at this incredible treasure and hugged her mother ecstatically. There is no telling what sacrifices the baroness must have made to buy such an expensive gift.

That Christmas, the baroness gave Audrey yet another generous gift: a ticket for a series of Beethoven's string quartets.

Every evening, whatever the weather, Audrey, who could not afford the electric tramcar, walked from her flat to the Concert-gebouw Hall. It was a very long walk of several miles there and back, and she had had hard hours of practice at the barre, but nothing could discourage her from going.

Then came a setback. Sonia Gaskell was unable to obtain government backing for 1947 because of new and highly Philistine elements on the Amsterdam and national cultural government boards. She had to tell her pupils that she was closing up and would soon be moving to Paris, where culture was appreciated and modern dance was not frowned upon.

This announcement spurred Audrey's previous ambition to go to London and try for a career in Britain. Then, by a miracle, she managed to get a job. A bilingual, British-Dutch travelogue was being made in Amsterdam, and on various Dutch locations, by Dutch director Huguenot van der Linden and H. M. Josephson. As a publicity gimmick, there was a casting call for a girl to play the KLM air hostess who would introduce and conclude the forty-minute movie.

The directors were told about Audrey by a friend who said he would speak to her and send her over for an audition. Van der Linden's family was moving to another house, and the only furniture in the rooms were packing cases. On the morning of the move, the bell rang and Audrey and her mother came upstairs. Van der Linden recalls that they cheerfully sat down on the packing cases and that "I stared at her [Audrey] while she was chirping away about her ballet work, and then I picked up the telephone and told my partner to stop looking for a girl, since she had just walked in. I remember saying, 'Did you ever see a dream walking? Well, I did.' Audrey was bright, cheerful and chummy and just emanated style, breeding, intelligence and good manners. She was wonderful. Her part took only three or four days to shoot. I tried to make another film with her, but I couldn't find the money."

H. M. Josephson recalls, "She was cheerful, charming, lovely . . . a little sun shone out of her — even then."

Although the picture was never heard of again, Audrey at

least had had the thrill of working in show business for the first time. She and the baroness then decided to take off for London and try their luck. They sailed with their tiny savings and arrived in London with a mere ten dollars between them. This was spent quickly on a room in a boarding house and, later, on a bed-sitting room with two beds in it, the rent paid in advance. The baroness obtained a job in a florist's shop, which earned her about ten dollars a week and kept the wolf from the door, while Audrey took a clerical job at night and managed to secure an occasional assignment modeling for advertisements.

At that time, the most important ballet school in London was run by the celebrated Marie Rambert. Audrey was determined to pass the rigorous auditions in order to obtain entrance to the very rigorous Rambert school and studio in Notting Hill Gate. On a wet fall morning, Audrey made her way to the school building, which was located in a seedy district. It was reached down a long, damp flight of steps at the rear of a building originally used as the refectory of a Protestant church, with an adjoining vestry. She made her way through a maze of corridors, small auditoriums, and a practice hall in the pale, gray, watery London light. Stained-glass windows gave a spuriously religious air to the hall; every sound of a voice or the loud banging of the practice piano rang out too loudly because of the high ceiling and the overpolished parquet floors, worn down by feet and filled with knots and wood joins that had never been fixed.

The barre ran the entire length of one wall; a large mirror glowed dully at the north end, and a fat stove erupted occasionally with disconcerting sounds, like those from a sleeping dog. The stove emitted virtually no light or heat. A Dickensian coal fire was equally useless. At the piano, a battered upright with cigarette burns on it, sat a woman with her hair in a bun, swathed in two cable-knit cardigans, dressed in a plaid skirt and sensible shoes, her chilblained fingers in shapeless mittens. To add to the picture, a tweed coat was slung over her shoulders, and her Tyrolean hat sported a small finch feather.

Marie Rambert appeared. Known to the world of music and

theater as "Mim," she was described by one of her admirers, the celebrated choreographer Agnes de Mille, as "Queen hornet, vixen mother, lady boss of Notting Hill." She was small, wrapped in a mysterious pink garment with ruffles around the hips, her legs in black tights with wrinkles and leg warmers and always on her head a veiled hat. Wildly eccentric, she taught without stopping and without inhibition in her flow of highly colored language, delivered in a rich, plummy Polish accent. Born in 1888, she was about sixty when Audrey met her. Audrey already had done her homework on this formidable *monstre sacré*. She knew that Madame Rambert had worked with Nijinsky on his notorious ballet set to Stravinsky's *The Rite of Spring*. Her troupe, founded in 1926, had moved into the converted complex of church buildings in Notting Hill Gate the following year. Part of the complex was converted into the soon-to-be-famous Mercury Theatre, which, although small (with only one hundred fifty seats and an eighteen-foot stage), boasted many fine performances including works of Frederick Ashton, Audrey's idol of the 1940 Sadler's Wells appearance in Arnhem. Another famous figure connected with the Mercury was the danseuse Andrée Howard, who was soon to play a major part in Audrey's career.

Madame Rambert looked Audrey up and down and asked her to exhibit her style at the barre. She probably felt more sorry for the girl than anything else. She pointed out to her that the life would be very difficult, but that if she worked hard enough the training would finally pay off. After much consideration, Madame Rambert offered her a scholarship but said she would have to provide her own living expenses. This was a blow to Audrey, because she had thought that the scholarship would give her at least a meager allowance.

Audrey was also snarled by immigration problems due to her mixed parentage, and it was some time before she could actually join the school. When she did, she was painfully aware that her technique did not compare with that of most of the other girls. With amazing kindness, Madame Rambert actually took her into her home at Notting Hill Gate and fed and boarded her so that she could continue, despite her knowledge that there would be little future for Audrey as a prima ballerina.

London was very depressing in 1948. Audrey could not afford its one consolation: the West End theater. There still was food and clothes rationing in an austerity Britain under the dismal Labour government headed by Clement Attlee. There were long lines at the grocery stores in the chilly rain, pathetically small amounts of meat or fish available, potatoes with black spots in them, poor quality fruit, and powdered eggs. Cake icing and marzipan were made from soya-bean flour and essence. Chocolates were Audrey's passion, and an hour's wait to buy a Mars or Crunchie bar was typical. The people were exhausted by the war — pale, irritable, nervous, and bad-tempered. The camaraderie of the war years had vanished, and Londoners bickered, fretted, and complained over their fish and chips wrapped in newspaper. Had they really won the war? Why did they see pictures of robust, prosperous Germans in magazines like *Illustrated* and *Picture Post*?

Audrey, at least, found in the damp Rambert practice room a world of discipline and beauty: the self-contained world of dance. She was a picture of dedicated seriousness: a blue-stocking. She gave up everything for dance and for Albert Hall or Wigmore Hall musical occasions. She had no boyfriends, no sports, no dances, no nights on the town, no fun like most girls of her age. And along with these sacrifices there were the physical problems of dancing in the thin ballet clothes in London's gloomy winter, with the sky like a low ceiling and the sulfur fogs creeping with yellow fingers through the doors and windows of the school. Sometimes the fog was so thick Madame Rambert could barely see her own pupils. Indeed, the feeble ceiling lights in their china shades had to be turned on in the middle of the afternoon. Audrey and the other students had to dress in lumber rooms, and even cupboards, and pile their street clothes several deep onto metal hooks. Few could afford the exorbitant London dry cleaning rates, so leotards remained stained with sweat and tights after washing had to be dried over the potbellied stove.

One pleasure was that the students were privileged to see the performances at the Mercury in dress rehearsal. They were not allowed to see the paid public performances because Marie Rambert needed every penny from box-office sales. The Mercury was a charming little theater, with a cardboard wicket at the entrance and the atmosphere of the court theater of an obscure European duke. It was a Punch-and-Judy show of marvels.

Audrey had to find enough work to keep going when at last she moved out of the Rambert home. Her mother had left the florist's to work in a firm of decorators and she and Audrey moved into a small flat together. Audrey worked in a nightclub for a time, holding up a placard that announced the acts: a uniquely seedy means of earning a living, and peculiarly English to boot. At night, there was that depressing assignment; in the daytime, there was the relentless slave driving of Madame Rambert. She would rap Audrey and other pupils over the knuckles or shoulders with a stick if they did not obey her commands. Irritable and impatient to a degree, she could inspire, aggravate, excite, and madden — all in her desire for immediate, polished perfection. The slightest laziness was punished with a violent rap of the stick, and even a point of criticism was emphasized by a blow against the long-suffering parquet floor. Audrey enjoyed the discipline, but she was not destined for Marie Rambert's special list of students. Then she had a stroke of luck: there was a casting call for dancers in a re-creation of a successful American musical, *High Button Shoes,* composed by Jule Styne. It had had a very successful run on Broadway, and was still being performed there. It was the story of a 1920s con man, Harrison Floy, whose escapades run the gamut from selling land in a swamp (a parody of the 1926 Florida land swindles), trying to get Rutgers to throw a football match (based on the famous 1919 White Sox baseball scandal), and tangling with the Keystone Kops and Mack Sennett's bathing beauties, to being chased off the stage by most of the cast. Boisterous, antic, and excessively noisy, the show was brought to London with some changes because Mack Sennett was suing the producers for plagiarism.

Audrey auditioned for the job of chorus girl without realizing what she was in for. This was no ordinary assignment to simply look pretty, perform high kicks, and roll her eyes. The Jerome Robbins choreography, re-created more or less intact, as directed under the aegis of British producer Archie Thomson, called for an extraordinary degree of skill and virtuosity on the part of the dancers. The climax of the show, in fact, was not a single solo number but the Bathing Beauty Ballet, in which the girls had to dance in fantastic arabesques, leap in the air, consort with bears and other animals, be chased in and out of bathing pavilions, bathhouses, and bathing beaches, and finally plunge into a frantic cops-and-robbers chase.

Fortunately, Audrey had seen silent films and knew exactly the mode in which she was working. Despite her painful thinness, she had great energy now, and wonderfully batted her eyes, danced the Charleston, and flung her arms about. She wsa actually as stiff as a board, but it didn't show, and Archie Thomson hired her on the spot. The show did reasonably well, enough to make her believe that if she could endure the foolishness of this new profession and the silliness of the nine girls with whom she shared a dressing room, she might have found her vocation. She now attended ballet school with the grim knowledge, once and for all, that she had no real future as a classical dancer.

The realization had dawned on her some time before, when Marie Rambert kindly but firmly made it clear to her that she simply did not have the necessary degree of talent. Much as she looked down on the burden of acting in a musical, she enjoyed the fun and laughter of the show and the task of working in it. However, she found it too exhausting to go to ballet school all day and work on stage at night. She needed the money to live; and at last she left the Rambert school, with good wishes from her mentor. In 1980, she returned to London to give tribute following Marie Rambert's death at a gathering of all the fabulous old lady's friends in the theater and the ballet.

Audrey did not see her father in those struggling years. He lived in Ireland, retired, and unheard from; her brothers went to work for various companies in the Netherlands.

Chapter Three

Excellent though she was in *High Button Shoes,* and wonderful though the training was, Audrey was very much a stranger in the world of show business. She was the odd girl out in the dressing room. She didn't know how to smile or laugh. The other girls would giggle, gossip, and exchange secret information about their boyfriends. Audrey still had no boyfriend, and she thought giggling was foolish. She didn't know the patois of show business. All she could think about as she sat away from the other girls were her earnings, and she would try to figure, penny by penny, how she could get through another week until the next payday. The few pounds were wrapped around a slip of white paper in a tiny brown envelope that, to Audrey, was like the pot of gold at the end of the rainbow, or Aladdin's treasure at the end of every week.

She decided to take acting lessons with Felix Aylmer, a delightfully pedantic, aristocratically mannered old British character actor who took a few pupils to eke out his income as a supporting actor in films and plays. He taught Audrey to speak in perfect English diction, to move correctly, and to use stillness and responsiveness in scenes so that an audience would watch her when she was doing nothing. She very much admired him in the play *Daphne Laureola* and on the screen as Polonius in Laurence Olivier's *Hamlet.*

When *High Button Shoes* closed, Audrey got a job in the chorus of the Cecil Landau revue *Sauce Tartare* as one of five girls dancing wittily through a pictorial travelogue of satirical scenes, from a tropical jungle to New York to a Rio beach and a lamplit alley in Paris. Audrey was greatly amused by the charming Moira Lister, delightful as a Theda Bara-like seductress, and she enjoyed Ronald Frankau as an ophthalmic surgeon who could not see beyond his nose.

Audrey went on to appear in *Sauce Piquante,* in which Moira Lister was a riot as Vivien Leigh in a burlesque of *A Streetcar Named Desire.* Douglas Byng, the celebrated female impersonator, played, with equal style, a belching volcano and a Montmartre cocotte who has seen better days.

In the meantime, Audrey appeared in small parts in films at Ealing Studios and Associated British Pictures. She had a walk-on in *Young Wives' Tales* and *One Wild Oat,* British farces filled with heavy double entendres, epicene leading men, and imposingly fat females. All this was very depressing, and she was still further put out when she lost the starring role in *Lady Godiva Rides Again,* in which she was to play the winner of a beauty contest, a part won by the now-forgotten Pauline Stroud, and in *Quo Vadis,* an MGM epic to be shot in Rome. But she was too thin for the first and too inexperienced and unknown for the second.

Audrey was earning five pounds a week, equivalent to the salary of a bookstore clerk or a factory hand. She was noticed by the brilliant young actor Alec Guinness, who was then the doyen of Ealing comedies. He gave her the opportunity to play a small but quite useful part in his film *The Lavender Hill Mob,* about a mousy bank clerk who robs his own bank and moves to South America.

Meanwhile, Audrey was still appearing in *Sauce Piquante.* Robert Lennard, the impresario, noticed her when he was helping to put together the cast for a picture to be shot in the south of France entitled *We Go to Monte Carlo.* He was struck by the fact that while the other girls in the chorus looked very bored as they highkicked with their arms interlocked, Audrey looked full of bounce and enthusiasm, her face radiated warmth and pleasure, and her eyes shone and sparkled with delight. She was the only thing on the stage that kept him awake, and by the time the final curtain came down, he was sure he had seen a star.

Lennard called the producer Cecil Landau next day and got her name and phone number. When he contacted her, she was very tense, anticipating a pickup. But when she understood that he genuinely wanted her for a good part in a picture to be made on the French Riviera, she became bubbly with excitement. The part he had in mind called for a bilingual actress, and Lennard was delighted to find that Audrey was as fluent in French as she was in English. This turned out to be crucial, since *We Go to Monte Carlo* was to be made in both languages.

The part was that of a motion-picture star involved in a chase after a missing baby. Ray Ventura, the bandleader, would be the center of the action. The script was ludicrous, but Audrey accepted it because she needed the work and wanted to see the Riviera. Ealing Studios reluctantly agreed to release her from her contract for this one movie, but first she would have to complete one more film.

While Audrey was making her brief appearance in *The Lavender Hill Mob,* Associated British Pictures was busy preparing a long-delayed movie entitled *The Secret People,* to be directed by the scholarly, bespectacled Thorold Dickinson. Dickinson had recently completed a very striking version of Pushkin's *The Queen of Spades* with Edith Evans.

The project had been discussed as early as 1940. Dickinson had become fascinated by the theme of illegal political organizations in England, and a story was developed in which a young terrorist plans the assassination of a general in London, using a café as headquarters. The story was rather like the plot of Alfred Hitchcock's *The Man Who Knew Too Much* crossed with his *Sabotage,* without the hair-raising suspense and thrills: it was just a touch drier, and more academic in content and tone.

In 1946, the gifted British novelist Joyce Carey, author of *The Horse's Mouth,* wrote a very intelligent screenplay. The picture was finally scheduled to be shot in the spring of 1951, and preparations began in October 1950. Thorold Dickinson interviewed Audrey twice for the part of Nora — the younger of two sisters who become involved with the terrorist group. The part of Nora as created by Joyce Carey called for a dancer of considerable skill, as well as an actress of power and authority. Nora's life as a ballet dancer was counterpointed by her tense existence in connection with foreign anarchism.

But much as Dickinson liked her, he felt that Audrey was too tall — not only to be a dancer, but also because the Italian actress Lea Padovani, who was supposed to play Nora's elder sister Maria, was quite short. It would look awkward, he felt, for an unknown actress to tower over the star and for a younger sister to physically dominate her sibling. He also had to bear in mind that Serge Reggiani, the pixieish leading man, although perfectly formed and athletic, was very short and would also be dwarfed by her.

However, Audrey had a powerful ally. Marie Rambert's former associate Andrée Howard, the accomplished choreographer and dancer, had been hired to direct the dances in which Nora would appear. She believed in Audrey, who was well aware of her background. Everyone knew that Andrée had a heart condition that had tragically shortened her career as a dancer, and that her famous appearance in *Death and the Maiden* as a younger girl making love to death was oddly prophetic of her condition: This beautiful woman wanted to devote her limited years to helping young talent, and since she saw great future promise in Audrey, she kept pressing Dickinson to take her on.

Dickinson still hesitated. On October 30, 1950, as preparations for the film continued, Dickinson, a clever, interesting man with untidy hair and a quizzical manner, interviewed Audrey again for the part of Nora. Impressed though he was, and despite his respect for Andrée Howard, he still felt that Audrey's height made her unacceptable.

The following month, Lea Padovani withdrew and Valentina Cortese was considered. She was a little taller than Signorina Padovani and therefore would match up to Audrey, but she was a long time in making up her mind. December and January dragged on with neither sister in the story cast.

Andrée Howard grew increasingly impatient. Meanwhile, Audrey had an unexpected distraction. She met a young man, James Hanson, who came from a wealthy truck-building family of Huddersfield, Yorkshire. He was a trustee of the D'Oyly Carte opera company, which produced Gilbert and Sullivan. He had served in the war, in the Duke of Wellington's regiment. He was a master of foxhounds, a keen horseman, yachtsman (the Royal Thames Yacht Club), and golfer. He was twenty-nine years old when Audrey met him. Slim and attractive, he was a typical Yorkshireman with his solidity, security, and strength. No doubt Audrey was strongly drawn to him and, in view of her extreme self-consciousness and her increasing feeling that her career would never take off, she very much wanted security and a man to lean on. Yet one side of her remained ambitious for herself, and she must have known that if she were to become seriously involved with Hanson, and move to Huddersfield and marry him, she would soon become part of a world to which she was completely alien. There would be no talk of ballet or theater in that world. Its members would be tweedy, dour, hunting, shooting, and fishing people, and she would be surrounded by nothing more interesting than stablemen and grooms and talk of the studbook and racing form.

She was very much torn between thoughts of the sober certainties of Huddersfield and the shining allure of popular success. Her mother, however, was not torn: the baroness adamantly opposed the relationship from the beginning. She wanted Audrey to have a career and, although she had carefully avoided the role of show business mother by not going to the Rambert school or watching Audrey on the set at Ealing, she could not tolerate the idea of Audrey becoming part of the world of horses and the trucking business. Thus, there was a conflict between the baroness and Hanson that could not be resolved, and Audrey and her mother had many tense conversations on the matter, which seriously affected Audrey's sensitive and nervous psyche.

It was a very difficult period. Andrée Howard was under pressure because she had been engaged to stage the Festival of Britain ballet that April; it was the biggest dance event of the year, and she could not forgo it. On February 15, at long-suffering last, Thorold Dickinson called Audrey in for her first dramatic test, to see how she would handle a fully played-out sequence. In the scene she was to enter the kitchen of the café that sheltered Serge Reggiani's terrorists. Valentina Cortese, who had just been cast, played Maria. Dickinson ordered the camera to turn. Audrey, very jittery, ran in from the left, hugged Reggiani and Cortese, and told them eagerly of a call she had received to dance at a party. She was to audition for the job along with two singers from Covent Garden and a clown. Audrey played the scene with energy and style, but Andrée Howard unwittingly ruined Audrey's big chance. She was so eager to push her that she broke the union rules — and went over the director's head as well — to do the unthinkable: she rearranged the lights to enhance Audrey's appearance. This, to say the least, was not what was called for in a choreographer. The cameraman was furious, and there was a scene followed by Andrée walking off the set.

Dickinson refused to be thrown by this, however, and in the meantime he found a partner for Nora in the Covent Garden Ballet's gifted John Field. On February 23, Audrey was tested again, this time in both a dramatic sequence and a dance number with Field's double. She ran through the work, and the entire unit exchanged meaningful glances: she was "it." Three days later, she was told she had been cast. She was ecstatic when Andrée Howard, who had worked so desperately hard for her, told her the news.

Rehearsals began, and problems arose at once. Audrey had passed her test with only a moderately good dancer, but now she had to perform the ballet sequences with John Field, a performer of the first rank. The rehearsals took place at the Bedford Theatre, which was fiercely cold and miserably damp. Audrey had to wear three sweaters to keep warm, and her legs got goosebumps in her tights. She added leg warmers, which helped. John Field danced in jeans. The choreography devised by Andrée Howard was hard enough, but even more difficult was the fact that the director decided to film the rehearsals, and every step had to be geared to the lighting and camera movements. This was a tortuously slow process. In one scene, with Audrey on stage performing a solo, the director diminished the light from that of early evening to night, and the light had to seem to come from the windows. Audrey had to stop and start dozens of times, until her feet and ankles were literally burning with pain, to secure the perfection of the shot.

As if that were not enough, the Philharmonia Orchestra arrived and sat in the pit, with conductor Ernest Irving in charge, so that the music could be matched to the choreography, the dancers' individual steps, and the lighting. It was nine days of agony before Dickinson was satisfied.

Then, on March 19, when the rehearsals were at last over, the theater was suddenly booked and the entire ballet sequence had to be shot perfectly in two days. Thorold Dickinson had to drag himself from a sickbed. He was coughing and snuffling with a miserable cold, and had to issue his instructions through a blizzard of sneezes. This scarcely helped matters; and the theater's chilliness was more intense now than ever. It was bad enough for the audience of extras, dressed in tuxedos and long gowns at 8:30 A.M., to have to leave their overcoats at the door; worse for painfully thin Audrey to perform without sweaters or leg warmers in the thinnest of ballet clothes. Even the athletic John Field had to struggle to smile under these conditions.

The orchestra played the same four or five minutes of music all through the day, while Audrey and John did dozens of takes, rushing to dressing rooms between them to warm their hands over electric fires and get quick rubdowns before they rushed back on stage. The corps de ballet had to sit miserably in the orchestra for hours, waiting for their turn to appear.

Not even the slightest variation could be shown in the dance movements as they were shot, because a crane carrying a camera swooped from a great height to focus on the stage and everything must flow together. At one point, the movement of the crane was mistimed, and the whole shot had to be repeated; at another, Audrey was seen to be shivering and that shot had to be cancelled; at yet another, John Field's wig flew off as he was pirouetting; and so forth, until everyone was exhausted.

The next day, Dickinson had the flu. Since the shot had to be finished without fail, he arrived on the set anyway, bundled in an overcoat, and full of penicillin and a sleeping draught. He could barely drag himself to work, and when he did, Audrey, John Field, the crew, and the corps de ballet had been waiting, with barely concealed impatience, for an hour. Even worse, Dickinson announced through his sneezes that all the effort of the preceding days' work was useless. The shot didn't seem right to him and he would have to start all over again. Andrée Howard and the production manager loudly blamed each other for the problems, and the production manager exclaimed furiously to all and sundry, "I'd sooner work with animals from the zoo!" After another bad day, the shot was at last achieved and everyone got home close to midnight through freezing rain.

Soon after, Audrey had to face another challenge. She had to play a dramatic scene in which she talked to her sister about a terrorist explosion, describing the dead and wounded that resulted from it. As she rehearsed the lines by herself, she remembered all too painfully the horror of war, the ordeal of Arnhem living in her mind. Perhaps because she could not face the emotion, could not find a way to use it, she froze as she came on the set and couldn't deliver the lines. She asked Dickinson what she should do to express the feeling in them. Dickinson was very shrewd. Knowing of her war experiences, he said, "Don't bother about how you're going to say it. Just think of the experience that lies behind the words. During the war perhaps you saw something like that. Not the same of course, but its equivalent. Get the feeling right and the words will look after themselves."

Audrey went into a corner, sat in a chair, and concentrated, closing her mind to everything else. It was typical of her to achieve this extraordinary amount of concentration, of focusing. It was an ability that would characterize her career and help her to become a star. Nothing else distracted her. She suddenly saw people dying in explosions, thought of her older brother being dragged off to a Nazi camp, of her younger brother being taken from her house to some unknown destination. The pain she could not speak about to others, the memories she refused to discuss with reporters, flooded her brain, and she came back on the set and delivered the lines, tears literally starting from her eyes. She delivered the words with great power. Her co-stars and director were riveted: it was her first moment of stardom.

People began talking, and the inevitable happened. Audrey began to be pursued for interviews, and she did not have the power to refuse them. When she needed all of her concentration and energy to focus her steely will and raw, exposed feelings on her work, she suddenly found herself having to pose for cheesecake shots, talk to inept and uninformed reporters looking for an angle, and tolerate questions about her occasional dates with James Hanson. She even submitted to such extremes of folly as a layout for the magazine *Illustrated,* in which she had to travel to the country of Sussex on her only day off to feed the ducks in a village pond, paddle barefoot, and walk in brogues along a hillside against the sky. She was most annoyed at all this attention because she felt that it was very premature, since the public had not seen her in anything significant. She told the later famous director Lindsay Anderson, who was present throughout the shooting as a kind of journalist-intern, "I'm worried they'll get sick of hearing about me. I'd much rather wait until I have something to show. Instead of risking a tremendous anticlimax when people finally do see the first little bits in films."

Many scenes of *The Secret People* were shot outdoors in that dreary April of 1951. Fortified by cups of tea and unappetizing cheese rolls in wax paper, Audrey somehow got through, though sitting on a damp log for a loveseat scarcely improved her temper. Many scenes were shot until 3 A.M. in a drizzle, with rain plopping on the cast members' heads through the trees.

Somehow, in her rare hours off, Audrey was reading the script for *We Go to Monte Carlo*. She had finally been offered it, and word of her good acting in *The Secret People* had proved influential in her getting the offer. However, she would not, she felt, find much sustenance in the absurd comedy, or in the part of the movie star involved in a chase after the where-abouts of a missing baby. But the lure of the Riviera, with its warmth and sunlight, was irresistible.

Audrey traveled to Monte Carlo just a day after completing work on *The Secret People* and began shooting in French and English, a most irritating procedure since she had to speak her lines in one language, and then the other, without losing the feeling. Furthermore, she might as well have been on the moon, since the hours of work were so long she couldn't take a minute to explore the French Gold Coast. To add to her annoyance, James Hanson's commitments to the trucking business in Huddersfield made it impossible for him to travel with her. The baroness's relief at his absence was not at all comforting to Audrey, but at least the baroness accompanied her to France.

Typically, she tried to give some characterization to her thinly written part. And she extracted much from the few hours she had off. She rather enjoyed the absurdly baroque Hôtel de Paris, though it was the antithesis of her spare and austere taste. The hotel was an extravaganza of marble, gilt, ginger-bread, and ornate mirrors that, if anything, enhanced its grotesque opulence.

Audrey was intrigued by a rumor, flying around the hotel, that the great French novelist Colette was staying at the Hôtel de Paris with her husband, the writer Maurice Goudeket, as the guest of Prince Rainier of Monaco. One day, she was shooting a scene in the dining room with the famous character actor Marcel Dalio when there was a sudden stir at the entrance.

A tall and hawk-nosed man appeared, interrupting the shot as he pushed a tiny, huddled figure of a woman with red-dyed corkscrew curls, a famished smile crinkling a round, rouged face, and a shapeless garment, in a wheelchair. The woman raised a tiny gloved hand to her eyes to shield them from the brilliant blaze of the arc lights, and the chair became inextricably caught in a tangle of wires. The woman grumbled loudly in French. The director, Jean Boyer, turned in fury at this untoward interruption of his work. But when he saw who it was, he was silenced and, instead, he advanced with outstretched hands, bowing profoundly from the waist. The French crew shrugged irritably and somebody called "Cut!"

It was Colette. She asked in her frail voice if she could watch the sequence being shot. Boyer agreed and placed her and her husband behind the camera, instructing them gently to be absolutely silent. She sipped a concoction called syrup of orgeat, and looked intently at Audrey and at Dalio. Goudeket kept his hands firmly on the chromium wheelchair so that it would not creak or squeak.

As the camera turned, Colette raised her eyeglass and peered even more closely at Audrey from her kohled eye. She was fascinated. Audrey was overawed: well read, she was of course completely familiar with Colette's works and loved them for their spareness and purity of style. Self-conscious over her silly lines, Audrey delivered them as best she could. Colette looked up at her husband and asked him to summon somebody from the crew. Goudeket called over the assistant director and Colette asked, "Who is that girl?" He replied, "Her name is Audrey Hepburn. She's accompanied by her mother, the Baroness van Heemstra, who speaks for her."

The man pointed out the baroness, who was seated in a corner of the lobby so that Audrey would not see her — she kept to her rule of not watching Audrey while she worked. The assistant director brought the baroness over to Colette. The baroness was overwhelmed by the invitation, for she never would have dared approach the novelist herself.

What Colette now told her impressed that stolid woman as much as had anything in her long life. Colette explained that she had promised Gilbert Miller, the distinguished Broadway producer who had bought her story *Gigi*, and its adaptor,

Anita Loos, author of *Gentlemen Prefer Blondes,* that she would do everything in her power to find a suitable actress for the starring role in the Broadway version. After looking at Audrey — *Oh mon Dieu!* She *was* Gigi! She was a colt! Half woman, half boy, unformed, unself-conscious as a woman, surely a virgin, perfection! The part of Gigi was that of a young Parisian girl who, untouched by men and innocent as the dawn, is trained by her grandmother and aunt, both former courtesans, in the ways of the fine world. When attempts are made to sell her to a wealthy young man-about-town, she resists and rebels, only to find true love with that same rake. It was a wish-fulfillment fantasy cloaked in a veil of realism, which proved intoxicating to readers both during and after World War II. The story was based on Colette's own experiences, sugarcoated by a master hand.

As Colette continued, she said, "Madame, your daughter is perfect for Gigi. We are preparing a stage production in New York. Would she be interested?"

The baroness tried to remain in control. Much had to be considered. For one thing, Audrey was under contract now to Associated British Pictures. She even owed a movie to Ealing. The baroness had to keep her head on her shoulders. Of course, Audrey herself had to be spoken to.

Discussion continued in Colette's suite. That afternoon, when shooting broke off briefly, Audrey came to the suite for a meeting. She listened carefully to the proposal, and there can be no doubt that her heart began to race. On the other hand, however, she felt she wasn't ready for Broadway or for stardom, and she said so: "But it is impossible, Madame. I haven't learned to act yet. I *cannot* be Gigi!"

Colette looked up at her husband and her husband looked at the baroness. All three felt like Gigi's grandmother and aunt in the story, when Gigi said she would not marry the Parisian man-of-the-world, Gaston. They were distraught; but at the same time, as they saw the tall, gazelle-like girl with her straight dark hair, huge brown eyes, high cheekbones, angular, severely tailored figure, and splay-legged dancer's stance, they knew there could be no other Gigi. They *would* convince her, come what may.

Audrey turned on her heel and walked stiffly back to the elevator to resume work. Colette waved the problem away. She told Goudeket, "Cheri, send a cable to Anita Loos at once. And then a letter, advising her. The cable should read, 'Don't cast your Gigi until you receive letter. Colette.'"

It was difficult for Colette to write because her whole body was twisted with painful arthritis. But she scribbled a note, which survives today, to Anita on her art nouveau flowered stationery, and Goudeket wrote that he and Colette had just seen an English girl of nineteen who would be perfect for Gigi. He gave her name and said she would be in London on July 7. Then Goudeket stretched a point and said that Audrey would be willing to play the part on Broadway; this was clearly intended to force Audrey on Loos and Gilbert Miller. He continued, "She is greatly thought of by film people generally and considered a future star of the first magnitude. I believe, however, she has had little experience on the stage. She is very pretty and has that piquant quality necessary for the part."

Anita Loos read the letter and, although she had never heard of Audrey Hepburn, called Gilbert Miller in London from her home in New York and persuaded him to join her in looking at Audrey in that first week of July.

Encouraged by the baroness, Audrey agreed to at least talk to Miller and Anita Loos when she returned to England from the shooting of the picture. James Hanson was not very encouraging. He wanted to marry Audrey as soon as possible and have her give up the theater and movies. She, loving him as she did, was still under great tension, and perhaps her feeling for him influenced her, adding to her reluctance to consider going to America.

But powerful forces were at work. Miller and Anita Loos had been having differences: Loos didn't like Miller, and was convinced that he wasn't really interested in the production, and was just looking for excuses to get out of it. She was wrong; in fact, he was very anxious to move ahead, since he had made his reputation, in part, by producing French plays in New York, and was a convinced Francophile and fan of Colette. He was not entirely pleased with Anita Loos, himself. He found her manner irritating, and he was quite immune to her celebrated charm. He had hired her for the adaptation chiefly because of her fame and the fact that she was bilingual, rather than because of any deep admiration of her or her talent.

Audrey came to see Miller at the Savoy Hotel. Probably the most powerful Broadway producer of his day, he was an overpowering personality. He financed his own shows, never touching the colossal fortune inherited by his wife, Kitty, from her father, millionaire Jewish banker Julius Bache. Miller spoke half-a-dozen languages, collected priceless French and Dutch masterpieces, could shoot elk or reindeer at hundreds of paces, owned an airline and a bank, lorded it over great estates in four countries, and was a close friend of several royal families. He was as big as his fortune. Enormously fat, at five-foot-ten and two hundred and eighty pounds, he looked not only as though he had conquered the globe but as though he had swallowed it. He sported three chins and a heroic stomach crossed by a gold watch chain. A champion traveler, he had crossed the Atlantic by ship or by plane close to three hundred times. He had had stunning successes with *Victoria Regina* starring Helen Hayes, *The Swan, Journey's End, What Price Glory?*, and *The Cocktail Party* by his friend T. S. Eliot. He was eccentric to a degree. He once bought two hundred ties at one dollar each from Cardinal of Fifth Avenue to take to London, and told everyone there he was selling them to stay alive.

Audrey entered his suite looking ravishing. She was very simply dressed in a man's white shirt, with the tails tied around her waist, and a flaring black skirt, bobby sox, and flat shoes, but the effect was stunning. She was surprised to hear that the great producer had a shrill, unpleasantly piercing voice — the last thing she would ever have expected. He asked her about her background and she spoke quietly and modestly about her dancing lessons and her first pictures. Miller may not have been an angel, but he was shrewd enough to know the genuine article when he saw it. When Audrey left, he told her to drop by Anita Loos's suite.

Audrey found Anita with Paulette Goddard, her great friend who was about to leave with her for the Continent. What a pair: the sophisticated, ageless, perky author and the beautiful and celebrated Hollywood star! Audrey strode in, splay-legged, and the two formidable women asked her to relax and chat for a few moments. Then she left. Meetings like this were always uncomfortable for actors. Only the strongest ego could resist the feeling that such an occasion was an exhibition, like a cattle show. But Audrey was lucky. Instead of a cold reading on a stage, with half-discernible faces and disembodied voices emerging from the house, she was being entertained in a great hotel by people of great fame and distinction. She was already one of the privileged, and she was destined to stay that way.

As she left, Paulette said to Anita, "There's got to be something wrong with that girl! Anyone who looks like that should have been discovered before she was ten years old!"

The next day, Audrey returned to Miller's suite and gave a reading of a key scene to him and Anita Loos. She lost her nerve halfway through and stumbled badly, but pulled herself together and proceeded to the most difficult speech in the play, the emotional outburst in which Gigi refuses to marry Gaston. Again, she became confused, even flubbed the lines but, despite everything, Miller and Anita knew she was all right. The only question now was whether she could project from the stage since, in those days, the infamous practice of "miking" was not yet being used by actors.

Miller arranged for Audrey to go over to a theater where his friend, veteran stage actress Cathleen Nesbitt, promised to listen from the back of the orchestra.

Audrey stepped onto the stage and gave her reading. Cathleen Nesbitt could hear nothing. It was obvious that Audrey would have to be very carefully coached, and as

Cathleen was leaving for New York she promised Miller that she would train Audrey at her country home just outside the city.

That was the only major problem for the moment. While Audrey was waiting for Miller and Associated British Pictures to sort out the business arrangements of her contract, she was spotted by scouts for William Wyler, the celebrated Hollywood director, who was trying to cast the leading role of the princess in *Roman Holiday* — originally a project of Frank Capra's — for Paramount. *Roman Holiday* is the story of the heiress to a Graustarkian throne who, young and restless within the constraints of her royal position, goes to Rome on an official visit. There, she meets a reporter who is on an assignment to write a story about her. He encourages her to escape from her entourage and enjoy the city with him as an ordinary citizen. Gradually, reporter and princess discover true love. It is a romantic, escapist comedy, originally scripted by the black-listed writer Dalton Trumbo, who passed it off under another name.

When Wyler traveled to Rome to select the locations, he left instructions in London with test director Paul Stein to give various actresses a special reading; the quest was publicized somewhat along the lines of David O. Selznick's search for the ideal Scarlett O'Hara for *Gone with the Wind*. Wyler had little patience with this method of casting, and said that he had not even cared to attend the auditions.

Audrey was quite uneasy when Paramount contacted the baroness, asking Audrey to come and test. After all, after much agonizing, she had now decided to embark on *Gigi*; she still wanted to marry James Hanson and settle down to raise a family; and how would she be able to play in *Roman Holiday* if *Gigi* had a long run? Her discomfort increased because Gilbert Miller was not very keen on her doing the test, since he was afraid that if she won the part she might be tempted to back out of *Gigi*. So she went for her test without the slightest enthusiasm and, indeed, she would not have cared if she had been turned down at once. Paul Stein, by contrast, was excited when he saw her. Before he began the test, he called Wyler in Rome. Wyler said that instead of ending the test with the last moment of the scene, he should keep the cameras running and see how Audrey looked when she thought she was not on film.

The sequence chosen for the test was that in which the pajama-clad princess sits up in an elaborate bed in Rome and stretches her arms kittenishly toward the ornamental ceiling. As Stein watched, Audrey deliciously and girlishly acted out the sequence and then, without telling her, he kept the cameras rolling. He said, finally, "That's it, you can get off the bed now."

"Oh, is it over now? Oh, good!" Audrey smiled and gave an infectious laugh that made the hardened crew laugh in response. The results were irresistible. Stein called Wyler and Wyler asked to see the test. It was flown to Rome, Wyler was enchanted, and Audrey was signed to play the part after the run of *Gigi,* no matter how long that run should be. This was a great risk for Paramount. The play could have run for years, and Gregory Peck had just been signed for the picture for the following summer. Also, William Wyler might not have been available when the play's run ended. Nevertheless, it was felt that only Audrey could play the part, and that was where the matter stood.

After she finished the test, Audrey took a ship to New York on loanout from Associated British. Her parting with James Hanson was difficult. Much to her sorrow, he was very upset at delaying wedding plans and was mollified only when she promised to marry him after the run of *Gigi.* He decided to come over to New York and visit with her as soon as he could.

She must have felt more and more that the situation was hopeless. Uneasy though she was over the challenge of playing Gigi, she was, after all, barely twenty and it was thrilling for a young girl to experience Broadway and New York for the first time. Unfortunately, the ship docked at 3 A.M. and, kneeling at the porthole in her nightdress, she could see just a blur of lights. It was only when she disembarked from the deck that the full glory of the Manhattan skyline emerged.

Miller's representatives met Audrey, checked her into her

hotel, and whisked her off to one of the last games of the World Series at Yankee Stadium, where she cheered her head off with excitement without the slighest idea of what was going on. Needless to say, photographers were there to take pictures of her cheering the team as it won the Series.

On her second day, Audrey went to see Miller in his lavish suite of offices at Rockefeller Center. He was alarmed at the sight of her. She had gorged herself on the ship and upon arrival with large amounts of cakes and puddings and already had gained a few pounds. She was no longer the gamine-like creature he had talked to in London only a month before. He issued her instructions to lose ten pounds on a crash diet. He sent her over to Dinty Moore's with orders that Dinty, the legendary restaurateur, should give her nothing but steak tartare every day for a week. She was forbidden her beloved chocolates, for which she now had a mania, and cake was strictly taboo.

Each day, she visited with Cathleen Nesbitt at her country home to extend her vocal range and projection. Miss Nesbitt would never forget her running down the platform from the train each morning calling, "Hello! Cathy dear! Here I am!" Men and women alike turned to look at her, not recognizing her but struck at once by her vitality, beauty, and charm.

Cathleen took Audrey into her garden and made her shout, speak in a whisper, and use every level of voice in between until at last she was perfectly audible. Cathleen then tested her in a rehearsal hall in New York City and more or less passed her, though Audrey still lacked true projection and would never gain it.

Next, Miller suddenly flew Audrey to Paris to work with the play's director, the gifted and innovative Raymond Rouleau. Rouleau saw her at the Hôtel Napoléon, where she was staying, and in his office at the Théâtre de l'Oeuvre. Rouleau was famous for his effective productions of surrealist theater and for his successful Théâtre de Minuit, a distinguished Paris attraction. He had just had a most successful long-running version in French of Tennessee William's *A Streetcar Named*

Desire. He was thirty-seven, but looked ten years older, a charmer, with white hair, pale blue eyes, and pink skin, almost like an albino. He spoke no English, but was delighted that Audrey spoke fluent French. He was fascinated by her, and she by him, and she rushed over for costume fittings, feeling she would get on with him perfectly.

She went to London briefly to see her mother and James Hanson, who said he was making arrangements to join his firm's office in Ontario, Canada, to be closer to her. She maintained her promise of marriage and, indeed, Huddersfield began to get excited over the match.

Back in New York, problems arose. Rouleau had managed to master a smattering of English from a phrase book, but he could not successfully communicate with the legendary actresses Constance Collier and Florence Reed, cast successively as Audrey's grandmother. (The part finally was taken by Josephine Hull.) To Audrey's delight, Cathleen Nesbitt was cast as her aunt. Luckily, everyone in the cast spoke French, but there were still arguments all through rehearsal because Rouleau had a nervous temperament, and Audrey was extremely on edge because, although French was her second language, she realized she would be speaking the part in English and she was uneasy about using the correct modulations and expressions without help from the director. The fact is that Anita Loos's version had to be translated back into French by Miss Loos herself and this, too, created a problem since the cast was rehearsing for a play in French but would have to act in English. In addition, the stagehands and stage manager had to try to cope with Rouleau's idea of English, which seldom reached even such heights of eloquence as, "Is better, my bluebird," or "Zhust acceptable de gloominess!"

Sometimes, Audrey herself or Cathleen Nesbitt would act as an interpreter when Miller obstinately refused to supply one. Audrey often irritated him and even dismayed Cathleen by shouting all her lines, slamming too many doors, and running rather than walking, or bounding onto the stage like a gazelle. She treated the play rather like a track meet, and when she jumped off a chair she fell on her knees to such jarring effect that she was in pain for days. Her part called for animation, but she was so overanimated that everyone was exhausted. Her biggest problem was with the scene she had stumbled through at the first reading, in which Gigi rejects Gaston. She was petulant and childish when she should have been angry and degraded, and neither Rouleau nor Cathleen was able to elicit from her the sense of a girl suddenly becoming a woman and acquiring confidence and a will of her own. She lacked confidence herself, and she was not yet sufficiently commanding to act beyond her own character.

Her phrasing too was weak. She had difficulty with long speeches and became ever angrier and more impatient with herself. Sometimes she was at her best around six o'clock at night, and in those days New York union rules forbade the stagehands to work one minute past that hour. Rouleau would scream with rage as Audrey would be suspended almost in midsentence and everyone walked out; he would call Gilbert Miller in desperation but Miller, who refused to pay "golden time," flatly declined to take his calls.

Audrey very much wanted her mother to be with her, but the baroness stuck strictly to her rule of not being too closely tied to Audrey's career, and she refused to cross the Atlantic.

In a letter to the author, Rouleau's widow writes:

The first eight days of work with Audrey were truly terrible: Audrey had no idea what she was doing. She was acting extremely badly, totally failing to understand the meaning of the text, going out late at night and arriving very tired at the theater in the mornings. Finally, my late husband, who was growing totally disturbed, on the eighth day took Audrey aside for a private meeting and told her quite firmly that she must improve, or else. She must work with more dedication, obtain enough sleep, eat properly, devote herself to the text and, in a word, become properly professional or he would decline all responsibility for her future on Broadway and in the production itself. He was very severe with her during this long and important conversation.

Next day, a new Audrey emerged. She understood everything that Raymond had told her. From that moment, she progressed steadily, an became better and better every day, using every bit of advice Raymond had given her, as though he had been in charge of a child-birth. Their conversations now acquired great affection and warmth, and she suddenly emerged as the fine professional she was to remain for the rest of her career. When Raymond was inspired by an artist, he became a magician. They worked in total happiness and confidence. And so, at last, did the reluctant crew, no longer fazed by the inter-preting necessary because of Rouleau's failure to understand English. At the last, Raymond said to me, "They all followed me so completely that if I had asked them to throw themselves in the Hudson they would happily have done so."

Allowing for this degree of vanity, it is true that Rouleau did weld everyone together expertly in spite of everything.

But then, further problems arose. Miller had reluctantly stretched the budget in order to have some beautiful drop curtains, suggesting various Parisian scenes, made in Paris, and a longshoremen's strike prevented them from being delivered, so Gilbert Miller's team had to search New York City for equivalents.

Paramount was giving Audrey a hard time. She had signed the agreement to appear in *Roman Holiday*, but now they wanted her to sign a seven-year contract. Contracts of that length were supposed to be things of the past, as the result of Olivia de Havilland's fight against Warner Brothers. Indeed, Paramount was so determined that, after trying bribes, flattery, and every kind of persuasion, they finally announced that another actress would replace Audrey as the princess if she did not yield. It was only a bluff, and Audrey finally won the struggle. Her steely resolution was remarkable in one so young. Her agents insisted that her name should be above the title outside the theater and Paramount agreed, for publicity reasons. It was a severe blow to Cathleen Nesbitt, much as she loved Audrey, because her name was pushed below the title in *Gigi* as a result. Audrey tried to correct that, without success.

Raymond Rouleau's struggles with the cast, Miller's uncertainty over her, Hanson's loving pressure, her mother's dislike of Hanson, her uncertainty about marriage versus career, Paramount and its stresses — the thoughts whirled around Audrey's brain, and she wondered if she would make it through the first night in Philadelphia.

But she did. The tough professional inside her fragile form won out. Every nuance of her performance was guided with the skill of a veteran. Not a trace of her anguish and doubt emerged as she skipped lightly onto the stage, the epitome of youth, buoyancy, and coltish charm. Her big eyes, spiky shoulders, thin but supple arms, and leggy dancer's stance captivated the audience, and even the doughtiest members of the Philadelphia Main Line gave her vigorous applause. Her very inexperience, awkwardness, and lack of sheer skill worked in her favor, and the audience took her to heart. None suspected the cool intellect that functioned inside the extraordinary machine that was Audrey Hepburn. They saw only the gamine.

The opening in New York did strike an icicle of fear through Audrey's heart. The Fulton Theatre suffered from acoustical problems, and she was very much afraid that she would not be heard beyond the sixth row. However, she disguised her fears and kissed the equally nervous Cathleen Nesbitt on the head before she ran to her dressing room, telling her not to worry. She was marvelous that night, and no one who saw her would ever forget her. She was best of all in the scene in which Cathleen, as Aunt Alicia, explains to her the virtues of a good stone. "What is that?" Cathleen would ask as she placed a jewel before Audrey. And Audrey replied "An emerald!" with all the rapture of a girl who had never seen an emerald before.

Even now, Audrey was not quite equal to the big renunciation scene in the last act, but nobody cared. November 24, 1951, was a night to remember. Richard Watts, Jr., the influential critic, wrote of her: "The delightful Miss Hepburn obviously is not an experienced actress. But her quality is so winning and so right that she is the success of the evening . . . Miss Hepburn is as fresh and frisky as a puppy out of a tub. She brings a candid innocence and a tomboy intelligence to a part that might have gone sticky, and her performance comes as a breath of fresh air in a stifling season."

Although he complained that the play was "very trivial and old-fashioned," the all-important Brooks Atkinson wrote in the New York *Times*: "Among other things it introduces us to Audrey Hepburn, a young actress of charm, honesty and talent who ought to be interned in America and trapped into appearing in a fine play."

The result was that Audrey was an overnight triumph, and the party at Sardi's was an ecstatic one. Even the difficult Gilbert Miller threw his hat in the air. The legendary Gertrude Lawrence came backstage and told Audrey she would like her to play her on the screen. But instead of luxuriating in the world's praise, Audrey typically kept a level head. Four days after the opening, she and James Hanson announced that they would be married as soon as the play's run ended. She would squeeze the wedding in between New York and Rome. Then, when *Roman Holiday* was finished, she would settle down with Hanson in Huddersfield. The baroness shuddered at the news.

Chapter Four

During the run of the play, Audrey never stopped studying. She not only spent every spare hour working with Cathleen Nesbitt on her phrasing and delivery, but she also concentrated hard on her dancing. She told one reporter, "I'm halfway between a dancer and an actress. I've got to learn. Ballet is the most completely exhausting thing I have ever done. But if I hadn't been used to pushing myself that hard, I could never have managed the tremendous amount of work necessary to learn in three weeks how to play a leading role in my first real acting job."

She took lessons at the Tarassova School of Ballet on West 54th Street. She knew she would never be a great dancer, but she needed the exercise (as well as the steak tartare at Dinty Moore's) to sustain her strength. She was greatly amused by Madame Tarassova's husband, Vladimir B. Bell. When she first saw him and asked him if he were an instructor, he told her: "Oh my dear! I have a sacroiliac condition and one waltz would dislocate my vertebrae!" Actually he was joking, for he had an alarming habit of pirouetting, despite his somewhat unathletic figure, in front of the class as well as consuming in their presence substantial quantities of cognac, whiskey, vodka, pichon, chablis, rosé, and eggnog along with buckets of black coffee and mountains of doughnuts.

During the Broadway run, Edith Head, the prominent Hollywood dress designer, came to see Audrey. They also had meetings at Edith's hotel. Miss Head had been hired to design the clothes for the princess in *Roman Holiday*. Edith Head was tiny, intense, hard as nails, and as precise as a clockwork toy. Her black hair was severely cut in a style that was combed forward to cover her forehead. Her manner was cool, tough, guarded, and smart. She had Audrey's willpower but not her warmth, her sudden gusts of amusement and charm.

These two remarkable women were to become long-term friends. They understood each other: each responded to the other's edge and precision of outlook. They were like runners or acrobats, sizing up each other's form. Audrey, who dressed with the utmost simplicity, admired the elegant severity of Edith Head's clothes. Miss Head, in turn, carefully noted the studied, seemingly effortless, but immaculate informality of Audrey's white, tailored man's shirt turned into a shirtwaist blouse, her full-bodied, pleated skirt flaring out from a twenty-inch waist, and her flat, almost balletic shoes — all bought off the rack. She was fascinated by the clean-cut, athletic lines of Audrey's body: no fat, no bust, almost no hips even, and the long legs. She was all angles, like a Braque painting. The danger would be to use her as a mere clotheshorse, or a mannequin.

Edith had to dress Audrey in two modes: as a princess and as a commoner. She was surprised to find that Audrey had very strong views on both, and had even made her own sketches. Edith showed her a rich brocade design for a royal gown, embellished with stars and other insignia of office, to be worn with elegant, elbow-length gloves. Audrey liked the designs but wondered how she could face up to wearing anything so pretentious. Edith suggested that Audrey wear falsies, only to discover that she was wearing them already. For the princess's streetwear in Rome, she settled on a modification of Audrey's own clothing. She used a little dark suit with white Eton collar and cuffs, which Audrey wore to one meeting, and variations of a man's shirt, rolling up the sleeves just below the elbow in an oddly masculine touch. Audrey herself suggested a heavy leather belt to emphasize her waist and, together, the two women devised a gathered cotton skirt that flared out fully, with bobby sox over stockings and, of course, flat shoes. Audrey also thought of a tiny detail: making the skirt of a particularly dull fabric and cutting it almost to ankle length, not fitting it perfectly to the hips, so as to suggest someone who was totally indifferent to fashion.

The result of these meetings, which took many hours and sometimes days, was not only a fastidiously designed wardrobe for the princess of the story but the forging of a powerful friendship between the two women. Just how adept Audrey was in managing her burgeoning career can be determined from their association. She had an instinct for the sources of power and at once knew how to form powerful alliances.

Not that Audrey was cold or calculating in her ambition; it was simply that she knew what was good for her. She was going to travel first class, come what may. Edith Head told me she had seldom been so impressed. She had worked with the greatest — Bette Davis, Joan Crawford, Barbara Stanwyck. But these were warhorses, long since streamlined by struggle. Audrey was a newcomer, but she had, as Edith Head described it to me, "the assurance of a veteran. She would laugh and curl up on the floor (which she always preferred to a chair) and tuck her legs under her like an adorable, naive, utterly innocent schoolgirl, and then she would say, with a sweetness that cut like a knife to the heart of the problem, 'I don't think the princess would be quite so shrewd, Edith darling, as to use that *particular* décolletage!' and I would think, 'Oh, my God, if she doesn't get to the top I'll eat Hedda Hopper's hats!'"

Gigi was still playing to packed houses in May when a very irritated Gilbert Miller was forced, by his run-of-the-play agreement with Audrey and with Paramount, to close the production, although he did retain his condition that Audrey would tour with the play that fall. She desperately needed a break; but so tight was the Paramount schedule and so impatient was the studio's production chief, Y. Frank Freeman, to get started, that she had to go straight from the closing night's performance of *Gigi* to her apartment, snatch a few hours' sleep, rise at dawn to pack, and then fly to Rome, with scarcely a chance to draw breath. She was very tired, but it was difficult to sleep on the plane during the long flight to Rome in those pre-jet days; and when she arrived, a mob of the ferocious Italian paparazzi, the scavengers of the local press, terrified her as she stepped down the gangway. It took all of her self-control not to flinch at the ceaselessly flashing bulbs.

She was asked about her marriage plans, but refused to answer. She had been forced to tell James Hanson that she could not consider the wedding until after *Roman Holiday* was finished, although she did say that she would try to squeeze it in before the *Gigi* tour. She still loved him, but she was tortured by her mother's dislike of him and about the thought of life in Huddersfield. Her career drew her, but she was so intensely self-conscious about the thought of appearing in a starring role opposite Gregory Peck, then at the height of his fame, that she also wanted to feel that she could fall back on marriage and children if her career as a star was to be short-lived.

The truth was that, even after her triumph in *Gigi*, Audrey was still unhappy with herself and with the way she photographed. Because of her irregular teeth, she was afraid of smiling with her mouth open; she knew how deadly the camera's eye could be, seeking out every possible flaw. True, her tiny proportions were protected by her own and Edith Head's wizardry, but she was jittery about her very thin arms, like the elongated arms of a fourteen-year-old girl rather than those of a mature woman; and about the fact that the styles of that period did not allow for long sleeves. Now, along with her self-consciousness, she had to cope with the needling questions, the tugs at her sleeve, the commands to turn around again and again and smile. Even the team of Paramount publicists could not quite shield her, and only halfheartedly tried to do so: they wanted as many stories in print as the traffic would bear. For the first time Audrey knew what it meant to be a star, and she wasn't entirely sure that she liked it. It was the first inkling that the price of fame was the sacrifice of an even greater privilege: the right to be a human being.

Audrey scarcely had time to powder her nose at the Excelsior Hotel before attending a very elaborate party organized by the studio in her own and Gregory Peck's honor. She was, as any girl in 1952 would have been, very excited to meet the great Hollywood star. He was then just past his thirty-sixth birthday: the very image of a tall, lean, handsome, all-American matinee idol. He exuded the qualities that were valued most highly during the Eisenhower era: moral integrity, clean-cut decency, and goodwill. He had made his reputation as the priest in *The Keys of the Kingdom*, the Florida farmer in *The Yearling,* and the crusading journalist in *Gentleman's Agreement*. At the party, Audrey was so overpowered by his handshake that she was speechless. She acted more like a fan than a co-star, and Gregory Peck was very amused. A kind, considerate man, he decided from the beginning that he would have to work to give this girl confidence. He also knew, in a spirit of cheerful resignation the moment he saw her, that once she was on the screen he would be reduced to nothing much more than a foil.

Audrey also met with William Wyler, whose stocky, jug-eared charm barely concealed a driving dynamo and a perfectionist of rare concentration and intensity. He was not in the best of tempers at the party. The studio front office had fought him savagely over his decision to shoot the entire picture in Rome. This was not only because Paramount felt it would be impossible to take over an entire city in days when American pictures were normally made in studios, but also because Wyler himself had always made studio-bound movies, and was not a part of the new school of Hollywood directors who were seeking realism by shooting on location. As part of his deal, Wyler had had to sacrifice filming the picture in color, which would have sent costs even higher, thus preventing him from showing Rome in all of its glory.

Although Audrey, Wyler, Gregory Peck, and everyone else

involved with *Roman Holiday* in that summer of 1952 strove to convince the crowds of spectators and the press that the production was without problems, making the movie was, in fact, something of an ordeal for everybody concerned. First, the assistant director and the production manager had to figure out the nightmare logistics of clearing the crowded streets for shooting at all hours of the day or night. Barricades had to be set up, taxi routes disrupted, trams stopped or diverted, buildings emptied of tourists, public monuments deprived of conducted tours, bribes paid to everyone. Above all, the greatest of challenges had to be contended with: the constant noise of Rome. The Klaxon horns, the screams of vendors, the yells of cabdrivers quarreling with their passengers over fares, the buzzing of planes overhead, and the constant babble of beggars — all had to be suppressed so that sequences would be audible. Even a temporary silence in Rome was not complete because of the constant splashing of fountains and the fluttering of the great army of pigeons that seemed to emerge from the very stone itself.

Moreover, it proved impossible to control or quiet the Italian crowds that came to watch the picture being shot every day and night. Ironically, the essence of the film's romantic theme was that the runaway princess and her journalist lover would find secret places in which to tryst — the base of an ornamental fountain, a statue's stone plinth, a small clump of greenery, the back of a museum — seemingly every public place in the city from the Baths of Caracalla to the Pantheon was used as a setting for romance. Yet while these intimate scenes were shot, it seemed as though half of Rome was present, shouting and yelling and pointing and making faces at the stars. Moreover, Audrey and Peck, who were supposed to be cool, relaxed, and enjoying their quiet affair, were, in fact, on edge, suffering from the intense heat of the worst summer in Roman history. The heat was so brutal that the makeup melted and ran down their faces. They often had to leave the scene to be washed down like boxers, and shooting usually began at dawn and continued until after midnight.

The actress Margaret Rawlings, today Lady Barlow, who appeared with Audrey in *Roman Holiday,* will never forget the heat in which the picture was made. It was so hot that although she and Audrey shared a room in a palazzo in which to change, they scarcely exchanged a word, even when a weird sort of packed lunch would be brought in. The work was so concentrated that both felt the need to conserve their energy — every scrap of it.

In one scene, a repeat of the test scene of Audrey waking up in bed, she was so overcome by the heat that she upset the breakfast tray, while what Lady Barlow calls "the rat Wyler" insisted on take after take. The candles in the wall brackets melted and hung down like limp bananas, whereupon the crew had to rush around replacing them. Lady Barlow noticed that Audrey scarcely ate anything, and allowed herself only a sip of champagne. To this day, she is full of admiration for the way the young actress disciplined herself and controlled her emotions.

To make matters worse, the political situation in the city was dangerous and violent that summer. All through the shooting, the Fascists and Communists were battling in the streets, and there were sudden explosions and rattles of gunfire. The May elections had just ended, and there were political incidents, killings and maimings, that left a blood-drenched wake when the Christian Democrats struggled for power. Communists were caught carrying TNT; five terrorists were discovered with explosives under a bridge scheduled for the next day's shooting; strikes constantly threatened to disrupt the work; and torchlight marches with everyone yelling in unison or singing populist anthems ruined the schedules. It was incredible that William Wyler should tell his biographer, Axel Madsen, that everything during the shooting of *Roman Holiday* was a joy; it was, in fact, unmitigated hell.

The work itself was slow and difficult. A joyous motor-scooter chase with Audrey and Peck was achieved only through the most heroic and exhausting efforts. Aside from the heat, Wyler was unused to location work and was fretful, often angry, at the lack of discipline of the Italian crew and the lack of control of an actual city after the airless, artificial world of the studio. He dragged Audrey and Gregory Peck through take after take, sometimes as many as sixty in an afternoon, but it says much for Audrey's nature that she did not resent this, since she, too, was seeking perfection and was only too painfully aware of her shortcomings that such repeated efforts might be able to overcome. In most work, Wyler had a maddening tendency to let the actors simply get on with the scene, give them no encouragement or praise (for which all actors hunger), and simply say coldly, while smiling his mischievous smile, "Let's do it again." But he did overrule himself in the case of Audrey, doing everything to bolster her assurance and unleash her naturalness and vivacity. He told me that what he had to do was have her forget to "act" and, instead, just "be." He was teaching her the first lesson of star movie acting: to respond with inner feeling and not to play "at" the camera, since that sensitive instrument would pick up every nuance of thought in a sincere and honest human being. Falsity or overt thespianism would be brutally exposed by the camera's probing eye.

Audrey was greatly irritated by newspaper reports linking her romantically with Gregory Peck. He was consistently thoughtful to her, sensing her insecurity and awe of him, and he unselfishly "fed" her scene after scene, resigned to the fact that she and not he — worthy, decent actor that he was — was already walking off with the picture. But there was no sexual involvement between them. Audrey was totally involved in her work, and was writing to James Hanson, who was now on his way to Canada to deal with the agents of his family trucking firm. Part of her still looked forward to the marriage, impossible though that might seem. Peck, too, was preoccupied — he was unhappy because his wife Greta was breaking up with him. He was making plans to move out of the villa the studio had rented for them to take their children out of town. With a crumbling marriage, Peck was in no mood to live out in real life the blissful romantic fantasy of the movie script.

It says much for the professionalism of the stars that, in fact, no trace of their discomfiture appears on the screen in a movie that still glows with effortless gaiety and charm. Wyler put the stars through their paces in memorable scenes: a dance on a barge on the River Tiber followed by a fistfight; a meeting at the Trevi Fountain; a tryst at the Castel Sant' Angelo and the Piazza Barberini. *Roman Holiday* was a perfectly sustained fantasy for armchair travelers.

During the shooting, cameraman Franz Planer, an Austrian of enormous charm and talent whom Audrey adored, fell out with Wyler and was replaced by Henri Alekan, on the invented grounds that Planer was ill.

Henri Alekan remembers his joy in working with Audrey in spite of everything. He writes, "My contacts with her were most amicable and I appreciated her intelligence and finesse during several dinners in her delicious company. Her charm and her great sensibility undoubtedly had much to do with the immense success of the film. She never complained, and I was impressed by her delicate will."

In one scene, which was being shot at 3 A.M. in a bower next to the Forum, a huge water cooler suddenly fell off the wall and Wyler screamed "Cut!" Audrey moaned and put her face in her hands. There were other difficult days. There was a sequence at the Colosseum that took twenty-two hours to shoot; it took place at the Wishing Wall, where during an air raid a man had asked to be spared from death. When a bomb had fallen nearby, it failed to explode. The man had put a plaque on the wall expressing his thanks to God, and when Audrey and Peck appeared they saw many such plaques. They told each other that shooting there might be a mistake, since this was a shrine, but, Peck recalled later, "Hundreds of people came with fresh flowers the first day we shot there — it was a steady stream to the shrine altar a few yards from the cameras. The people prayed, then watched in silence as we shot the scene."

The picture was finished at last in September. Audrey was not allowed any rest. Because of the delays caused by the change of cameraman, she had to go straight into the exhausting road tour of *Gigi* for which Gilbert Miller had contracted her; theaters had been booked all across the country and the bookings had to be held firm for limited runs. Audrey longed to fly to Canada to see Hanson, but it was hopeless, and it became clear to her that there could be no marriage now. Hanson, however, optimistically still made plans.

Audrey embarked on the tour quite worn out. Most young people would not have hesitated, but she was so frail, so weakened by the privations of the war, that she felt much older than her years. The baroness did her best with nostrums and vitamins. She kept up her pressure on Audrey (according to Cathleen Nesbitt) to end her relationship with Hanson once and for all. At last, Audrey gave up the struggle and announced on the play's opening in Chicago that it was all over. Miss Nesbitt recalled: "The wedding dress was waiting and the whole of Huddersfield was agog with excitement. How relieved her mother was! 'Imagine Audrey living in a huddle of horses in Huddersfield,' she moaned . . ."

Meanwhile, word was leaking out that Audrey was a sensation in *Roman Holiday.* Wyler told me, "As I saw the rushes (which Audrey would not see, so uncomfortable was she with her appearance in photographs), I had that rare gut feeling that I was witnessing something very special, indeed. She *was* a princess — she had so much poise, no doubt from her experience as a dancer and from her mother's aristocratic background. But she was also every eager young girl who has ever come to Rome for the first time, and she reacted with so natural and spontaneous an eagerness that I, crusty veteran that I was, felt tears in my eyes watching her. Audrey was the spirit of youth — and I knew that very soon the entire world would fall in love with her, as all of us on the picture did." One of those who would never forget her, and who was to work with her again and again, was Franz Planer, whose "illness" was relieved by Audrey's constant gentle concern and affection.

It was immediately time to prepare another vehicle for Audrey. While briefly in New York before the tour of *Gigi,* Audrey had read *Sabrina Fair,* a slight but appealing comedy by Samuel Taylor about a Long Island chauffeur's daughter who is tranformed from goose to swan after a trip to Paris. It was soon to be played on the stage by the mercurial and difficult Margaret Sullavan. Although Audrey was not yet a star, with great boldness, she asked her agent Lew Wasserman to have Paramount buy the play as a vehicle for her. When they got wind of her potential and ran the picture, the Paramount executives decided *Roman Holiday* would launch her spectacularly, and agreed to do as she asked.

Billy Wilder, the tough, cynical, and supremely self-confident Austrian director who had achieved a great triumph with such films as *Double Indemnity, The Lost Weekend,* and *Stalag 17,* was hired to direct the screen version of *Sabrina Fair.* A rather peculiar and not very inviting studio publicity release at that time read as follows: "The man who brought you *The Lost Weekend* and *Stalag 17* now brings you a new romance . . ." However, the choice of Wilder was not as strange as it might have seemed. He had grown up as a writer for Ernst Lubitsch, the great German director who specialized in bittersweet romantic comedies spun from the imaginary lives of a highly romanticized European upper class. Wilder decided from the outset to take the rather feeble drama of *Sabrina Fair* and turn it into a romantic comedy of manners in the Lubitsch mold.

Audrey was pleased to hear that Edith Head — the reigning queen of Hollywood fashion and a contractee at Paramount — had once again been engaged to create her costumes. Miss Head flew to San Francisco to visit with Audrey, who was completing the run of *Gigi* there. Edith took with her tiny drawings of Audrey, plain stick figures on which she and Audrey could together sketch a wardrobe for a young girl with no money, before her transformation in Paris. Audrey once against overflowed with exciting ideas. The sessions were long and concentrated, designer and actress achieving an even deeper rapport as they discovered each other's unlimited discipline and perfectionism.

On days when there was no matinee, Edith and Audrey would go shopping together, delighting store clerks as Audrey would try on her size eight or nine, celebrating the discovery of a particular dress with a whoop of delight and an unexpected announcement of a treat she had in mind. Usually, the treat would make diet-conscious Edith quail: five chocolate éclairs would be consumed by stick-thin Audrey in one go, or she would eat a jumbo-sized banana nut sundae or a coconut cream pie. Edith would gingerly nibble a few bites while Audrey cheerfully consumed eight hundred calories at a clip, confident that she would never gain an ounce. She would talk nonstop about starving in Arnhem as she bought a large box containing several pounds of richly filled chocolates. By 1953, she had already become a hopeless chocoholic.

This pleasant interlude was followed by a disappointing blow. Edith Head was convinced that she would naturally be designing Audrey's entire wardrobe for *Sabrina,* as the picture was now called — most importantly, the costumes for the Paris sequences and the clothes that the young girl would bring back with her to make a conquest of the son of the rich Long Island family. But Miss Head was cooly informed that Mr. Wilder had reached a momentous decision: the costumes would be designed by a leading Paris couturier, Hubert de Givenchy, and Miss Head would ignominiously be confined to the clothes of Cinderella *before* the transformation scene.

This was a severe blow to the egotistical little woman who thought she was empress of the rag trade in Hollywood. Audrey was also shocked, but with her customary steely logic she saw the wisdom of the decision and of course, as most young girls would have been, was excited by the idea of being dressed by a Parisian designer. With great and genuine apologies to Edith, Audrey flew to Paris for a meeting with Givenchy.

The Marquis Hubert de Givenchy had just turned twenty-six in 1953, and he was already providing formidable competition for the even younger Yves St. Laurent. Givenchy was a case of the man who has everything. He was descended from the wealthy owners of the Gobelin and Beauvais tapestry companies. Extremely tall — about six foot six — strikingly handsome with perfectly formed features, dark hair, and romantically dark eyes, he had begun his career as a law student but, before obtaining his baccalauréat, had abandoned the course suggested by his parents and had, with their backing and blessing, started working in fashion houses. He began with the House of Lelong as a slender teenager of eighteen, and then proceeded, driven by high ambition, money, and talent, to successive positions with Piquet, Jacques Fath, and Madame Elsa Schiaparelli until he formed his own salon on the Avenue Georges Cinq just exactly a year before Audrey arrived in Paris.

When Audrey met Givenchy for the first time that summer of 1953, she could not have known that he would forever be as closely associated with her as her own skin, that he would be as much a creator of the Audrey Hepburn persona as her own remarkable will.

Givenchy's designs, which reflected his love of classic art and sculpture, were drawn from the simple lines of Greek friezes. Since Audrey herself had a figure of geometric spareness, she was ideally suited to Givenchy's creative approach. She responded equally to the designer's austerity of nature, to absolute simplicity of style reflected in straight lines, boxed or bowed shoulders, subdued off-whites, blacks, and delicate pastels that ideally complemented her angular figure. Givenchy's designs most subtly and cleverly feminized Audrey and gave her a sexy quality that a less-adept designer might have failed to do.

Pictures of Givenchy at the time show him alighting from a glittering black Citroën, in a handmade French suit that impeccably fit his fineboned, slender frame. Fond as he was of tennis, riding, and the country, where he was soon to acquire a beautiful farmhouse, he was to Audrey a supremely urban animal — the very expression of wealth, cultivation, and good breeding.

Givenchy, in turn, was captivated by Audrey's informal man-tailored shirt, self-designed skirts, and ballet shoes which, together, created an extremely feminine effect. He discussed with her her own excellent ideas for the designs that would express the Long Island Cinderella's metamorphosis. He designed one very effective cocktail dress of black silk with a small, square-cut neckline fastened by tiny bows at the shoulders that discreetly asked to be undone. The bateau neckline thus accentuated was complemented by a tiny jeweled hat. Givenchy also captivated Audrey with his sketches for a ravishing white ballgown of fairy-tale elegance and beauty. By a delicate irony, Edith Head was awarded an Oscar for these two dresses, and Givenchy was too much of a gentleman to make a public complaint. It is probable that the formidable Miss Head had it in her contract that she and she alone would receive screen credit for each and any of the clothes in the picture, shrewdly foreseeing the possibility of being double-crossed in a manner that would be something along the lines of what actually did take place. Audrey flew back to Hollywood after just one week in Paris, carrying with her Givenchy's portfolio of sketches which Edith Head would now physically execute with her own team — an arrangement with which the infuriated designer had to be more or less content.

During the making of *Sabrina*, Audrey had immediate rapport with Billy Wilder, who confirmed her feelings about herself when he gave an interview to a reporter to which she took not the least exception, speaking of "the peculiar ugly face of that dame." Of medium height, stocky and muscular, with a face like that of an aging troll, Wilder may have looked like a boxer but had the brain of a wit. He was dangerously sharp and ruthlessly on target. For example, Ray Milland once claimed that while making *The Lost Weekend* he had disguised himself as a patient at Bellevue Hospital in New York and had himself admitted as an alcoholic. He then fled the hospital in the middle of the night in pajamas and robe, just as the failed writer Don Brinam had done in the novel. Asked about this, Billy Wilder smiled. He said, "Very interesting. It's the first I heard of it, but who am I to contradict a fellow director?"

Audrey had always had a delightful sense of humor, and was very amused when somebody she knew asked Wilder his opinion of her. He said, "She gives me the distinct impression she can spell schizophrenia." That said it all.

Audrey was looking forward to making *Sabrina* more than ever, now that she had met the director. But it would not have been a Hollywood movie, nor any movie, had it not been fraught with aggravation from the first minute of shooting to the last.

Chapter Five

One of *Sabrina*'s chief problems was Humphrey Bogart. Cary Grant had originally been offered the part of the older brother who finally falls in love with the chauffeur's daughter (Audrey) and marries her, instead of the part of the playboy younger brother. But Grant didn't want to play a stuffed-shirt business-man, and Paramount cast Bogart in his place. Unfortunately, Bogey was at his very worst that year. He had just finished playing Captain Queeg in *The Caine Mutiny* and still identified with the suspicious, miserable ship's commander of Herman Wouk's celebrated novel. Bogart was so much on the defensive you could almost see the snarl on his face.

Audrey was shocked to find that Bogey was the exact opposite of the laconic, indifferent, super-cool Rick in *Casablanca*. He was irritable, edgy, still somewhat paranoid. He was drinking more than was good for him, and he emphat-ically did not like Audrey. As far as he was concerned, she was simply a rank beginner and an unknown who had no right to appear with him in a major film that he hadn't wanted to do in the first place. It is possible that he also hoped Lauren Bacall, whose career in 1953 had taken a dip, might have played Sabrina — a part to which she would have been quite unsuited. Insult was added to injury when Wilder told a reporter the reason that Bogart, not William Holden (who played his younger brother), wound up with Audrey in the last shot. "Because," Wilder characteristically replied, "Bogart gets $300,000 a picture and Holden $125,000."

83

Mrs. Billy Wilder recalls: "Bogey was forbidden access to the regular after-hours drinks we all enjoyed together. The reason was, we just didn't think he was fun to be with. Excluded, ostracized, he reacted with anger and became worse than ever. This caused extreme tension on the picture."

While Bogart disliked Audrey, and she had most coolly to tolerate this disdain, William Holden, by contrast, utterly fell in love with her. She was, in turn, very strongly attracted to him. He was then at the height of his career after his Academy Award-winning performance in *Stalag 17* and his extraordinary portrayal of the disillusioned-writer-turned-hustler in *Sunset Boulevard,* in which he made an ideal foil for Gloria Swanson's bizarre and eccentric old silent-movie star. He was a "man's man" — naturally athletic, broad-shouldered, with a boxer's hands — who exuded a deceptive aura of security and masculine certainty. Audrey was drawn to Holden's tweed jackets, knitted ties, slight aroma of cigarettes and Scotch, crinkly brow, and kind, deep-seeing eyes. He of course was drawn to Audrey's complementary qualities of frailty, delicacy, and quiet femininity. The result was inevitably explosive, and a real problem existed.

Holden was very much married. His wife Ardis, whose screen name was Brenda Marshall, was a statuesque brunette with striking good looks and presence. He also had a family of two handsome boys and an older daughter — pictures of the time show Holden, sleeves rolled up, talking to his sons while the young girl perches on a coffee table.

The Norman Rockwell-type living room of the Holdens' Toluca Lake home exuded Middle American solidity, with white scrubbed-pine walls, chintz, overstuffed furniture, and crackling open hearth. There were family games everywhere. And it was all part of a myth, because even before Audrey's advent the home was torn apart by Holden's anxious hunger for ego gratification in the arms of admiring women. The smiling Brenda Marshall, the very picture of the Hollywood housewife, was in fact a miserable woman — tormented by Holden's promiscuity and shocking habit of bringing women home to meet his wife.

As Audrey was soon to discover, behind Holden's rugged exterior was an anxiety-ridden and deeply neurotic (though warm and generous) individual whose nicotine-stained fingers and liquor breath spoke of many tormented midnights. A hypochondriac, he worried about his sexual performance, nibbled on health pills, used sunlamps to sustain a winter tan, struggled with severe ulcers, and was convinced he had a heart problem which, in fact, he did not. He would rush to doctors every time he felt a chest pain, which was usually caused by nervous indigestion. He was the type of man who would board a plane with the total conviction that the free drinks would wind up in his lap — and more than once they did.

Holden was therefore not the ideal man with whom to have an affair. He had a tendency to blow his lines and, as a result, he unsettled Audrey, who allegedly blew hers. Bogart, who was letter perfect, was furious, complaining in a loud and grumbling voice to all who would listen that Audrey was just a snit who thought she could act; who couldn't do a scene in less than twelve takes; who was conspiring with Holden against him because she was giving Holden a tumble; and who, as he directly charged her more than once, came to him with rings under her eyes because she was visiting with Holden night after night. He detested Holden, who insisted on going through an ultra-macho trick of rolling his own cigarettes with a well-licked forefinger, using a disagreeable variety of Gaulois tobacco, and then puffing the smoke directly in Bogey's face. Audrey herself smoked Goldflake cigarettes brought from England and put into a filter holder. The air resembled London in a sulfurous fog. To make matters worse, Bogart was a physical coward, and when Holden told him to put his fists up he wouldn't. Even worse, Bogey kept calling Wilder a Nazi; this "Kraut bastard, Nazi son-of-a-bitch" was in fact Jewish and had lost several of his family at Auschwitz.

In competition with the others, Bogart also began to forget his lines, grumbled about the homburg and pepper-and-salt trousers he had to wear, and told reporters that *Sabrina* was "a crock of you know what."

Given this degree of tension on the set, Audrey sought

relaxation by wearing the Givenchy gowns, pedaling a chrome-and-aluminum bicycle from Wilder around the lot, and enjoying the welcome arrival each afternoon of her beloved waiter Herman from Lucey's, the famous eatery near Paramount, with tea on a tray and Dutch cookies sent by her mother from London, where the baroness was now living. On weekends, if Holden was with his family, she would enjoy that pleasure for a celebrity of being entirely alone from Friday night until Monday morning. In her pleasant two-room apartment on Wilshire Boulevard, she would relax in old clothes, listen to Sinatra records, steam a chicken with water, onion, and a sprig of tarragon, drink tea, and just loaf. She would also intermittently study her lines. These were the times when she could refuel, collect her thoughts, and consider the future.

During the shooting of *Sabrina*, an episode occurred which lightened the tension of the work. The king and queen of Greece visited the set. Wilder, with typical humor, got hold of the thrones used in the Bob Hope picture *Monsieur Beaucaire*, obtained a red carpet, and placed the thrones at the top of a flight of steps in the Long Island mansion set, with the red carpet leading up to them. The king and queen were embarrassed into laughter by this absurd arrangement. Feeling very awkward, Audrey led her fellow players up the steps, not knowing whether to curtsy or not. Suddenly, just as she reached the thrones, an electrician called out to Her Greek Majesty, "Hey, Queen, where were you last night when I needed you to fill a straight?" Everyone burst out laughing.

In contrast with this amusing episode, Audrey soon faced another major problem. *Sabrina* was shifted to Glen Cove, Long Island, for the sequences that were shot outdoors at the house. Shrewdly, Paramount used the estate of its own chairman, Barney Balaban, an arrangement which also provided a convenient tax deduction. While staying at a local hotel, Holden made a painful confession to Audrey: he could no longer have children. He had had a vasectomy, and he felt acutely guilty about it. In his biography of Holden, Bob

Thomas says that Audrey was so affected by this news that she decided she could not contemplate marriage with him. It is doubtful that this interpretation is correct. Given her character, it is much more likely that she never seriously contemplated marrying Holden in the first place. Even though his marriage was a wreck, she was not the type of person to destroy what was left of a marriage, deal with a grown daughter and two grown sons — all of whom might well resent her — and face the public calumny that would result from charges of encouraging adultery and being a homewrecker. She certainly could not cope with anything as sordid as this. Another possible reason for her reluctance could have been that Holden was prone to travel extensively, and their schedules would have torn them apart again and again. Given the logic that had caused her to sever her relationship with James Hanson, it would be reasonable to assume that she decided with equal firmness that there was to be no future with Holden.

Her decision not to go ahead with Holden affected him very profoundly. Years later I was on a talk show with him in Chicago when the host, rather boldly, asked him with whom had he been most deeply and truly in love? His face, deeply creased and pouched from years of heavy drinking, suddenly became more intensely sad than before, and through a cloud of cigarette smoke he said two words, "Audrey Hepburn."

Henry Gris says that Audrey would never have married Holden because the one consuming ambition in her life, apart from her career, was to become a mother. It was almost an obsession with her, and she especially wanted sons. Therefore, she needed not only a husband who was capable of fathering children but also one who had the correct combination of mental and physical qualities. Even if Holden had been fertile, his neurotic personality and heavy drinking would not have been the answer to Audrey Hepburn's dreams. In fact, Henry Gris, who is very close to Hepburn, says that he very much doubts if she even went to bed with Holden. It seems unlikely at first glance because Holden, whatever else he may have been, was then at the height of his physical prowess, youth, and attractiveness, and Audrey Hepburn was in the first flowering of her beauty. But it seems that Holden suffered from recurring potency problems and Audrey, if Henry Gris is to be believed, had very little sexual drive.

Within days of completing *Sabrina,* which wound up on a New York location, Audrey, weary of the Holden situation, flew to London for the premiere of *Roman Holiday* on August 20, 1953. She had tried not to think about the reviews or the public reception of her as a star during the making of *Sabrina,* because such thoughts could have affected her performance. Now she was pleased to learn that the advance reviews had appeared in Hollywood and were on their way to her in London. The trade papers were talking of a new Garbo. They were ecstatic about her vitality, beauty (still disliking her image, she shrugged with amazement at that), and unspoiled charm and style. It was agreed that there was nobody quite like her in pictures. She was like a marvelous changeling rather than a creature of flesh and blood. She had the quality of someone who came from a better, purer world. Her gazelle-like eyes, high cheekbones, attractively irregular smile (how she still hated those misaligned molars!), and elfin chin dazzled men and women alike. The newspaper reviews were equally enthusiastic and, wonder of wonders, even the intellectuals embraced Audrey. She was perhaps more highly thought of by critics than any other star of her period, and still continues to be. Bosley Crowther of the New York *Times* wrote that she was "alternately regal and childlike, in her profound appreciation of newly found simple pleasures . . . ," and most critics concurred. Doubtful as she was about her own accomplishments, and convinced that she was not photogenic, Audrey could scarcely fail to be delighted by all that was being said about her. Within a week she was internationally famous, her image relayed on newsreels all over the world. Television, then in its first bloom, celebrated her as well. Without meaning to, she also brought off a master stroke — by avoiding publicity, passing up most interviews, and refusing to be excessively swamped by the press, she became even more special and did not suffer from the deadliest of dangers for a newcomer: overexposure.

At the premiere in London, she was seen to hide her face throughout much of the screening. Indeed, it is likely that she would have hidden in the ladies' room throughout if she could. She found it extremely unnerving to watch herself walking and talking on the screen, and she was far too intelligent to display the blind, empty-headed narcissism of so many stars. Indeed, in her self-criticism and discomfort with her image, she laid the groundwork for perfection. She was like a young athlete who starts with physical disadvantages that may not be visible to others and relentlessly works to overcome them.

At the elaborate party after the premiere, Gregory Peck introduced Audrey to a great friend of his — and a partner in the La Jolla Playhouse — the director, actor, and writer Mel Ferrer. Audrey had seen Ferrer twice in what had become one of her favorite movies, *Lili*, in which he played a puppet master in love with a plain but sweet-natured young girl played by Leslie Caron. Audrey adored Ferrer's performance, and she told him so. She also was, to his surprise, fully familiar with his work at La Jolla and with his impressive performances as the celebrated torero in *The Brave Bulls* and the black-clad villain of the costume drama *Scaramouche*. On the rebound from Holden, Audrey felt an immediate attraction to this charismatic leading man.

Ferrer was then just thirty-five years old. He was tall, with a carved, El Greco face, deep-set dark eyes, high cheekbones, and a beautifully chiseled jawline. His spare, tough body was well coordinated; he was a skillful fencer and tennis player. He was also gifted with considerable intelligence, far above that normally possessed by Hollywood leading men. The problem was that he was a man of too many parts: he was adept in so many fields that no single achievement placed him quite in the first class. He was fragmented, and frustrated by the very range of his own abilities. This eclecticism made him restless, volatile, and high-strung; he could not settle into a semblance of a mold.

Ferrer had dropped out of Princeton in his sophomore year,

upsetting his Irish-American heiress mother (one of the O'Donahues of New York) and his Cuban-Spanish father. He was too edgy and restless to concentrate on his studies. He dabbled in summer stock, went off to Taxco in Mexico to struggle with a first novel, turned up in a printer's shop in Vermont, danced as Clifton Webb's protégé on Broadway, worked at various odd jobs, and emerged as the author of a children's book entitled *Tito's Hat*. He was making some headway on Broadway when he was stricken with polio and his right arm shriveled. He worked out with a flatiron to return the arm to normalcy. He shifted to Hollywood, under the spell of the director D. W. Griffith, directed screen tests for David O. Selznick, worked for Howard Hughes, and at last achieved success as a black doctor passing for white in the movie *Lost Boundaries*.

Unfortunately, Ferrer lacked the warmth, sheer animalism, and brute force that would have ensured him enormous popular success. He failed to cross the great gulf between leading man and star. There was a certain stiffness about his acting that didn't exactly spell woodenness, but didn't spell electricity either. He failed the all-important test — he did not provoke sexual longings in millions of women; he did not evoke fantasies. He seemed a bit above the crowd.

But in 1953, Mel Ferrer was still something of a name to conjure with, and Audrey could not help but be impressed by his sharpness, quick humor, and good looks. And she was soon to discover his ultimate attraction — he spoke several languages, and could converse with her in French.

Audrey flew on to the Venice Film Festival, her head buzzing with excitement. Indeed, had she not been so realistic, cool, and controlled, she might have lost her head at the combination of sudden success, rave reviews, a glittering premiere in London, and the advent of a man whom she liked so much. But she kept her counsel, and the baroness, as always, was there to disapprove of any romantic thoughts and to discourage Audrey from any relationship with a man. She hadn't approved of Holden, and Ferrer was certainly not in his class; there was no way she would approve of him. Or of any other man, for that matter, in the future.

The excellent public reception of *Roman Holiday* was followed by a great stroke of luck. The newspapers picked up a useful parallel in the fact that England's Princess Margaret had everybody in a spin because she was going to marry a commoner, society photographer Antony Armstrong-Jones. This earned an untold number of column inches. However, surprisingly, *Roman Holiday* did not do quite as well in the domestic market as everyone had hoped. Perhaps part of the problem was that it was set in Europe, and many Americans in that pre-jet age, who had not been in Europe, were puzzled by the unfamiliar accents, characters, and settings. By December, *Variety*, the show-business bible, was reporting that *Roman Holiday,* which had been expected to gross five million dollars in domestic rentals, was now expected to make only three million. *Variety* said, "This is strong coin, of course, but forty percent under the amount anticipated. Reason for the less-impressive returns is puzzling . . . observing that business was good but should have been better, a circuit operator in the East commented. 'The picture was very delightful. Maybe the public isn't high on delightful pictures anymore.'"

However, Audrey became hugely popular and her short haircut achieved an international vogue. Outside of the United States, *Roman Holiday* was a smash hit. It was an outright triumph in Japan, where it became legendary and where Audrey Hepburn haircuts were especially the rage. In the Scandinavian countries, it was the most successful Paramount picture released up to that time, surpassing even Cecil B. De Mille's circus spectacle, *The Greatest Show on Earth.* By early 1954, it was clear that the picture would make ten million dollars worldwide — earning substantial profits for the studio and fully justifying its gamble with its new star.

Time magazine's publisher Henry Luce responded to Audrey so strongly that he advised his editors to profile her on the front cover of the issue of September 7, 1953. This was almost unheard-of for a complete newcomer. *Time* described

Audrey as "exquisitely blending queenly dignity and bubbling mischief," a "stick-slim actress with huge, limpid eyes and a heart-shaped face" who was "teaching U.S. moviegoers . . . a lesson they already knew and loved — i.e., that the life of a princess is not a happy one."

Time went on: "Audrey Hepburn gives the popular old romantic nonsense a reality which it seldom had before. Amid the rhinestone glitter of *Roman Holiday's* make-believe, Paramount's new star sparkles and glows with the fire of a finely cut diamond. Impertinence, hauteur, sudden repentance, happiness, rebellion, and fatigue supplant each other with speed on her mobile, adolescent face."

Billy Wilder told *Time*: "After so many drive-in waitresses in movies — it has been a real drought — here is class, somebody who went to school, can spell and possibly play the piano — she's a wispy, thin little thing, but you're really in the presence of somebody when you see that girl. Not since Garbo has there been anything like her, with the possible exception of Ingrid Bergman."

Audrey returned to Hollywood for some interviews and a couple of dubbing sessions on *Sabrina*. Meanwhile, on a flight from London to New York, Ferrer read the play *Ondine,* by the late playwright Jean Giraudoux. Audrey had told him at their meeting in London that she would like to do a play with him if he could find one that was suitable, and now he had lit upon what would undoubtedly be the ideal vehicle.

Ondine had first been performed with the great Louis Jouvet and the magical actress Madeleine Ozeray at the Théâtre Athenée in Paris on April 27, 1939. Based on a medieval text, it was the story of Hans, a handsome knight-errant caught in the rain who takes refuge in a fisherman's hut in a mythical kingdom. The knight discovers that the fisherman and his wife are sheltering a fifteen-year-old changeling, the water sprite Ondine, who falls in love with the knight. He, in turn, is captivated by her. Ondine is warned by the King of the Water Folk that if Hans deceives her by behaving like all mortal men and proving unfaithful, death will follow; but she doesn't listen. Ondine eventually realizes, however, that Hans is all too mortal, too flawed. He turns against her, confounded by her innocence and unable to bear such purity of feeling. He becomes betrothed to another woman and tries to have Ondine destroyed as a witch. The trial is a black farce and, later, Hans dies according to the laws of the water kingdom. Ondine escapes mortal judgment by fleeing to the aqueous world, which is part of neither life nor death.

By all accounts, the original production was exquisite, irradiated with beauty and conveying the author's master hand with consummate artistry. The play was a symbolic fable of the inability of human beings to deal with innocence and their ultimate need to destroy it. It was at once romantic and disillusioning, realistic and fanciful.

Ferrer was captivated by the play, which he read in French, and flew to Hollywood to tell Audrey how perfect she would be as Ondine. Before he left New York he had already talked The Playwright's Company, a cooperative venture, into financing the play, and he had begun negotiations with the exceptionally difficult Giraudoux estate. He had also obtained the provisional agreement of Alfred Lunt to direct the play. Lunt had starred with his wife Lynn Fontanne in Giraudoux's *Amphitryon 38* before World War II.

Ferrer took Audrey out to dinner. She was fascinated by the idea of playing Ondine, but there was a problem: Paramount naturally wanted her to begin another picture right away. It was not customary for new screen stars to return to the stage — particularly in highly intellectual works that might distance them from mass taste.

With great difficulty, Audrey and her agent managed to persuade the studio to delay any further preparation of vehicles for her in order to allow her to appear on Broadway. At last Paramount yielded on the conditions that the run be limited to six months and that Audrey agree to appear in a picture version if the play succeeded.

Very excited, and already attracted to Ferrer, Audrey flew to New York in the harsh winter of 1953. Almost at once she discovered yet another individual who was to play a crucial role in her career: the celebrated couturiere Valentina.

Valentina, who had been invited to design Audrey's costumes for *Ondine,* had been associated with the Lunts before. She had been the model of, and had designed the costumes for, the character of the eccentric and fake White Russian countess played by Lynn Fontanne in Robert Sherwood's well-known play *Idiot's Delight.* She had also designed the costumes for *Amphitryon 38.*

Valentina and her celebrated husband George Schlee, a man of great wit and style who managed the affairs of his intimate friend Greta Garbo, had escaped the Bolsheviks during the Russian revolution. After a shaky start, Valentina had finally emerged as a couturiere of daring originality and flair. It was often said that her costumes made entrances along with the stars. Among her most imposing customers were the Duchess of Windsor, Queen Marie of Rumania, and Hollywood stars Rosalind Russell, Norma Shearer, and Paulette Goddard.

Valentina had an intensely theatrical personality, living to the hilt her role of high priestess of fashion. Tall, fair and hypnotically beautiful, with a volatile temper and colossal ego, she dressed with melodramatic authority, making sweeping entrances at her celebrated fashion shows wearing a black turban or purple headdress, flowing classical gowns, and dead white makeup.

Audrey paid many visits to Valentina's salon on East 67th Street. The house was as theatrical as its owner. It was arranged like a stage set, designed to impress the visitor and ensure that he got his money's worth. Audrey had to climb from the semicircular reception room, with its polite but frosty receptionist, up a richly carpeted spiral stairway, to the upstairs rooms, where Valentina, in turban and flowing robes, was waiting. There was an elaborate crystal chandelier that added a royal touch to the scene, a beautiful French floral screen, and numerous eighteenth-century French antiques. But the eye was more completely held by a life-size papier-mâché mannequin that stood facing the door. This model of a tall thin woman, sometimes rumored to be based on Garbo, wore an odd brown linen dress, with a stole thrown around its shoulders that trailed all the way to the floor. On the figure's head was a Garbo-type floppy hat. Valentina told Audrey that this was her guinea pig — she tried every new dress on it as an experiment.

At her cluttered desk heaped with drawings, unanswered letters, telephone messages, and receipts, Valentina dramatically explained to Audrey in her Russian accent her visions for *Ondine*. Like others before her, she was amazed to discover that this twenty-four-year-old girl had very strong views of her own. Surrounded by a puzzle of clothing boxes, and flanked by two draped tables covered in gold and pink cloth, Valentina was a marvel of sparkling energy as Audrey's measurements were taken — 34, 20, 34 — and explained to her what she had in mind for the water nymph: a radiant succession of garments of net, shells, and seaweed suggesting a watery world of pale colors and aquatic motifs. She told Audrey that all human beings could be divided into creatures of fire or water; Audrey, of course, was most conveniently of water. She made a mannequin of Audrey out of unbleached muslin, which made Audrey feel slightly uneasy as she saw her likeness join figures of, among others, Lillian Gish, Lilli Palmer, Liz Whitney, and Jennifer Jones in the fourth-floor workshop, where forty-five workers toiled under Valentina's exacting guidance.

Audrey stood without movement or complaint through very long fittings, which were necessary since there had to be a suggestion of nudity in her costumes without the slightest loss of taste. The fishnet covering for one dress actually had to be sewn over her square by square as she stood, and she fretted over the tiniest flaw even more than Valentina. Fortunately, her many hours of dance practice had firmed and strengthened her, giving her an extremely straight, steely back that allowed her to stand for long periods of time without feeling weak or exhausted. Valentina attended all the fittings, personally supervising every stitch, while keeping up a flow of high-powered conversation, usually in a monologue with very few rounded vowels or finished sentences.

At last, the couturiere and her perfectionist model were more or less satisfied. The clothes had the abstract beauty of an illustration by Edmond Dulac for a Hans Christian Andersen fairy tale. In the midst of all these fittings, Audrey was very busy with rehearsals. Director Alfred Lunt was a gentle and tasteful guide; he was courtly and good-natured to a degree. His only differences were with Mel Ferrer, who he felt was usurping the part of director, as well as playing the leading role of Hans. Maurice Zolotow, then with the New York *Times* and today a free-lance journalist and biographer, recalls that Lunt, whom he later commemorated in a biography, complained to him constantly that Ferrer was acting as Audrey's Svengali and simply would not allow her to follow Lunt's direction uncritically. There was constant tension backstage and out front from the first day of rehearsal to the last. Lunt obtained consolation from creating an atmosphere of pure magic that would survive even the New York critics. Lunt told Zolotow: "All the actors are pure because they're not distracted, not worrying about reviews or publicity. They can give themselves up to the illusion, feel what the playwright wanted them to feel. Oh, I promise you a performance so beautiful you'll not be likely to forget it as long as you live."

There was a major problem over Audrey's hair in *Ondine*. Lunt felt that she, being a creature of the watery deep, should be blond, since saltwater bleaches the hair. Audrey was opposed to this, in spite of the fact that, as Lunt pointed out to her, Madeleine Ozeray in the original production had been ash blond. Audrey argued with Lunt over the hair all the way up to the opening night in Boston, and Mel took her part. Then, just a few hours before the Boston opening, she gave in and had her hair bleached. Ferrer hated it as much as she did: it looked false and unreal, and added to her already washed-out appearance. She later had her natural color restored after the first night, and changed to a blond wig. She disliked the wig even more, however. She still looked washed-out, and she told Mel Ferrer that the wig felt "stuffy and hot and horrible," and "dead in the back," and, above all, that she couldn't scratch it without its moving. The arguments with Lunt continued until, at last, she found the solution — she tinted her hair with simulated gold dust each night and washed the dust out after every performance.

On the night *Ondine* opened in Boston, Audrey was in her dressing room making up, feeling butterflies in her stomach. Only fifteen minutes before curtain time, her agent called her from Hollywood to tell her that the first preview of *Sabrina* in Long Beach, California, had been a success; the audience comment cards had raved about her. She tried not to get excited, since excitement could ruin the effect of the first act. It was not until that act was over that Mel Ferrer heard the news and said to her, "Isn't it wonderful?" "Yes, it's all very nice and all very fine," she replied coolly, "but didn't you think the first act went a little too slowly?"

Elliot Norton, the dean of Boston theater critics, gave the first nod of approval and the Bostonian audience was most enthusiastic. When *Ondine* opened in New York, Brooks Atkinson of the *Times* abandoned all his customary caution and unabashedly threw his hat in the air. He described the production as "Ideal from every point of view. Ideal literature, ideal acting, ideal theater — it hardly matters how you approach it." He went on to say that Audrey's performance was "tremulously lovely," and that Mel Ferrer made "the perfect counterpart. We are lucky. There's a magical play in town." Warming to his theme, the distinguished critic added: "Everyone knows that Audrey Hepburn is an exquisite young lady, and no one has ever doubted her talent for acting. But the part of Ondine is a complicated one. It is compounded of intangibles — of moods and impressions, mischief and tragedy. See how Miss Hepburn is able to translate them into the language of the theater without artfulness or precociousness. She gives a pulsing performance that is all grace and enchantment, disciplined by an instinct for the realities of the stage."

While Audrey's cup was running over with notices of this sort, and her affair with Mel Ferrer was becoming even more intense, she heard the news about which everyone except herself had been certain — she had been nominated for the Academy Award for *Roman Holiday*.

Much as she feigned indifference or told herself she had no chance against the other contestants, Audrey was extremely nervous waiting for the outcome; and playing Ondine night after night became exceedingly taxing to her limited strength. She kept going to Dinty Moore's for her steak tartare. She was so dehydrated after the performances, and utterly exhausted, that she grabbed at anything, from ice cream to beer, to steady her nerves and give her some nourishment. Beer — a remedy known to many in the theater as well as to nervous bride-grooms before a honeymoon — was especially helpful in settling her butterfly stomach. She received good news from Italy that helped to buoy her up. Ingrid Bergman had been to see *Roman Holiday* and had come out crying. "What were you crying for?" her husband Roberto Rossellini had asked her. "I was so touched by Audrey Hepburn," the great star replied.

Then at last came the night of the Oscars on March 25, just six weeks after *Ondine* opened and Audrey had been nominated for a Tony. The awards were held at the Center Theater, with a linkup to Hollywood to accommodate the East Coast nominees. Feeling very rundown, Audrey had to leave the theater in the savage March chill in her fishnet costume, wrapped in an enormous black coat. Protected by patrolmen and sergeants from the vast crowd of fans outside the theater, she ran, followed by the baroness, through the lobby with its reporters, admirers, and blaze of lights, to a changing room where a white lace Givenchy dress was waiting for her. She dressed in an instant, and once again flashed as quick as a water sprite through the crowd to the VIP row in the orchestra that also included Lena Horne, Steve Allen, and the Arthur Murrays.

The results were more or less a foregone conclusion. When Fredric March stepped onto the stage and said, "The winner is — Audrey Hepburn!" even then Audrey could not believe her ears. To a great burst of applause, she almost ran up the aisle, then in her excitement lost direction and turned left instead of right, winding up in the wings. There was a roar of affectionate laughter as she reappeared, made a charming frown of displeasure at herself, waved to everyone, then dashed up to March and almost ran into him head on as she grabbed the award. After a brief thanks she then fled the stage.

On her way to the press conference that followed, Audrey was so petrified that she lost the Oscar: she had put it down somewhere and nobody could find it! She therefore couldn't pose for photographs with it, and finally someone emerged with another. After a search, hers was found in the ladies' room. By now, Audrey was so completely jittery that she didn't know what she was doing. Her usual cool had deserted her completely. She kissed Academy president Jean Hersholt on the lips instead of on the cheek, and then, perhaps fortunately, went home. But she couldn't sleep, and spent the night tossing and turning in a state bordering on ecstasy, thus giving the baroness a restless night. It was all too much — but then a few days later she heard good news again, that she had won the Tony. She was far more assured when she accepted that award. There was no doubt about it: she was, whether she liked it or not, on top of the heap. But trouble still lay ahead.

Chapter Six

By early April, Audrey was suffering from anemia and total emotional exhaustion. The baroness kept issuing statements that Ferrer and her daughter were not romantically involved, while the couple, in fact, planned to marry as soon as *Ondine's* run was over. Each night after the curtain fell, Audrey had to retreat to her apartment where her mother and a doctor were waiting in attendance. She never missed a performance. Her love for Ferrer, her desire to please him in every way, and the tension in which she lived wore her down still further. The mother she loved so much was certainly very dominant in her life, and that too caused many problems.

Another headache was that the columnists, backed by many in the theatrical profession, became more and more critical of the fact that Ferrer would not allow Audrey, who was of course the supreme star of *Ondine,* to take her last curtain call alone. This was against rules, and it made Ferrer extremely unpopular in the business. It was felt, perhaps unfairly, that he was hitching his wagon to a star in the most blatant manner, although no doubt his response would be that since he had discovered the play for Audrey and certainly influenced her performance in private, he was entitled to break protocol and share her exceptional triumph. The matter is still open to debate.

When Audrey finished the run of *Ondine,* she was utterly drained by New York's humid and suffocating summer; she felt

she had to have a complete rest or she would be seriously ill.
Ferrer had been offered a picture in Italy, and reluctantly
accepted it — it was *Madre* (The Mother), and it offered him a
very good part. He and Audrey agreed that she would go to
Switzerland because she was developing asthma, a very serious
disease that could kill her, and the clear Swiss air was thought
to be good for the ailment. They would marry as soon as she
was sufficiently recovered, and Ferrer obtained permission in
advance from the Italian film production company to take
leave when the marriage was to take place.

Switzerland was clean, orderly, beautiful, peaceful, and
virtually devoid of interest. It had no scars from World War II.
It offered succor for the spirit as well as a tax haven and a Swiss
bank account. From every point of view of health and practi-
cality, it would make an ideal retreat for a very exhausted
young woman.

Audrey flew to Switzerland and began with a hired car and
driver to drive to Gstaad, where she had booked at the Palace
Hotel. On the way, she began to feel very drained and sick, and
the chauffeur suggested they take a detour — to the Burgenstock.

Going to the Burgenstock was one of the most significant
decisions of Audrey's life. It was one of the most luxurious and
civilized mountain retreats in the world, a private kingdom
equipped with its own police, who were armed against intru-
ders. It boasted three splendid hotels, the Grand, the Park, and
the Palace. The Burgenstock was the creation of the Frey
family, whose present scion had just assumed his imperial
office in 1954. Just over a quarter of a century before, the
family had bought five hundred acres of the three-thousand-
foot-high mountain peninsula that jutted into Lake Lucerne.
They had transformed this wilderness into not only three
imposing buildings, but also a golf course, three tennis courts,
a beach, a swimming pool, an outside glass elevator, a funicular
railway, and a forested park. The Burgenstock was staffed by
hundreds of craftsmen and servants, and even had a fire
brigade. It was a favorite resort of kings.

The drive up to the Burgenstock was almost perpendicular, rising three thousand feet in twenty minutes and marked by several hairpin turns. When another car approached Audrey's, her driver had to back up to the edge of the road to let the other vehicle by. Afraid of heights, she kept her eyes closed during most of this journey, but once the car reached the high plateau, she opened her eyes to a scene that was to be familiar to her for many years.

Below lay glittering, blue-gray Lake Lucerne, surrounded by mountain peaks shining in the midday sun, with a single steamer silently traversing the still water, a wisp of smoke emerging from its funnel. Across the lake shone the beautiful small city of Lucerne itself. Ahead were rolling green fields with perfectly groomed cows that rang cool silver bells as they shook their heads. Children played with their nursemaids or bounced colored balls on flawlessly groomed lawns in a formal park dotted with firs and pines. Suddenly, guards emerged and checked the limousine; then the road swept up to the three palatial hotels.

Audrey felt she was in Shangri-la. She entered the Grand, which had an enormous lobby furnished with Louis XV and Maria Theresa antiques and paintings by Rubens, Tintoretto, Correggio, and her countryman Vandyke, and was quite overcome. Then at lunch she was approached by the gracious owner, Fritz Frey, who was already among the most famous hoteliers in Europe. He was to become one of her closest and dearest friends. Thirty-eight years old, good-looking, with slightly receding, graying dark hair, clean-cut features, and an elegant suit and tie, he exuded great charm, energy, and dynamism. He was, in every way, an impressive and genial host. He told Audrey that the Burgenstock was intended to be far more than a trio of hostelries for the super-rich — it was a retreat, a haven for the injured or broken in spirit, the old, the sick, or the neurotically disturbed. No matter what the guests' tastes were in food or wine, they would always be satisfied. There was also a staff of electricians, plumbers, gardeners, paper-hangers, and mechanics on call all year round; one man had spent thirty years doing nothing but washing the crystal.

Frey expressed admiration for Audrey's work on the screen and said to her, "I see you are not registered as a guest. Where are you going?"

"To Gstaad," she said.

Privately, Frey thought she was making a mistake. She would hate it there, since it was much too fashionable, and full of celebrities and tourists. But instead of warning her, he sensibly said, "If you don't find peace in Gstaad, call me. I can assure you, you will find peace in the Burgenstock."

She thanked Fritz Frey and touched his hand. Then she proceeded to Gstaad. As soon as the car approached that famous resort, the worst possible thing happened. A huge crowd of international reporters and photographers had been tipped off to her arrival by an overzealous hotel publicity man. The crowd descended on her, beating on the windows until she opened them, and yelling when was she going to marry Ferrer? When would Ferrer finish his picture in Italy? What picture would she be doing next? Why was she not in Italy with him? Had there been a rift?

It took all of her great self-control not to scream. She felt distraught; somehow, with the aid of the hotel staff, she managed to struggle through the lobby to an elevator. Some reporters slipped in with her, but at last she managed to get to her suite and lock the door.

She sank down exhausted and instantly called Fritz Frey. She wanted to return to the Burgenstock, where reporters would be forbidden and every telephone call would be monitored by the switchboard. She told him what she was going through, and he explained to her that he would not only protect her but also would give her a house to lease next month, when the Burgenstock would close for the fall and winter seasons. He told her that she could have his wife's summer home, a small wooden chalet of not much more than fifteen hundred square feet at the back of one of the hotels. He would move into his father's house, since his father had recently died.

Audrey somehow made her way back to her car and driver. She was so close to a breakdown that she cried during most of the journey back to the Burgenstock. When she arrived there for the second time, Frey was shocked by her appearance. She was literally gray with exhaustion. He said to her, "My dear Miss Hepburn, you're ill. I'm going to get a doctor. We have our own. He will visit you as often as you want. In the meantime, we're going to disconnect the phone to your house. Just call the hotel on the house telephone for anything you want, and my wife and I will take care of your slightest request. Nobody will be able to reach you unless you want them to. You are here for peace. The Burgenstock is a place to which people come for peace."

Indeed, the little chalet was ideal. It was furnished in a cheerful, attractively feminine style, with overstuffed chintz chairs, glazed chintz curtains, and comfortable, informal furniture. It was almost Californian in its modernity and cheerfulness, and lacked the heavy opulence of so many Swiss interiors. Audrey felt instantly at home. Each day there were fresh flowers, the view of Lake Lucerne (unless the fog closed in), the scent of firs, meals with delicious coffee, farm eggs, freshly baked warm bread, delicious little cakes and petits fours — everything Audrey's heart could desire. Above all, bliss of all blisses, her heart and mind could rest in privacy. The only sound at night, apart from the occasional faint tootle of the Lake Lucerne ferry, was the gentle ringing of the cowbells. Audrey slept like a babe in arms.

Even though the sudden, drenching rain of the Swiss mountains tended to beat down, her health started to improve. It was literally the first rest she had had from the moment she was cast, seemingly centuries before, in *The Secret People*. It was now time to take stock, and she and Mel spoke to each other as often as they could on the long-distance telephone to Sardinia, a colossal but worthwhile effort at communication.

The wedding date was set for September 25, 1954. Mel flew from Sardinia, breaking off shooting for the occasion. The unhappy baroness reluctantly flew in from London for the service. Mel's sister Julia was to be bridesmaid and the British diplomat Sir Neville Bland — a close friend of the baroness and former Ambassador to the Netherlands — was to give the bride away. A very few reporters, led by the inevitable Reuters, were allowed to attend the ceremony. The wedding was conducted to the ceaseless drumming of heavy rain, which competed with the organ in the small Protestant chapel owned by the Burgenstock that directly overlooked the lake. Ferrer broke tradition by escorting Audrey to the chapel in her exquisite white Givenchy wedding dress, white hat, and veil. She carried a tiny bouquet of lilies of the valley and pink sweetheart roses, and an elegant satin-covered prayer book.

Unfortunately, because Mel had to return to shooting in Italy, the couple had to honeymoon there, which meant running into more reporters. Ferrer had found a perfect honeymoon retreat, however: a restored farmhouse of the Garibaldi era in the beautiful Frascati vineyard country on the way to Anzio, in the heart of the Alban hills. It was a dream house — surrounded by vines and well-tilled fields, with a fine view of the valley; it was fashioned in Italian granite and pink stucco, festooned with night-blooming jasmine and the richly scented, multi-colored bougainvillea that flourishes in the region. Inside, the house was cool, with echoing tile floors and sudden flights of stone steps. There was a spacious kitchen, with brass pans and tureens and colanders hung from hooks, trailing plants, and large wooden platters from which to serve cheese and cold vegetables on long summer evenings. Even more delightful, the house contained a perfect Noah's ark of creatures, including a donkey, two dogs, nine cats, and two fluttering and moaning fantailed doves. It was heaven on earth, and well worth the struggle of fighting through more reporters at the Stazione Termini in Rome and the further obstacle course along the Appian Way.

As long as they could avoid the press, Audrey and Mel were ecstatically happy. They began to plan a film version of *Ondine,* while Ferrer completed his picture and began discussions with producer Dino de Laurentiis about appearing as Prince Andrei in a version of Tolstoy's *War and Peace.*

After a month in Italy, the couple returned to Switzerland. Even at that early stage in their marriage, there was talk in social circles of Mel "using" Audrey to further his career; that she had forced him upon Dino de Laurentiis because, without him, the Italian producer could not have had her. Nothing, of course, could have been further from the truth. As we know, Ferrer had been hired several months before Audrey. Unhappily, this nonsensical gossip became rife in the winter of 1954, and there seemed to be a resentment in the press toward Ferrer, who did not try to suppress it because of his rather difficult and remote personality. He never felt compelled to flatter and cajole the columnists, and he tended to aggravate them by failing to send flowers, champagne, or other bribes to ensure that he would be given consistently supportive treatment. Ferrer was not an easy man, and the general feeling (which grew) was that he exercised far too much control over Audrey. There was a reason for this, however. Audrey had become increasingly insecure, and began to change from a somewhat innocent and jittery girl propelled into enormous fame overnight into an authentically recessive and neurotic personality. She clung to Ferrer in a relationship in which she was totally dependent on him for every move and every decision. In addition, the relationship was curiously ironic in that her talent far surpassed that of her husband, and her sensitivity and delicacy of nature were more refined than his. But, not without a degree of conscious control, he asserted his masculine authority by overpowering her completely. His purpose was not questionable in any sense; he simply allowed his instincts to operate without control, except to give Audrey mutual power of decision when it came to discussing all of their future script projects. It was one of those marriages in which there was a degree of strain even when it seemed most comfortable. Audrey, too, possessed her own will and determination, and she had to suppress these in order to satisfy what was perhaps a too carefully devised program for mutual happiness. Both actors were playing out their own psychodramas, and to visitors it often seemed that they were making too conscious an effort when a more relaxed and natural friendship between husband and wife would have been more appropriate.

In October 1954 Audrey became pregnant for the first time. She was deliriously excited, since she desired a child far more than success in motion pictures or the dubious attentions of a sensation-hungry press. She saw in a child the prospect of releasing her own nature in selfless love, and no doubt wanted to give a child the life of luxury that she now enjoyed and of which she could not even have dreamed when she was a child herself. All of those days of starvation and desperation would be swept aside for the comfort and ease of a Swiss upbringing. She seriously wondered whether she shouldn't even abandon the making of *War and Peace* the following spring. But her powerful Dutch sense of duty overcame that instinctive feeling and made her realize that she could not betray Dino de Laurentiis's confidence in her. Besides, she was very fond of the mercurial, tiny, and extravagant Dino, with his endless stream of Italian anecdotes, and of his wife, the ravishing Silvana Mangano. Mangano, who had created a sensation in *Bitter Rice,* was now the mother of a gorgeous brood of little Italian children with enormous dark eyes and curly black hair, who would fling their arms around Audrey in a manner that made her heart almost stop beating and tears of happiness well in her eyes. Evenings at the de Laurentiis home were wonderful, and Audrey felt a strong empathy for the Italians, with their warmth, their outgoing, slightly crazy humor and energy, and their fits of sulking, laughter, and tears. Always controlled herself, she loved their lack of control and envied it. Like so many people raised with extreme discipline under conditions of hunger and privation, Audrey was captivated by people who lived at the center of life, free of anxiety, with a full expression of their natures in terms of food, wine, family life, and sex. Beside the vitality of the de Laurentiis family and their friends, she could not help but feel almost dried up, driven back, even in her youth, to a sense of deprivation and inferiority. But when she could forget herself, she joyfully realized that she had begun to find a new country and a new family.

As for Dino, he was fretful. Although he wouldn't say it, Audrey's pregnancy was perilously close to being a disaster for him. He had planned to start shooting *War and Peace* in the late winter of 1954, in northern Italy, when Audrey would be seen in fur hat and muff against the background of the icy snows of Moscow or St. Petersburg, but now, because she was going to bear a child, he would have to delay the entire production until the late summer, since Natasha could not appear to be heavy. She had to be slender and light, and even a hint of pregnancy would ruin the effect of a virginal girl let loose in the extraordinary atmosphere of Napoleon's invasion and the threatened world of the Russian upper class. Audrey would not deliver the baby until July. Nor could he put the picture forward, shooting immediately, before Audrey was in the fourth month. He was still mustering up the Italian Army and securing large numbers from Italy and from Yugoslavia, Sardinia, and Corsica, for use according to his schedules. He had only just succeeded through endless wheedling, bribery, and cajolery, in wresting a promise from the government that he could have thousands of able-bodied soldiers by March. He had also scheduled the making of thousands of uniforms, and each soldier had to be fitted individually, which was a colossal job of organization. Moreover, he would have to weed through the ranks of extras, because many would be physically unsatisfactory to dress as hussars or infantrymen and others might not be able to ride horseback — a crucial factor in the scenes of the retreat from Moscow. All of these exhausting logistics were literally turned upside-down by the prospect of Audrey's longed-for child.

Two of Mel's children, who had been present at the wedding, came to visit in Switzerland during their school holidays and, once more, Audrey loved being a surrogate mother for them. She refused to accept the title of "stepmother," and insisted they call her Audrey. She extinguished any fears they might have had that she would be like the wicked stepmother in fairy tales, or that she would in any way try to alienate them from their real mother, whom Ferrer had so recently divorced. Audrey was at her best in coping with the difficult situation and in making the children feel at home in Switzerland while remaining loyal to their own home in the United States.

Ferrer had to fly to London twice for discussions on his next picture, *Oh! Rosalinda!*, a version of Johann Strauss's *Dei Fledermaus* by the great British director Michael Powell. Audrey was alone for a while, which she hated, but she loved the wild and deafening storms that roared about her chalet, and would gaze out at the lightning and the driving rain sweeping the pine forest, as enraptured as a little girl gazing at a Gothic scene in an illustrated Victorian novel.

Meanwhile, she read and rereared *War and Peace,* and felt herself becoming more deeply involved with the character of Natasha. She studied biographies of Tolstoy, coming to understand how he had drawn from his intimate knowledge of the Russian aristocracy, and absorbed herself in the very task he had undertaken through so many years of dedication and concentration. She steeped herself in the Russian author's great novel until she felt part of it herself. Of course, the wintry Swiss setting of that late fall season was perfect for an appreciation of the novel.

Audrey flew to Holland for a special tour for a local charity — something that she dreaded because of her hatred of publicity and reporters, but one that she felt a moral obligation to undertake. The Dutch public was ecstatic over her return, because she was unquestionably the most celebrated person other than the queen in that country. When she and Mel arrived in Amsterdam, a crowd of fans stormed her; they terrified her as she got off the plane and, later, she was involved in an incident while she signed photographs at a department store to raise money for victims of World War II. The crowd literally broke windows and display cases and surrounded her until she started back in terror. The police had to break up the mob. For one of the rare occasions in her life up to that time, Audrey realized the extreme danger of popular success: she could not help but think that such manic enthusiasm was only the turn of a coin away from the mood of a lynch mob. Much as she loved her success, she had a residual fear of crowds that never left her.

Audrey and Mel returned to the Burgenstock for the Christmas holidays, planning to fly to London when Mel would begin work on *Oh! Rosalinda!* They had a joyous time, and with great ceremony presented each other with gifts under the Christmas tree, with the Fritz Freys in attendance. Audrey gave Mel two handsome cashmere sweaters, and he gave her some very fine Irish linen because she always felt, no matter how much she had, that she did not have enough linen in the house. Just before New Year's Day of 1955, the couple flew to London and moved into a comfortable apartment in Portman Square, a cozy neighborhood which also housed the Poetry Society of London. The apartment was typically British, with wall-to-wall carpeting and several large rooms, and they were very happy there. Their chief problem in London was the baroness. She was far from happy with the marriage, and had never approved of Ferrer any more than she had approved of any other man in Audrey's life. Surrounded in her own apartment by photographs of Audrey, the baroness was simply not at all comfortable with this great rival of a tough and resilient husband. Of course, since she had been raised as an aristocrat and thus had perfect manners, she would present no direct confrontation, and refused to express her real feelings. But the frosty tension of her manner was unavoidable, and there is no doubt that Audrey suffered from the failure to reconcile the two most important people in her life.

Audrey decided to thwart the baroness's dire prediction that two actors married to each other would be a disaster by programming her life to the finest detail so that she and Mel would literally never be apart for more than a few days. Most marriages of show-business people (unless they formed a team) would suffer from the fact that the couple would be split by separate shooting schedules, often, in those days of location shooting, in different countries. Instincts and emotions would surface, sexual opportunities would occur, and unless the individual qualified for sainthood, there would be the tempta-tion of an affair with an attractive leading man or woman. Thus, the prognosis for marriage in the field was usually poor. Audrey was determined to overcome the problem. She pressed her agents to obtain parts which would involve her co-starring with Mel in the future. She turned down the role of Joan of Arc in Otto Preminger's movie version of Shaw's play, a part which was soon to make the unknown Jean Seberg world famous. The reason for this is believed to be that Preminger refused to cast Ferrer in the role of the Dauphin, which was subsequently played by Richard Widmark.

Meanwhile, during those weeks in London, she and Ferrer badgered everybody in the motion-picture industry to make *Ondine*. But people were afraid of it, because what had been successful as a fantastical theatrical presentation would be harder to realize in the more realistic world of color and CinemaScope, which was then all the rage and, indeed, the only acceptable medium in Britain and Hollywood. Ferrer took his mind off the problem by playing in *Oh! Rosalinda!* He once again earned himself a reputation for being difficult with the press when he refused to allow Audrey to appear with him in photographs when she came to watch him work with the director Michael Powell on a difficult sequence. Powell recalls that Ferrer was overprotective of Audrey, but he may not have realized the degree of Audrey's delicacy and her fear of being photographed. Without the protection of the carefully flattering lighting of a Hollywood cinematographer, the results could be disastrous to her face. British cameramen were usually particularly brutal, and would place the lights right next to the camera, in front of the face, so that the results were harsh, garish, and ruinous to all but the most exquisite human faces.

Audrey returned to Switzerland in the very late winter, and in early spring, she waited for her baby to be born. She had one favorite place above all others — a café, or Konditorei, in a little street that ran off the Schwanenplatz, or public square, near Lake Lucerne. She was very fond of the lady who ran the café, and the waitresses, and felt almost as though they were her own family. They always addressed her as Mrs. Ferrer, which was very important to her, and they treated her as one of their own, with warm, sweet smiles and generous hugs, whenever she walked through the door. Even the solidly detached Swiss customers would look up from their tables and their delicious coffee and cakes to see her, but they wouldn't stare. The security they offered her was necessary to her, now that she was pregnant. It was essential, the doctors told her, that she somehow calm her exceedingly nervous nature. Otherwise this tension, which never seemed to leave her, might possibly affect her unborn child. What was more, the genuine love that surrounded her was a welcome respite from the artificial affection of so many people in the motion-picture business.

Audrey enjoyed a world in which doctors still made house calls and people took care of sick neighbors, shook hands with each other every day, inquired with sincere concern about the baby, and made useful suggestions on baby clothes and toys and comforters. Audrey told her friend Henry Gris, "There is no other place in the world where I feel so much at peace. It's my very private stomping ground. I've become one of these people. And we're loyal to each other. It's a very human thing. We haven't signed a pact, we simply understand each other."

But this idyll, like most idylls, was of short duration. In March 1955, with *War and Peace* now firmly set for shooting in July and some sequences already shot in the Dolomites in Northern Italy, Audrey began to have painful, unsettling, frightening symptoms. She was in pain and felt sick, and then, one horrible day, she realized that the life inside her was dying. She underwent that ordeal of ordeals for a young woman in love: she developed premature labor pains and was rushed to a hospital, where she miscarried. The reasons for the miscarriage were not disclosed; it is possible that her frail body, with its narrow hips and tiny pelvis, could have caused the problem. The agony of the discovery had only one advantage: it drew her and Mel even closer together. His extreme protectiveness and masculine desire to control her, to exercise his will on her, probably sprang more and more from the suffering he knew she was undergoing. That was a nerve-wracking spring, and Dino de Laurentiis (who had several young children of his own) and his wife Silvana were full of sympathy. De Laurentiis had to admit he was privately relieved, guilty though he might have felt about that, because now he could embark on *War and Peace* earlier, as soon as Audrey was physically and psychologically up to the job.

But Audrey still felt ill and distraught and despite her professional spirit, might even have contemplated canceling *War and Peace*. Ferrer, however, felt that it would be good for her to proceed with the film, since the challenge of playing Natasha would provide a release from her anguish and occupy her mind, so that she would not brood. Her increasing delicacy and fragility, poised as always against the steely strength of her nature, emerged more clearly than ever. Indeed, while she struggled to make up her mind, Dino and his Italian backers, and director King Vidor in Hollywood, wondered if she would be able to face the tedious costume-fittings and long grueling months of work in Rome's notorious summer heat.

Audrey rallied. But she was Dutch-stubborn and determined to show no strain. If there was any single thing that moved her even more than her grief, it was an old-fashioned sense of duty to Ferrer, his career, and her producers. She and Mel moved to Rome in the late spring of 1955 and together they rediscovered the charming house in which they had spent their honeymoon, which Mel, as a great gift to her, had persuaded the farmer-owners to lease to them once again.

Audrey was back in paradise. The garden was in full bloom, ablaze with hydrangeas and rich plantings of lilac and roses, shaded by the spreading branches of the fig and olive trees. Water gushed enticingly from an antique carved stone head of a woman at the center of the bluegreen pool that brought a touch of freshness to even the most severe Roman heat. The grapes flourished and supplied good wine. Chickens and sheep provided meat, and fresh fish were brought from the coast and prepared by Audrey and the good cook. Audrey had an especially light touch in the kitchen, preferring not to indulge in the heavy cuisine typical of the region. Guests were enchanted by her various creations, and her pasta with herbs was outstanding. The Italian cook rejoiced in Audrey's recipes and gradually Audrey, busy chopping and boiling and roasting, with the fine brass pots and pans hanging from the ceiling, glittering against the whitewashed walls, grew joyful and recovered her strength.

Rehearsals and costume-fittings began that spring. Audrey would drive from the farmhouse, with its private zoo of donkeys, dogs, cats, and doves, to Cinecittà, the massive studio in Rome which was constructed like a small city — with rooms for Silvana's children and a large complex of dressing rooms, cutting rooms, laboratories, and sound stages. The movie city-within-a-city was run with a mad, inspired inefficiency, and hectic noise and bustle typical of Rome. Unlike a Hollywood studio, where under a surface of good fellowship there was often an atmosphere of tension, Cinecittà was cheerful — in a frenzy of activity from morning to night. Audrey found it stimulating to work there, and liked the fact that at lunchtime, when the crew and movie extras were forbidden wine, they would immediately threaten to strike. It pleased her to see the crew members heartily eating spaghetti during their various breaks, and consuming large quantities of espresso or cappuccino — all far removed from the plastic cups and hasty hamburgers of Hollywood.

During the preparatory work, Audrey put her foot down and demanded the Albert Di Rossis, a team whom she admired as hair and makeup artists. When she was unable to get hold of her favorite cameraman, Franz Planer from Vienna, she insisted upon having Jack Cardiff, whose work she had admired in such fine films as *The Red Shoes* and *Black Narcissus*. What Audrey wanted, Audrey got. Few would dare to cross her once her mind was made up. Her will conquered every obstacle. Indeed, she somewhat aggravated the costume designers when she flew Givenchy from Paris to approve every stitch, despite the fact that he was not an authority on period custome.

Audrey was tireless in her supervision of the details of her clothes. She read books of illustrations of the early nineteenth century, ensuring that every particular was accurate down to the last strand of hair, cut of skirt or bodice, stockings, and shoes. She would stand for hours, surprising everyone with her strength, lucky in having one of those backs that is absolutely straight. So strong were the muscles supporting her spine that she never faltered, and her dressers marveled at her. She also controlled her makeup, insisting on the nearest possible foundation to that which would have been applied in Tolstoy's day. Thus, her face never looked "modern."

While she exercised her power with gentle but firm authority, Dino de Laurentiis's exhausting work continued. He was in a frenzy from dawn to midnight.

The logistics of *War and Peace* were staggering: fifteen thousand Italian soldiers, the cream of the Army's crack troops, had finally been hired. All those with even the slightest physical or postural flaw or problem of weight had been ruthlessly weeded out. In the increasingly oppressive heat of June and July 1956, de Laurentiis and King Vidor had to stage snow scenes, with snow machines blowing corn flakes dipped in gypsum as imitations of the real article. Moscow of 1812 now stood incongruously upon the banks of the Tiber: onion domes, towers, churches, and winding streets were remarkably authentic. One afternoon, Audrey stood on a small hill watching an impressive sight as production assistants went about with torches, setting the imitation city alight. It was Dino's attempt to outdo David O. Selznick's fabled burning of Atlanta in *Gone with the Wind*.

During the scenes of war and carnage, Audrey was plagued by nightmares, waking night after night screaming with terror. She was reliving the horror of her childhood, and so fragile was the state of her unconscious mind that even a hint of violence could trigger the most terrifying memories. It was painful for her to watch the war scenes, but she knew that in playing Natasha — a young girl engulfed in historic events, aware of the contrast between the spectacle of an invaded Russia and her own still, small world — she had to confront the realities Natasha faced and be part of the experience that Natasha had known. For Audrey, mere playacting was not enough. Although she was far removed from the Method school of acting, she did believe in digging deeply into the character she was playing, into motivations and emotions, and she could never act superficially. Nor could she act without believing that the character she portrayed was convincingly real. It was a misfortune that the script for *War and Peace* — written by far too many writers — was a classic case of too many cooks spoiling the broth. In fact, because of rewrites and adjustments to accommodate the schedule shifts and logistics of the production, much of the detail of character in Tolstoy's writing had had to be sacrificed.

Audrey struggled to give depth and resonance to the somewhat monotonous and colorless delineation of Natasha in the screenplay, and she could do so only by expressing strong emotion in the delivery of each line; she moved skillfully from innocence to experience, from the virgin girl of Tolstoy's imagination to the full-fledged woman. She kept trying to reintroduce lines from the book, but it was difficult and took all of the concentration she could muster. It was almost impossible for her to relax during this ongoing struggle with the part.

She was much annoyed by a number of distractions during the shooting, despite the fact that she had issued orders to everyone, producer and director included, that there must be little or no press and that she would not tolerate visitors on the set. The reporters flooded Cinecittà. When the famous old gossip columnist Louella Parsons turned up during the shooting, and occupied a large suite at the Excelsior Hotel in Rome, Audrey shuddered. She usually went to enormous lengths to avoid Louella, and the last thing she wanted was a gossipy journalist watching her on the set. When it became obvious that Louella was furious she couldn't watch Audrey at work, Audrey tried to appease her. She had her gardener send Louella bouquets of flowers from her garden, delivered by special messenger to her suite. Louella had to be content with these, and with a mere telephone interview. She burbled in her column: "[For Audrey] Italy is enchantment, but there is no place like home, and home to an American is the United States, so I look forward to see [*sic*] both [Mel and Audrey] return to the land of the free."

Throughout the shooting, Audrey refused all other interviews. She had had to bend to the press agents during the making of *Roman Holiday* and *Sabrina*, but now she was feeling her oats as a star and would not tolerate the prying questions, banning even the most superficial discussion of her life with Mel. She was on her way to becoming one of the most private of stars — almost the equal of Garbo in her anxiety about the press. She was so very fretful that she requested the crew remain as unobtrusive as possible; seeing people moving within her range of vision irritated her to the point that, on more than one occasion, it took all of King Vidor's powers of persuasion to prevent her from walking off the set.

Unfortunately, it proved impossible to control the Italians in the studio. They simply refused to accept discipline of this sort and heads would pop up without warning, making her flub a line. Members of the crew would argue hysterically with each other, ruining a shot. King Vidor told me it was like trying to run Italy single-handed.

It was impossible to control the stream of visitors to the set, many of them Italian nobility. When pretentious women in large hats stood and chattered as they watched her, ignoring all attempts to silence them, Audrey at last went to Dino and demanded that they be removed at once. These visitors were not even film exhibitors, for whom, under constraint, she might have made an exception. They were just there to stare and comment, and it was unbearable. It was equally infuriating when still photographers would visit the set and try to photograph her when she was acting to the camera, and she refused to have any stills taken until the entire picture was finished. Moreover, she demanded that she see every still and approve it personally. More often than not, Audrey hated pictures of herself, particularly those that emphasized what she felt to be her wide jawline, the almost visible bones in her eye sockets that created deep shadows, her thin neck, and her worst bête noir, her nostrils, which she thought flared too wide.

Audrey's nerves were in shreds after a few weeks of Cinecittà. Another problem was that she had to do the scenes out of sequence, and she vowed she would try to take movies in consecutive time order in the future — a vow she was to keep. It was hard for her to maintain the thread of emotion and inspiration for months of work when crucial sequences were thrown out of order by the endless changes in the schedule. She once told Henry Gris in anguish, "Nobody realizes what I had been going through. That I had been frantically saying to myself for minutes on end, 'I must remember that line, I must summon the tears.'"

Finally, matters came to a head. Audrey was playing a very important scene with Henry Fonda, who was cast as the intellectual Pierre. Audrey was, as usual, fretting about the scene — whether she would blow a line, whether she would play the emotion too strongly — and the kindly Vidor was patiently guiding her through take after take while Fonda (who was going through severe marital problems) grew more and more upset. Suddenly, two friends of the producer literally walked onto the set and shook her hand. Audrey forced herself to smile, but the instant they left she went to her dressing room and refused to come back. Vidor went to see her, but she told him on the verge of tears that no power on earth could make her summon up the emotion needed and Vidor was in despair.

Unhappily, these distractions affected her performance. She looked the perfect Natasha, but the feeling, the consuming force that animated her was frittered away and her acting never reached the core of the character. She was not satisfied with her performance and told Henry Gris, "Acting doesn't come easily to me. I put a tremendous effort into every morsel that comes out. I don't yet have enough experience or store of knowledge to fall back on. Many of my reactions stem from instinct rather than knowing. So I must work very hard to achieve what I'm after."

In the midst of all this turmoil, however, there were at least some pleasant distractions. In the final weeks of shooting in the fall of 1955, Audrey was offered two new pictures.

Chapter Seven

The first movie Audrey was offered was the film version of Tennessee Williams's celebrated play *Summer and Smoke*, about a frustrated schoolteacher in a small town who discovers love in middle age. The part was ideal for her, and she asked to meet the producer, Hal B. Wallis, and Williams to discuss it. They flew to Rome and drove up to the farmhouse on a Sunday night when Audrey was not working. Wallis would never forget the experience. First, they had to wait until 10:00 P.M. when Mel Ferrer returned from location. Meanwhile, Audrey kept up a stream of amusing conversation. At about 10:30, two servants wheeled in a large cart on which sat a heavy platter bearing a single enormous fish without any dressing, not even sliced tomatoes. The fish's eyes glared accusingly at Wallis and Williams, and Wallis's associate Paul Nathan went a light shade of green and said he couldn't eat the thing. While Audrey and Mel were talking to Williams, Wallis whispered to Nathan, conspiratorially, "I have a feeling if you don't eat that, there won't be anything else. It's obviously the entire dinner." It was. According to Wallis, the Ferrers served no soup, dessert, or coffee; the guests nibbled gingerly at the fish and then, murmuring politenesses, put it aside. Wallis says, "Audrey, dainty as a Dresden figure in a Givenchy original, consumed a large portion of the sea beast with great relish."

As the guests finally drove off, they looked back and saw the Ferrers framed in the front doorway. As if in a movie scene,

Ferrer picked Audrey up and held her high as she waved good-bye. Williams grunted sourly, "The Lunts did it better." The others laughed. They simply didn't believe that the intimate, charming gesture was genuine. This attitude reflected the overall (although unfounded) skepticism in the industry about the couple's relationship.

Audrey never made *Summer and Smoke*. Negotiations between Wallis and Audrey's agent Kurt Frings finally broke down because she unwisely insisted upon Givenchy designing her a spinster schoolteacher's wardrobe. Also, Wallis could not see Ferrer in the part of the man who deflowers the middle-aged virgin, and insisted upon selecting Laurence Harvey for the part. When Audrey refused to begin the picture, Wallis became convinced that she would not allow the harsh realism of the writing to be preserved and would try to glamorize the drabness of the character. He cast Geraldine Page instead.

The other part Audrey was offered was quite appealing. She was to play a young bluestocking working in a bookstore in Greenwich Village who is discovered by a fashionable and successful magazine photographer who then turns her into a model and whisks her off to Paris to shoot a layout for a magazine modeled on *Vogue*. The part offered her a wonderful opportunity to dance, and she was delighted to learn that the great Fred Astaire was eager to have her play opposite him in the picture, to be entitled *Wedding Day* (later changed to *Funny Face*).

The concept of *Funny Face* had originally been proposed by writer Leonard Gershe, who had been a close friend in the merchant marine of celebrated photographer Richard Avedon and who had long dreamed of making Avedon's life the point of departure for a musical comedy. Gershe developed a libretto, *Wedding Day,* with a score by Vernon Duke. However, there were a number of complications, and it was decided that the picture would be made at Metro-Goldwyn-Mayer with a Gershwin score instead. Gershe dared to rewrite a number of the Ira Gershwin lyrics, and the title *Funny Face* was drawn from a Broadway stage show in which Fred Astaire had appeared in 1927.

Astaire would consider only Audrey for the part of the bookworm-turned-model and, in order to accommodate him, when Paramount refused to loan Audrey to MGM, the entire production was shifted over to Paramount. (Coincidentally, Astaire had signed a multi-picture contract at that studio.) The complicated situation was resolved after much negotiation, but then Audrey held up the proceedings herself. Much as she wanted to act with Astaire, she and her agent were laying down very rigorous financial and other conditions, and the negotiations dragged on through the last weeks of *War and Peace* and well beyond.

Yet a third project was mentioned — *Ariane* for Billy Wilder — in which Audrey would play the daughter of a detective in Paris who redeems an aging playboy through true love. But this was delayed again and again, the reason being that Wilder was having numerous problems with weather conditions for *The Spirit of St. Louis,* the story of Charles Lindbergh's pioneer flight across the Atlantic, and *that* picture was held up.

To try to iron everything out, Audrey and Mel flew to Hollywood in October; they were greatly cheered by the reviews of *Sabrina.* Bosley Crowther in the New York *Times* was captivated by Audrey's performance, sharing his colleague Brooks Atkinson's rapture at the very mention of her name. When I interviewed Crowther in 1962, he told me that Audrey was his favorite actress in the world, and the former critic admitted ruefully that he was actually in love with her, though they had never met.

During discussions in Hollywood, *Funny Face* was developed and rewritten extensively. One of the main characters was a manic magazine editor, based on Diana Vreeland of *Vogue* and tailored for Kay Thompson, author and nightclub star, who was new to pictures. Stanley Donen, director of such hit musicals as *On the Town* and *Singin' in the Rain,* was hired to direct the picture.

Audrey was still not totally committed — even then — because she was nervous about the schedule. It was decided in Hollywood that *Funny Face* would be shot, in its entirety, in Paris. This might have meant separation from Mel. By sheer pressure, the studio and all concerned managed to have Mel's next picture, *Elena et Ses Hommes,* to be directed by Jean Renoir, delayed until Audrey could go to Paris; *Elena et Ses Hommes* coincidentally called for a Paris shooting schedule. These endless problems occupied almost the entire fall of 1955 and, indeed, without this solution *Funny Face* might never have been made. The intention was to create a movie that would reflect the glittering world of fashion photography. Richard Avedon was hired as visual consultant, to give the picture the look of *Vogue,* with extremely bright colors, classical compositions, luscious effects, and a highly glamorized Paris background. It went without saying that Audrey would get to wear a Givenchy wardrobe in the fashion show and other display sequences; and Paramount shot the bankroll to have her beloved designer prepare the most dazzling costumes he had ever created.

Audrey returned briefly to Switzerland, rather tired by the endless negotiations; then she went to Hollywood for dance rehearsals. The director of these was Eugene Loring, a man of great charm and distinction, but Fred Astaire was the real creative influence. Audrey worked at the barre with grueling intensity, week after week — stretching, limbering, painfully aware that she was no longer a teenager and that, even in her mid-twenties, she was stiffer than she had been in her earlier days. In fact, the painful problems she had faced at the Marie Rambert school were increased by her age, and she had to work fiendishly hard to manage the necessary movements.

At last she was ready to meet with Fred Astaire. She was nervous at the prospect, despite her adoration of his screen image, chiefly because she had heard that he was a perfectionist and extremely tough on beginners or semi-amateurs. He told me that he was overjoyed by her, and he was fascinated by the fact that she behaved more like a normal human being than almost any actress he had worked with since Ginger Rogers. He knew that he would have to overcome her extreme self-consciousness and shyness, before he even began to adapt to her, by modifying his own techniques.

In her turn, Audrey felt that she had turned to solid lead, and her feet seemed rooted to the floor. Fred sauntered in, impeccably slender, fine boned, delicate as a boy, with a perfect, light, dancer's body though he was in his late fifties. He was wearing a yellow shirt, immaculately pleated gray flannels (held not by a belt but by a crimson scarf knotted three times), pink socks, and white felt moccasins. He was smiling in the warmest possible manner.

Astaire's personality combined devotion and concentration with a seeming shyness and diffidence. His beloved wife had recently died of cancer, but he would not allow anything to interfere with his single-minded dedication. Dance for him was a supreme expression of body and spirit — although he would never tolerate such a high-flown description. He was a man of few words, and was as spare and lacking in hyperbole in person as he was in performance. Seeing Audrey standing there shaking, he acted promptly. He embraced her gently and swept her into a dance routine on the spot. She said later, "I experienced the thrill that all women at some point in their lives have dreamed of — to dance just once with Fred Astaire."

Although Astaire prepared a geometric plan for every dance, he helped to ease Audrey's insecurity by telling her that he would rely greatly on her judgment and would even ask her what she thought about certain steps and movements. This was flattering, of course, and Audrey was intrigued to hear Astaire tell her of how he had first come to agree to work with her. Roger Edens, the genial producer and pianist-composer-arranger, had run into Astaire at a party at the home of actor Clifton Webb. Edens had asked Astaire what he was doing, and Astaire had said, "A picture called *Papa's Delicate Condition*." Edens had told him, "You can't do it. You've got to do my story *Wedding Day*. Lenny Gershe has done it, and it's great. Audrey Hepburn likes the story and wants to do it — she *will* do it if we can get you!" Astaire recalled that he had asked Edens to run that statement by him once more. Edens had done so. Then Astaire had said, "What do you mean *if* you can get me! I'm already ready! Audrey Hepburn! That's the dream of my life!" As Astaire told Audrey this, she blushed like a schoolgirl and they both broke out laughing. The rapport between them was instantaneous.

One of Audrey's capacities was her ability to learn; she had the intelligence not to be self-contained, and she learned much more than dancing from Fred Astaire. Because of Fred, and his consideration, thoughtfulness, and discipline, Audrey learned the necessary minimalism of screen acting. Astaire contributed just as much to the choreography as Eugene Loring and Stanley Donen, who monitored everything with a very sharp eye. Audrey attended meetings with the director and writer and with Richard Avedon, fascinated by the way the entire movie was depicted on storyboards by these brilliant collaborators. Each shot was pictorially worked out on paper, because it was a picture in which nothing could be casual or accidental: it was as meticulously designed as any of the fashion layouts it parodied in *Vogue* or *Harper's Bazaar*.

Every sequence was choreographed even when dancing was not involved. Audrey was to appear in an opening scene in a bookstore, swamped by a loud gang of fashion-magazine types who were using it as a setting for a layout. Dick, the photographer suggested by Avedon (Astaire), pushes a wheeled ladder the entire length of the shop to clear the scene, not realizing that Jo (Audrey) is huddled on top of it. She screams as the ladder hits the wall. Audrey, who was very much afraid of heights, was uneasy about the sequence, and only when the ladder was very carefully secured by wires was she able to go ahead with it. Much of the picture was framed within the atmosphere of the fashion magazine being parodied. Even when Audrey was not in the sequence, she wanted to see it designed.

The fashion editor Maggie (who was to be played by Kay Thompson) was featured in the opening in a number entitled "Think Pink!" in which, with manic intensity, she announces that her staff must "banish the black, burn the blue, bury the beige," and at the end of the scene, she hurls a pink linen bolt of cloth literally at the camera.

Audrey had a keen sense of color, and, with the aid of Givenchy and Edith Head (who once again had to suffer the humiliation of doing only the early, drab clothes, before the goose is tranformed into a swan), she was able to work with Avedon and the others on the use of special tints in her clothes. For example, a lemon, orange, and lime straw hat was made to contrast with her dull artist's or bookclerk's smock; in one scene she runs with the hat, waves it, and uses it as a dancing partner. The effect is beautiful.

After the work in Hollywood, the cast, crew, and unit publicists shifted to Paris, Audrey's beloved city. She and Mel (who was about to start work on the Renoir picture) checked into the Hotel Raphael, an old and favored hostelry with sumptuous decorations and grand marble hallways. It was on this trip that Audrey instituted a custom that caused widespread comment in the industry. First, her secretary called the hotel and announced that Miss Hepburn would not be accepting the furnishings of the suite, elegant though they might be, as she needed to feel completely at home. She broke the hotel's protocol by shipping, in overflowing cabin trunks, a collection of favourite candlesticks, china, books, pictures, vases, lamps, pillows, and silverware, while the contents of the suite had to be removed and stored in the hotel's basement.

For anyone as tightfisted as Audrey (who became anxious when she had to make a long-distance phone call), the sheer extravagance of this was surprising. But she had learned this custom from the hallowed traditions of the very rich in Europe — a tradition that went back centuries. The task of packing and unpacking all this material was daunting. Hour after backbreaking hour, she and her staff wrapped or unwrapped every item themselves, since Audrey was too much of a perfectionist to trust movers to do the job. She labeled every package, the list running to sheet after sheet of meticulously enumerated items, so that she would be able to find everything; she would upon leaving repack the contents in exactly the same order. When she walked with Mel into the suite at the Raphael, no fewer than twenty cabin trunks stood awaiting them, almost filling the living room, and within seconds Audrey, with undaunted determination, began unpacking and placing everything in its position to resemble as closely as possible the living room of her chalet in Switzerland.

She was to continue this habit for the rest of her life, and for years had her possessions stored in various hotels at great cost, to be shifted from place to place, sometimes just for a matter of weeks, so that she would never be without her own things. Eventually, this extravagant custom would be rewarded: when her house was burglarized some years later, many of the most precious items were spared.

With everything unpacked, she was still busy, working with the French dancer and choreographer Lucien Legrand of the Paris Opera Ballet Company to improve her dancing, continuing working with Astaire, and in every way devoting most of her waking minutes meeting his challenges. She also spent hours in fittings with Givenchy, who combined colors in order to satisfy the requirements of the color photographer Ray June.

As far as possible, to alleviate her uncertainties, Audrey was satisfied by the studio in terms of shooting in sequence. The big number "Bon Jour, Paris!" was staged from a TWA flight from New York to a bustling scene at Orly Airport in Paris, and thence to scenes at three hotels, one of which, of course, was the Raphael. Audrey was seen in an alleyway in Montmartre, and other scenes were shot at the Arc de Triomphe, Notre Dame, and the Eiffel Tower. It was difficult shooting in a busy and overcrowded Paris, so the cast often had to rise at dawn. Always difficult for entertainers, this was particularly so for Kay Thompson, who was a nightclub star and a night owl.

In another sequence, "Let's Kiss and Make Up," there was an encounter between Dick and Jo during which Dick sits on the limb of a tree and serenades her. One of the most difficult sequences was "On How to Be Lovely," in which Maggie (Kay Thompson) explains to Jo how to give interviews. A big fashion show was a highlight: Rex Reed once said it was the finest on the screen. Givenchy excelled himself, and Audrey never looked more stunning, with the classical elegance of vivid ivory whites and golds shimmering against a salon of Second Empire grandeur.

The weather remained a consistent problem throughout the shooting. It was an uncommonly cold and miserable spring season, and the damp and chill continued into the summer. The movie called for a fantasy version of Paris: clean, drenched in sunlight, and without even a hint of rain or fog. Again and again, Audrey would leave the Raphael in the morning only to return an hour or two later feeling disappointed because the weather simply wouldn't allow for what the director wanted. Donen had to reorganize the shooting schedule, shooting with desperate speed in the rare moments of sunshine when a public monument could be cleared of tourists through sheer force. One particularly difficult scene was at the country churchyard of Chantilly just outside Paris, in which she and Astaire were to dance, she in a wedding gown and he in a cardigan, in the fairy-tale number "He Loves and She Loves." The scene had to be a romantic vision of dark green trees, fluttering doves, and swans sailing on dusky amber-colored water. The sequence was supposed to have a luminous, soft-focused radiance, but it was delayed again and again until finally it had to be shot. When Audrey and Fred arrived, the ground had turned to mud. According to choreography worked out weeks before in Hollywood, the two of them had to dance down a lawn, through a walled garden, across a small ornamental bridge, and onto a moored wooden raft. Every time they began, their feet became dirty in the mud and they slipped and slid until they were reduced to a combination of exasperation and laughter. Everyone was tense until Audrey suddenly said, grinning, "Here I've been waiting twenty years to dance with Fred Astaire, and what do I get? Mud in my eye!" Everyone broke up and the work recommenced.

The picture on the whole was a happy one, and on weekends Audrey seldom had a dull moment. Her French was excellent, but she took lessons to improve it still further, she read and reread the script for her next movie, *Ariane* (reworked as *Love*

in the Afternoon), which was sent to her by Billy Wilder and
I. A. L. Diamond. She read French verse, pursued further
ballet lessons, or took long walks, blessedly unrecognized,
through the parks with a bright umbrella in the rain. Mel could
join her on Sundays. Only one incident jarred her happy breaks
in work: she was in a store in the Rue de Rivoli when an
elderly woman tourist seized her by the elbow and brutally
swung her round to face her, snapping aggressively, "Now
come on, admit it, you are Audrey Hepburn, aren't you?" She
told the woman in no uncertain terms that she was not, left the
woman aghast, and fled into the street.

Audrey was fascinated by museums, and went as often as she
could. She thought once again of filming *L'Aiglon*, the story
of the son of Napoleon and the Empress Marie Louise, a
project she had dreamed of for years. Indeed, she would have
been a convincing boy, with her square shoulders, flat chest,
and slim hips. But unfortunately, she was not destined to make
the film.

Astaire had a wonderful talent for brilliant improvisation.
Sometimes, the pre-planning of the picture was broken up
because he had a sharp and unexpected idea. Arriving at the
studio one day in a trench coat in the rain, unfolding his
umbrella, he danced in front of Audrey at a big rehearsal
mirror, pulled off the coat, shook out the raindrops, and used
it as a bullfighter's cape.

Shooting continued into the summer, and Audrey became
exhausted once more. She lost fifteen pounds (her weight was
now below one hundred), and she felt very weak and worn out
at night. But the relentless schedules at Paramount permitted
her no break at the end of shooting; she had to start immediately on *Love in the Afternoon*, and the only consolation was
that she could stay on at the Raphael. Mel luckily was cast in
another picture set in France, *The Vintage*, but this would take
him away from Paris for periods and Audrey worried about
that.

Love in the Afternoon was the culmination of many years
of dreaming by the practical and cynical Billy Wilder. It had

been delayed again and again, and only now was it ready to go. The original novel by Claude Anet was set in pre-revolutionary Russia. It told the story of an aging man of the world who falls in love with a very young girl; she pretends to be inexperienced in order to win him. Billy Wilder and Diamond added the part of a detective, father of the young girl Ariane, who is preparing files on the roué. The part was written for Maurice Chevalier.

Originally, Wilder and Diamond had written the part of the rake as an Aly Khan character, with Yul Brynner in mind. But the more they researched Aly Khan, the more boring they found him; all he could talk about with men was horses and with women clothes. So they decided to change the character to a worldly wise American with whom audiences in the United States would more easily identify. Cary Grant would have been the ideal actor to play him, but instead the director settled on Gary Cooper who, although an elegant dresser with his tailored shirts and ascot scarves, scarcely suggested a European-American exile, and still carried with him the aura of a leathery, aging cowboy.

Once again, Audrey took a keen interest in the production. She observed the elegant designs of the great Alexandre Trauner, who took over almost the whole of the studios of Boulogne to re-create the entire second floor of the Ritz Hotel in Paris (with working elevators and a fully furnished suite, filled with the hotel's own linen, silver, and crystal), and who, with camera trickery, re-created the Paris Opéra house in performance.*

Audrey was greatly cheered during that time by a gift from Mel, the most thrilling one she had ever received. It was a Yorkshire terrier puppy, with sparkling eyes, long, silky brown hair, and the characteristic nervous excitability of the breed. Audrey made of Famous,† as she called the lovely pup, a

---

* Billy Wilder and I. A. L. Diamond still fret at Pauline Kael's *New Yorker* summary — run whenever the film is revived in Manhattan — in which she misrepresents the staging done by Trauner.

† Also called Mr. Famous.

surrogate child, giving the little creature all of the love and attention she was precluded from giving because of her miscarriage.

Famous's Sunday morning walk from the Raphael was always a tremendous occasion. It was like an old movie comedy as the hour approached: the hotel staff — from boot-blacks to maids, valets, waiters and elevator operators — was alerted to clear the way as rapidly as possible as Madame descended with the pooch, which was decorated with bright red ribbons and toddled as rapidly as his tiny paws could carry him along the corridor, into the elevator, and through the lobby to the busy street. Audrey went to great lengths to ensure all of the attention normally given to a star performer of the canine kingdom: shampoos by the finest dog hairdressers, every hair combed with minute attention, claws clipped, and new dog collars and ribbons as often as possible. Christmas and birthday gifts were lavish, and the rapport between Audrey and the dog reached *Private Lines* proportions.

Despite the stimulus provided by Famous, she was tired then, because she usually liked to rest between pictures, and the weather delays on *Funny Face* had not given her a chance to do so. As always, she became easily exhausted, and was not really in a condition to start work. She was especially edgy and fretful; and she insisted to Herb Sterne, the unit publicist, that she should see and approve all the stills. She told Sterne that she forbade the cameraman to shoot her at too low an angle because she again suffered the thought her nostrils were too large and would flare on film. Sterne was amazed at her obsession with her own face.

After a brief period in Hollywood and in Switzerland, Audrey and Mel moved back into the Raphael. Once again this involved the colossal extravagance of moving all of her furniture, crockery, linen, silverware, and even vases to the suite. Billy Wilder and his wife Audrey also moved in, but moved out after only a few days because the bartender couldn't make a martini. They lived briefly in an apartment in the same building as Marlene Dietrich in the Avenue Montaigne, and then moved to the Tremouille, where the bartender specialized in American drinks. Now that he was happily ensconced, Wilder and his co-writer, Izzy Diamond, embarked on the picture.

Since her part called for perfect fingering as a cello student, Audrey took lessons from a cellist. Gary Cooper arrived from Hollywood to work with her. At fifty-six, he looked at least ten years older, but Audrey was fascinated by him. He was impeccably tailored, with wonderful ascots and blazers and suits of Savile Row elegance. He was surrounded at all times by very attractive women, his wife Rocky conveniently and traditionally left at home to suffer in silence and take care of their daughter, Maria.

Despite his elegance, however, Cooper had one problem playing the part of an aging man-of-the-world. He was a very poor dancer. Wilder had to teach him with a professional partner until he managed to move with something approaching grace on his very large feet.

He had loved Audrey in *Gigi* on the stage and was as excited to be working with her as she was to be working with him. Maurice Chevalier, cast as Audrey's detective father, was a different animal entirely. Whereas Cooper had a carefully cultivated, shy, and sleepy charm, Chevalier was charming only on the surface. He was essentially a cold man, very self-contained, and quite egocentric; Audrey Wilder recalls that his only topic of conversation from morning to night was himself. If the conversation veered away from him, his eyes turned to glass. He was on his best behavior, admittedly, because he was still under a shadow eleven years after the war because of charges that he had collaborated with the Germans. Marlene Dietrich, who had rejected an offer of marriage from Hitler and whose sister had been held as a hostage in Belsen in consequence, had stood up for him, saying that all he had done was entertain at the prisoner-of-war camps. According to I. A. L. Diamond, Chevalier had joined the Communist Party to clean up his position vis-à-vis the Fascists, and this had scarcely been helpful to his image during the Cold War. He was delighted to be working with Audrey, whom he had met at a party given by Sam Spiegel in New York; and although she, like everyone else, found him boring, he was almost literally in love with her and there were even improbable rumors of an affair.

One important ingredient in the picture was a recurring gag in which a group of musicians from a gypsy orchestra was paid by the roué to follow him and Audrey around wherever they went. At one point, the serenaders even had to navigate a lake. Wilder and Diamond, with their wives and Audrey, went to the famous old World War II Nazi hangout, the Shéhérazade nightclub, with the music director Matty Malneck, an amusing little man, and talked to the gypsy orchestra there. The leader said, "Are you people from Hollywood? I'm not a gypsy, I'm a Dutchman!", thus losing himself a very profitable job. Everyone laughed and took a cab to the Monseigneur, where they hired that famous nightery's gypsy band.

They all took off in a very good humor for location work at the Château de Vitry, a romantically beautiful castle built on a hill overlooking a lake, not far from Paris, on the River Loire. This was where the scenes were to be shot of Gary and Audrey rowing on the lake followed by the serenading gypsies, and of a picnic on an island. They drove to the location through ground fog, proceeding with the fog lights on while heads of cattle emerged through the swirling haze and issued low, booming moos. Everyone giggled at the sight.

They arrived at the château and shot some scenes inside by prior arrangement with the owners. The elderly countess who owned the château, the housekeeper with her traditional long, clanking chatelaine of house keys, the live-in servants, the bright-faced children, and even cousins and in-laws gathered silently on the stairs, as though posing for a family portrait, to watch the proceedings below with wide-eyed fascination. The gypsy violinists would play, Audrey and Gary would dance, and everyone would applaud at the end of the scene as though watching a play. They were unable to understand why this had to be repeated several times, and were quite exhausted by the time it came to the aperitifs, and everyone could relax.

Audrey in the 1950s
(Charles Higham collection)

A beautiful early portrait
(Culver Pictures)

Audrey in the late 1950s
(Culver Pictures)

Cogitating in *Gigi* on Broadway
(Culver Pictures)

With her beloved Cathleen Nesbitt, in Gilbert Miller's Broadway production of *Gigi*
(Culver Pictures)

Above: As Princess Anne in *Roman Holiday*, the movie that made Audrey a star *(Culver Pictures)*

With her fiancé, trucking heir James Hanson (whom she gave up for her career), in 1951 *(AP/Wide World Photos)*

With Gregory Peck in *Roman Holiday (Culver Pictures)*

On the Spanish Steps with an ice cream in *Roman Holiday (Culver Pictures)*

Facing page, top: As the water sprite in Alfred Lunt's exquisite production of *Ondine* on Broadway. Mel Ferrer is the beleaguered knight errant *(Culver Pictures)*
Bottom: Mel Ferrer courted Audrey onstage—and in private—in *Ondine (Culver Pictures)*

Audrey dressed by Givenchy in *Sabrina (Culver Pictures)*

Facing page, top: As the chauffeur's Paris-struck daughter in the unforgettable *Sabrina (Culver Pictures)*
Bottom: Sabrina—the cooking school scene *(Culver Pictures)*

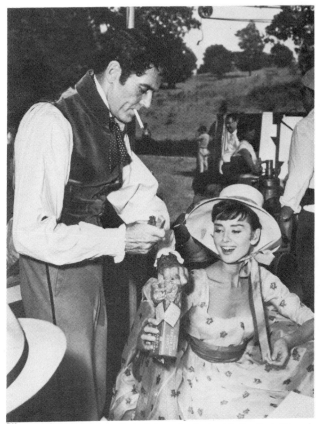

An off-the-set chat with Henry Fonda during a shooting break in the classic *War and Peace* (*The Museum of Modern Art/Film Stills Archive*)

Facing page: The famous Givenchy bateau-neckline dress in *Sabrina*. Millions of women imitated it (*Culver Pictures*)

Left: As Natasha in *War and Peace (Culver Pictures)* *Facing page, top:* On the bicycle Billy Wilder gave her, Audrey chats with Fred Astaire on a shooting break during the filming of *Funny Face (The Museum of Modern Art/Film Stills Archive)* *Bottom:* La Vie Bohémienne. *Funny Face (Culver Pictures)*

Below: With Mel Ferrer—whom she had just married—and Henry Fonda in *War and Peace (Culver Pictures)*

As the bluestocking in *Funny Face (Culver Pictures)*

Facing page, top: As the detective's daughter in *Love in the Afternoon (Culver Pictures)* *Bottom:* May–December romance with Gary Cooper in *Love in the Afternoon (Culver Pictures)*

A Givenchy again. *Love in the Afternoon (Culver Pictures)*

Below: Husband Mel Ferrer directing Audrey when director Billy Wilder was off the set—in *Love in the Afternoon (The Museum of Modern Art/Film Stills Archive)*

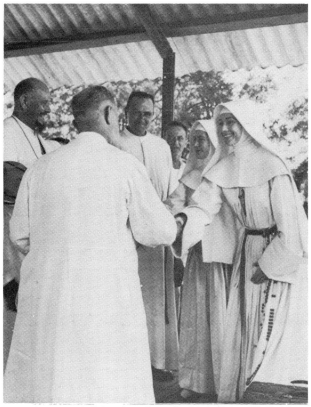

Meeting dignitaries in the Belgian Congo during a break in the filming of *The Nun's Story*
(Culver Pictures)

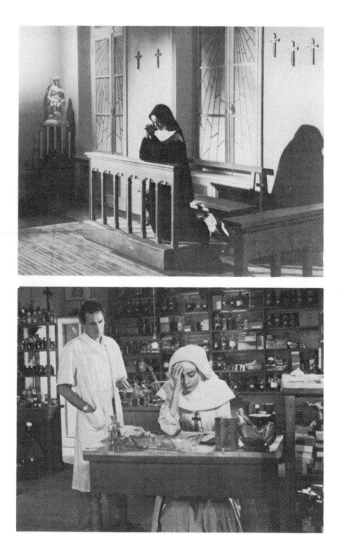

Facing page, top: Audrey as Sister Luke, praying in *The Nun's Story (Culver Pictures)* *Right:* In the dugout canoe at Stanleyville—*The Nun's Story (Culver Pictures)*

Facing page, bottom: With a young Peter Finch in *The Nun's Story (Culver Pictures)* *Right:* Conferring with Kathleen Hulme— author of *The Nun's Story* —and director Fred Zinnemann *(The Museum of Modern Art/Film Stills Archive)*

With her mother, the remarkable Baroness van Heemstra *(The Museum of Modern Art/Film Stills Archive)*

Facing page, top: In the beautiful *Green Mansions*, directed by her husband, Mel Ferrer *(Culver Pictures)*
Bottom: With the pre-*Psycho* Tony Perkins, in *Green Mansions (Culver Pictures)*

This page: As the immortal Holly Golightly in *Breakfast at Tiffany's (Culver Pictures)*
Facing page, top: Kissing George Peppard in the *Breakfast at Tiffany's* famous love scene in the rain *(Culver Pictures)*
Bottom: There were rumors of an off-screen romance with George Peppard in *Breakfast at Tiffany's (Culver Pictures)*

The famous Ascot scene—dressed by Cecil Beaton—in *My Fair Lady (Culver Pictures)*

Facing page, top: A Paris location for *Charade (Culver Pictures) Bottom:* With Cary Grant in *Charade (Culver Pictures)*

He grew accustomed to her face. With Rex Harrison in *My Fair Lady (Culver Pictures)*

Facing page, top: Eliza Doolittle as a lady—hat and costume by Cecil Beaton. *My Fair Lady (Culver Pictures) Bottom:* Eliza Doolittle turns into a swan. The magical coming-out scene in *My Fair Lady (Culver Pictures)*

Astride the white stallion in *The Unforgiven*. Later, the horse threw her, breaking her back *(Culver Pictures)*

Facing page, top: With Audie Murphy (the most decorated war hero of World War II), in *The Unforgiven (Culver
Pictures)* *Bottom:* A dramatic scene from Audrey's Mex-
ican Western, *The Unforgiven (Culver Pictures)*

Beautiful in her late thirties—*Wait Until Dark (Culver Pictures)*

Facing page, top: As the blind, tormented heroine of *Wait Until Dark*, with Richard Crenna *(Culver Pictures)*   *Bottom:* Fleeing from a demented Alan Arkin in *Wait Until Dark (Culver Pictures)*

Top: With her second husband, Dr. Andrea Dotti of Rome, around the time of an attempted kidnapping of him *(UPI/Bettmann Archive)*   *Bottom:* With her son, Sean, at a New York art exhibition in 1979 *(UPI/Bettmann Archive)*

The lake scenes were tricky, because the camera crew and director had to follow the boat with Audrey and Gary and also the one carrying the gypsies; this required great concentration to keep them all within the camera lines. A picnic was set up on the island. Audrey had to eat chicken, but unfortunately she was allergic to garlic, and there was no way that anyone could persuade a French chef to leave garlic out of a fowl recipe. So, she stuck a piece of pear to a chicken leg with toothpicks and the audience didn't know the difference.

There were piles of French bread, sausages and hams, and heaps of cheese. Ninety people gathered round washing down the heavy food with wine, coffee, beer, and milk from the cows grazing in a nearby pasture, while swarms of mosquitoes attacked the stars. With self-control, Audrey stopped herself from beating them off and ruining the shot.

Love in the Afternoon was a happy picture for everyone. Back in Paris, Audrey, Billy and Audrey Wilder, Izzy Diamond, Cooper, and almost everyone except Chevalier went to a little boîte in an unfashionable quarter for drinks at the end of each day. The only unpopular one was Mel Ferrer, who was regarded generally as a party pooper. He watched Audrey like a puppet master, not seeming to want her to have any fun. Audrey Wilder remembers that one evening Audrey was reminded that she had to leave the next day for a quick hop to London to attend the premier of *War and Peace*.

Audrey had had slightly too many drinks. She had tried, along with the others, English, French, and Russian vodka. According to the Wilders, she said, very loudly, when she was told that a couple she knew were fussing about their tickets, "What a crock of shit about the tickets." This was amazing coming from the epitome of fifties purity, and everyone looked up amazed. Audrey Wilder remembers that Mel Ferrer was furious: his wife had put a dent in her image, and the dreaded public was actually present when they were all enjoying a drink. "You're leaving here now!" he exclaimed. Everyone was annoyed as they walked out.

Once again there were widespread comments in the industry

that Ferrer was holding Audrey on far too tight a rein. Even the slightest hint of her being human rather than saintly allegedly seemed to annoy him, and he would whisk her away on the spot. Ferrer was not liked for this. Yet it is easy to understand his motive: he was Audrey's protector. Every star needed one so that the public, fed on fantasies, would not suspect the truth. He sheltered her completely. Her fragile, jittery personality had to be hidden so that people would think her as cool, composed, and lighthearted as she was on the screen.

Once again the variable weather of Paris, shifting from rain to sunshine, from fog to gusts of wind, proved to be a problem in the making of the picture. Finally Wilder realized that the light fluctuated too greatly to permit him to shoot exteriors all day, so he transported two interior sets — a Paris café and a hospital room — from the studios of Boulogne to the woods of Gambais. He found all kinds of ingenious ways to overcome the many problems of the production. As during *Sabrina*, Wilder was a constant source of amusement; he was a mischievous Katzenjammer Kid among directors, with his witty face, more interesting than handsome, and his jug ears. He rejoiced in mentioning to Audrey that the film's theme tune, the well-worn "Fascination" waltz, an old Paramount stock-in-trade, had been the music that accompanied his first sexual experience. Nobody believed him, but it was good for a laugh all around. The movie turned out to be a delight, marred only by Cooper's aged look, which made people feel rather uneasy about the romantic sequences. His leathery face kissing Audrey's unlined features seemed more than a little embarrassing, not to mention the fact that he had to stoop over for the task.

At the conclusion of *Love in the Afternoon*, Billy Wilder decided to give an elaborate Hollywood-style wrap-up party. It took place on the set of the Ritz suite, and Herb Sterne sent out fifteen hundred invitations. A red carpet led into the studio of Boulogne, and there were arc lights and bleachers for the fans. The party was catered by the Ritz itself, with actual waiters instead of extras, and the famous Ritz silver and glassware.

Audrey was apprehensive about the party: she dreaded it, as she dreaded all such events. Then, the worst possible thing happened. She had hoped to avoid it or at the very least take a back seat to Cooper and Chevalier. But Gary was stricken with influenza and could not attend for more than a minute or two, and Chevalier was unavoidably booked to appear at the Olympia. Herb Sterne recalls that he was at his wit's end. Louella Parsons was supposed to be talking to the stars on the telephone from Hollywood for the millions of readers of her Hearst newspaper column. Audrey was not keen to talk to her, and never had forgotten her appearance in Rome during *War and Peace,* when she had so desperately needed her weekend solitude at the farm.

Sterne told Audrey that Louella would be on the phone. She groaned inwardly. Ferrer brought her to the set to wait for the mob to arrive. Louella came through in the line, and Sterne went to Audrey and told her. But Audrey completely ignored the call and told Sterne she was going to check the place cards out. Sterne began tearing his hair out and begged Mel to intercede. Mel said it was hopeless, but Sterne kept begging him until finally he spoke to Audrey. Even so, she refused to come back. Sterne says, "There was no rushing her. There Louella was sitting on her ass, tapping her foot."

Soon afterward, Paramount's New York office called Sterne for some color stills of Audrey. There was no Chinese paper to use as background in Paris at that time. Silk was in short supply, and Sterne was desperate to find backings. Finally, somebody suggested balsa-wood flats, which could be sprayed in different colors. But again Audrey proved difficult. She hated doing the stills and couldn't make up her mind which clothes she wanted to wear. This made it impossible to spray the flats. Finally, Sterne had a rack of forty costumes brought onstage. After much hesitation, Audrey would bring herself to choose a particular garment; then one of the crew had to spray the flat. A minute later, Sterne had to order the sun arc lights switched on to dry the flats. It was a nightmare from beginning to end. Audrey's finickiness and insecurity took their toll on everyone who worked with her.

Audrey and Mel had a heavy travel schedule after the completion of the picture. They flew to Hollywood and then took a brief vacation in La Quinta, a pleasant resort in the California desert near Palm Springs. Then, on New Year's Day of 1957, they traveled to New York, where they made a version of *Mayerling,* the old chestnut about the love affair of the crown prince of Austria and the tragic Marie Vetsera, which, according to some accounts, culminated in a double suicide. The director, the colorful White Russian Anatole Litvak, had directed another version of this story with Charles Boyer and Danielle Darrieux, almost twenty years earlier, in pre-World War II Paris. That version had been something of a classic, but this one emphatically was not.

It was made for NBC-TV's *Producer's Showcase,* and there is no question that Mel Ferrer was entirely miscast as the young and dashing prince. The part called for a beautiful and athletic youth obsessed with romantic daydreams, and although Boyer had been even more physically wrong, he had somehow managed to convince the audience that he was romantically obsessed. Ferrer was not only too old, and too gaunt; he was too dry, cold, and matter-of-fact as a performer. Audrey was, of course, ideal as Marie Vetsera, with her heart-stopping prettiness, vulnerability, and essentially aristocratic poise. The problem in making the picture was that it also provided an unsympathetic portrait of Crown Prince Rudolf's nervously edgy attitude toward his young love. Litvak told *Life* magazine (February 4, 1957): "When Audrey plays Maria, speaking to the prince, she is also Audrey speaking to her husband. It is very difficult to get Mel to treat her roughly. I had to work with him to get him to do it."

He had to teach Mel other things as well. There is an amusing photograph in *Life* showing a quite elderly Litvak embracing Audrey while Mel stoops to look at them. The caption reads, "Litvak as lover shows Ferrer how he should hold his wife, Audrey, to get best effect at romantic moments."

While in New York, Audrey finally yielded to the persuasions of Kurt Frings and signed a contract for the motion-picture version of *The Nun's Story* by Kathryn Hulme, a novel which was then high on the best-seller list. Audrey had held back because there was no part in it for Mel, or so Warner Brothers, which was to make the film, asserted. To do the picture would involve a separation, since Audrey would have to go to Africa for a long period of shooting, and it was likely that Mel would have to accept commitments in America or Europe to avoid a hiatus in his career. Also, with her fragile health, Audrey was nervous about a sojourn in Africa, in the intense tropical heat of the equatorial regions; and she had heard of the health problems suffered by Katharine Hepburn while making *The African Queen* on an identical location some six years earlier. Still, the part of Sister Luke was far too important for her to turn down. Moreover, it had resonances which echoed those in her own life. Sister Luke was Belgian, and Audrey had been born in Brussels; one of the reasons Sister Luke left the convent was that she was not permitted to work in the Belgian Underground. Nothing could have been closer to Audrey's heart.

The book opens with Gabrielle Van der Mal in the anteroom of a cloister, with a group of farm girls putting on hooded black capes. She is thinking about Lourdes, its cures and candles. She is about to become a postulant and dwells on the physical world she is about to depart. "It was, Gabrielle thought, like being in quarantine before a border crossing into a country of silence." But, she wonders, how is she to quell her memories, her senses, her sexuality? How is she to suppress her pride? Hulme examines, with precise, concrete details and simple language, the ordeal of self-sacrifice, penance, deprivation. The culpa, the de profundis, the kissing of the feet of the eldest nuns, the begging for soup, the once-a-week bath, the devotions that made the knees ache, the hunger for salvation, the itineraries and litanies that stripped the soul bare — all are driven home to the reader with clinical exactness and scrupulous documentation. Vivid scenes occur in the school of tropical medicines, in a château in a suburb of Brussels — not unlike the one in which Audrey spent her early childhood.

Sister Luke struggles to master the deadly diseases that plague the staff. There are lectures on the mosquito, the examinations of the deadly shapes that cause leprosy, sleeping sickness, yaws, malaria, and elephantiasis. She is in training for a journey to the Congo.

She also works in a madhouse, a purgatory filled with a dull, subhuman roar of the dangerously demented. Again, her training is for the Congo. She struggles with an insane patient in one very powerful scene. And now at last she goes to Africa, to the heat, the dusty streets, the local convent, and the challenge of Dr. Fortunati, the chief surgeon, obstetrician, and specialist in tuberculosis and cancer. Dr. Fortunati is an almost Graham Greene figure of a dirty jungle saint, dedicated to medicine despite the stench of his body and the squalor of his thoughts. Always, Sister Luke is portrayed as a creative personality — building, learning, and developing in a world that is static and immutable. At one stage, Mother Mathilde is so concerned by Sister Luke's interest in the doctor that she asks her whether she has fallen in love. She replies that she only cherishes him "for his skill and selflessness when there's a life to be saved."

War comes. Sister Luke returns to Belgium and is to be appointed to the Dutch border. Sister Luke envisions the Nazi parachute troops: "Small puffs of white dropping from the skies which would look at first like clouds and then, as they neared the earth, would turn into parachutes with Nazi storm troopers dangling from the invisible cord."

Now, Rotterdam is bombed and Belgium bombarded. Artillery fire resounds; refugees pour into the convent. The author evokes an atmosphere of a country under siege that is a mirror image of Audrey's own experience. Sister Luke even protects a British flier. She hides him in a private room. The tension becomes extreme. And at the same time there is the deeper tension of knowing that her work is a test of courage and a threat to her necessary humility. At last, she realizes the extremity of her problem. Reality impinges on her. And here the novel becomes almost uncanny in its parallels with Audrey: Sister Luke's brother, like Audrey's, is a prisoner in a concentration camp, while another brother is trying to harass the occupation forces within the country.

Sister Luke feels that she must leave the convent. She can no longer offer blind obedience. She needs to serve mortals on her own initiative. The Reverend Mother begs her to change her mind, but finally it is made up. She obtains permission to re-enter the world. There is a marvelous description of the fear, the unease that suddenly comes with the first act of choice (in clothing), and the first thought that she will have to make decisions for herself. It is a powerful conclusion to a novel that was deeply and sincerely felt.

However, Audrey was very uneasy about acting out the war scenes she had lived, and it seems that the deal was made on the understanding that they would be omitted. It was agreed that Robert Anderson (at that time famous for his play *Tea and Sympathy*) would write the script while Audrey traveled with Mel to St. Moritz and to Spain and Mexico for *The Sun Also Rises,* a film version of Hemingway's novel in which Mel was cast.

After two weeks of skiing in Switzerland, Audrey and Mel flew to Madrid, where an extraordinary collection of people was gathered to make the movie — among them, Errol Flynn, Tyrone Power, and Ava Gardner. Later, the shooting in Morelia and Mexico City was exciting, charged with the electricity of the people involved in it. Ava Gardner was having an affair with the Italian comedian Walter Chiari, having lost the celebrated screenwriter and novelist Peter Viertel to Joan Fontaine, who was in turn to lose him to Deborah Kerr. Darryl Zanuck, the producer, was having an affair with Audrey's friend Juliette Greco, the nightclub star and toast of the Left Bank. Flynn had dumped his wife, Patrice Wymore, and was becoming involved with prostitutes; and there was tension between Flynn and Power because they had formerly had an affair.

Often at night, Audrey and Mel would meet with Ava and Tyrone and do the town, and on weekends Audrey and Ava, who adored each other, would go shopping, Audrey bringing along Famous, with his red ribbons, jumping up excitedly on his leash. Henry King, the director of *The Sun Also Rises*, recalls that Audrey seldom came on the set or the location, realizing that her presence would be distracting for all concerned; it was not customary for stars to watch each other working if they were not in the picture. So she stayed home, tending her health, until she flew to Hollywood with Mel to visit his children in Santa Barbara and then to Long Island to visit his family there. She decisively turned down parts in *A Certain Smile* and a story of the von Trapp family which later became *The Sound of Music*; she also declined to replace Diane Cilento in the London West End musical *Zuleika*, based on the famous Max Beerbohm novel *Zuleika Dobson*. She returned to Switzerland in the early spring and was pleased to hear that society columnist Cholly Knickerbocker, followed by British society photographer Antony Beauchamp, had named her one of the world's ten leading women.

In Switzerland, Audrey read Anderson's final draft of the screenplay for *The Nun's Story*. She was restless and unhappy at the time, disappointed because she had not become pregnant again despite every effort by herself and Mel and still uneasy about Africa, but consoled by the Burgenstock once more. In the years she and Mel had intermittently been there, the local people had, to her great pleasure, paid no attention to her. She was just another foreigner. Only that spring were they recognized, not so much as a tourist couple back at their favorite resort, but as two members of their community. They were greeted as they walked through the fields. They had never been recognized before. One old man particularly fascinated them. He was a peasant with a weather-beaten sunburned face, a pipe dangling from his mouth whenever they saw him. He would never so much as glance at them when they ran into him on the forest paths they frequented. It was impossible to make him smile.

One day, after rain, Famous toddled beside them in the slush, looking like a pathetic rat with his hair all wet. As he jumped up, the man caught sight of him and his sour face cracked into a grin. Mel and Audrey hugged each other delightedly. They had made a conquest.

An episode took place that seemed to come from the pages of a fairy tale — or a publicity release — but Audrey told the story herself, to Henry Gris. One afternoon, her beloved pet canary escaped from its cage when she inadvertently left the door open as she went to fetch the birdseed. The bird flew out of the door, and Audrey was devastated. A child at heart, she cried like a little girl. She called Fritz Frey, who, trusted friend that he was, came to the rescue. He summoned every able-bodied man of the Burgenstock to search the mountain, concentrating on trees where a canary might perch.

One man in particular was said to be able to find anything that flew or walked, for he frequently had recovered the pets of neighborhood children. He was equipped with a lumberjack or linesman outfit, with steel hooks attached to a belt and many lengths of wire and cable. This man went from tree to tree, day after day, night after night, climbing, searching. At last, a miracle happened: he saw the canary perching on the low branch of a fir tree. He climbed the tree with a series of grappling hooks, but the canary flew away. At last, he located its resting place; then it flew off again.

Audrey was told the canary had been traced and came from her house to watch the search. She said later, "A whole afternoon went by. It was miserable. I pleaded with the man to give up, to forget the whole thing as he went from tree to tree. But at dusk the canary settled on a lower branch and at last the man caught and rescued him. I was overwhelmingly happy and grateful." Audrey offered a reward, but the man refused to take it. That was the Burgenstock.

During those weeks in Switzerland, Mel Ferrer decided that he wanted to direct Audrey's next picture after *The Nun's Story*, which was to be *Green Mansions: A Romance of the Tropical Forest*, based on a novel by W. H. Hudson. While in Mexico, Mel had rediscovered the book, which he had first read at Princeton.

Ferrer loved *Green Mansions,* and so did Audrey. Hudson

had spent part of his early life in South America, and as a naturalist he understood the reality of the jungle. Living in London in great poverty at the beginning of the twentieth century, he wrote the fantastic book to alleviate his drab and depressing surroundings. *Green Mansions*, set in Venezuela in the late nineteenth century, is the story of an explorer, writing in the first person, who feels the atmosphere of the jungle as part of an inner landscape. In the jungle, the explorer meets a strange girl, Rima, who has a magnetic, soothing quality on all living things. He describes her thus: "Her figure and features were singularly delicate, but it was her color that struck me most, which indeed made her differ from all other human beings. The color of the skin would be almost impossible to describe, so greatly did it vary with every change of mood — and the moods were many and transient — and with the angle on which the sunlight touched it, and the degree of light."

In Rima, Hudson creates an unearthly being, a creature not quite human who converses with birds and every living creature with intense sympathy. But the legend has a puritanical touch: the adventurer does not experience Rima as a man experiences a woman, and he fights his passion for her fiercely. When at last he holds her she is as elusive as the mist, leading him into the world of the forest like a guide. In the second half of the work, a sense of threat emerges and, finally, the story evolves into something not unrelated to the theme of *Ondine*. Because Rima is too perfect to live, the Indians burn her to death as an evil spirit.

Mel and Audrey agreed that Audrey should be Rima. The character was ideal for her: a strange, remote creature who loves all living things and is betrayed by the evil of man. It is easy to see why Mel, still madly in love with Audrey, would want to present her under his own direction in his vision of her: a lovely creature who was above the crowd, who had a quality of fineness that was seldom discovered in human beings.

Mel and Audrey flew to Hollywood to try to put *Green Mansions* together. Mel was surprised to find via Kurt Frings that there was a history attached to the property. In 1932, RKO-Radio Pictures had bought the book as a vehicle for Dolores Del Rio, but it had never been made. It had lain on a shelf at the studio for eleven years, gathering dust, when independent producer James L. Cassidy bought it for a song. He sold it to MGM in 1945, netting almost seventy thousand dollars more on the deal than he had paid for the book. Writers struggled for eight years to satisfy Louis B. Mayer, MGM's boss, but failed; then, in 1953, Alan Jay Lerner wrote a script for Vincente Minnelli to film in South America. Pier Angeli was to be the star, and Minnelli, art director Preston Ames, and unit manager William Kaplan flew to Venezuela to select backgrounds. But then a change of policy and management at the studio killed the project.

Ferrer realized he had much to cope with in trying to get the picture off the ground. But he found a sympathetic producer, Edmund Grainger, who decided to go ahead, and Preston Ames agree to resume the job of designing the picture. Dorothy Kingsley, a writer Mel admired, agreed to do the script, and after some considerable delay, the studio agreed to proceed with Mel as the director and Audrey as the star. Executive-level doubts about the story's potential box-office appeal were partly assuaged by the conviction that Audrey had so secure a box-office record she could carry anything to success. And indeed, in 1957 she was among the most beloved of stars.

The chief problem Audrey and Mel faced was that of scheduling. How would it be possible to make *Green Mansions* before *The Nun's Story*, which by now, the spring of 1957, was in full preparation? Audrey fretted that she would greatly disappoint Mel if *Green Mansions* had to be delayed for more than a year, the time it would take to set up, shoot, and cut *The Nun's Story*; Mel would have no place in the cast of the latter picture, and his career might suffer accordingly. She even thought for a time of withdrawing, but Frings and Ferrer begged her to reconsider, and she yielded to their pressure. Mel pointed out that while she was in Africa, Rome, and Belgium shooting *The Nun's Story's* on diverse locations, he would be in South America selecting material for background shots and deciding if the conditions would be feasible for Audrey and the rest of the cast.

Much of the spring was spent in long discussions between Mel and Dorothy Kingsley and the front office at MGM, and between Audrey, Fred Zinnemann, Henry Blanke, and Robert Anderson on *The Nun's Story*. In April, Audrey shot black-and-white photographic tests for cameraman Ted McCord at Warner Brothers, characteristically fretting over the contact sheets and ruling out all except three. She asked for the *War and Peace* team, as always feeling more secure when she was surrounded by the people she knew, including cameraman Jack Cardiff, assistant director Mario Chiari, makeup team Alberto and Gracia Di Rossi,* and unit manager John Palmer. A high spot of that spring was meeting with both Kathryn Hulme, author of *The Nun's Story*, and Marie-Louise Habets, the Belgian former nun who inspired the character Sister Luke in the novel. According to publicity releases, Audrey met Miss Habets only once, and sat tongue-tied before her, in Miss Hulme's living room at Wildwood Place, Eagle Rock, near Los Angeles, unable to utter a word. This story was a pure fabrication. In fact, the studio files show that Audrey worked closely with both women as she studied, with typical intensity, every minute detail of her role.

In visits to Eagle Rock, she learned much of how the writing of *The Nun's Story* had begun. Miss Hulme had been a nurse in 1945, at the end of the war, working in a high school near Cherbourg which housed about three thousand United Nations Relief Organization employees. They were concerned, as Miss Hulme was herself, with aiding the innumerable refugees living in displaced-persons camps in a ruined Germany.

Miss Hulme and her fellow workers lived in hastily converted dormitories, filled with some forty army cots, in what

---

* The only members of the team who finally worked with her on the new production.

had once been schoolrooms. Privacy could be obtained only by stretching a blanket in the form of a wall between one cot and another.

Miss Habets's cot was inside a set of double doors near the washrooms and the noisy stairway to the mess hall. Kathryn Hulme noticed that this lonely woman, who spoke to no one, spent most days lying exhausted on the bed, stretched out like a figure on a tomb with the toes of her army boots pointing upward. Everyone passed her by with noisy voices and feet clattering on stone, and she never moved an inch. Miss Hulme told Audrey that she was baffled by the woman's incredible power to sleep motionless in the midst of such a disturbance; Kathryn actually had to step over Marie-Lou's form on the cot when she went to have meals or attend briefings in the lecture hall. The ribbons on her army uniform carried the Belgian colors; a further mystery was why she didn't have any part in the Belgian contingent of UNRRA. At last Miss Hulme met the Belgian nurse. The team was due for transfer to Germany on army trucks, and Miss Hulme observed her coolly placing her first-aid kit in the second truck. Five days out on a harrowing, bumpy journey with very low-grade rations and unpleasant weather conditions, one of the English secretaries fell from a truck and suffered a fractured clavicle. Kathryn Hulme was amazed when Miss Habets instantly and calmly located the fracture, immobilized it, and asked for a stretcher.

In Germany the two women worked together closely in a displaced-persons camp. Marie-Lou worked devotedly on double duty while others went on furlough. She worked long and grueling hours in a savagely cold winter to sort and inventory children's clothing for the many pathetic refugees in the camp.

After hours of this work, Kathryn said to her, "You're a saint, Marie-Lou." Miss Habets started back in horror. She said that Kathryn had stepped completely out of line in calling her that. Then she drew her aside, her face a picture of anguish, and said with extreme shame, "You have seen too much. I was a nun once. But a nun who failed her vows."

Kathryn Hulme tried to reassure her. She said — not quite correctly — that there was no shame attached to failure in America. Many people failed their marital vows just as they failed in their marriage to Christ. She urged Marie-Lou to tell her more. Gradually, painfully, Marie-Lou told her everything. Audrey was once again magnetized by the fact that Marie-Lou, like Audrey, had helped British flyers to safety when they landed in the fields. She understood more and more what agony of spirit Miss Habets had suffered when she was forbidden by her mother-general to engage in patriotic activities.

As time went on, Kathryn and Marie-Lou became initimate friends, and the idea of writing the book became more and more consuming. First, Kathryn wrote *The Wild Place*, which was about displaced persons, and then at last "Sister Luke" asked her to write her story; the rest was history. Marie-Lou Habets moved into Kathryn Hulme's house near Malibu, and they worked together on every page. Later, she moved to Eagle Rock and worked at the Santa Fe Railroad hospital in Los Angeles. She suffered from high blood pressure and had to transfer to private nursing in consequence.

Indeed, it was kept very quiet that Audrey worked intimately with Marie-Lou Habets on every detail of her nun's habit, her coif, the way she would mount and dismount a streetcar, how she would perform her orisons, Hail Marys, and other offices, how she would say her rosary, and how she would approach an altar or kiss a silver crucifix. Marie-Lou told her all about the conditions in a convent, and Audrey told Zinnemann and Blanke she was quite resolved to spend several days and nights in a selected convent in Belgium in order to enter into the spirit of the part completely.

Audrey also learned surgical techniques from Marie-Lou, and she attended operations at local hospitals in order to observe the handling of instruments. Yet all through the work, she was not totally at ease and still kept fretting about the schedule that might delay *Green Mansions*. The matter was further complicated when Mel was suddenly compelled to go to Germany to prepare the movie *Fräulein*, and she was to go with him late that summer.

In the meantime, Zinnemann and Blanke flew to Africa, Rome, and Belgium to select the locations and prepare the bases of shooting. Securing the cooperation of the Catholic Church was a problem, not only in Belgium but in Italy and Africa as well. Habets's story was not liked in many church circles, chiefly because there was general disapproval of a nun who had broken her vows making commercial capital out of her story. There was also much criticism that she had exaggerated the harshness of convent life, and there was controversy surrounding her description of kissing her superiors' feet, undergoing flagellation, and being ordered to fail her examinations to teach her humility.

With great shrewdness, Jack Warner and the Warner Brothers front office selected John J. Vizzard, second under Geoffrey Shurlock of the Motion Picture Producers' Association (designed to protect the industry's moral standards) to represent the studio vis-à-vis the Catholic Church. Since Vizzard had worked with the celebrated Monsignor Devlin, head of the Legion of Decency, he was perfectly chosen for the task. But he ran into severe difficulties from the moment he arrived in Belgium. The bishop of Bruges was totally opposed to the project and flatly refused to allow the shooting to take place in the original convent of the Sisters of Charity at Ghent. The mother-general of the sisters failed to respond to Vizzard's careful reassurances and blandishments. She said that much of the book was false and deliberately invented, and that she especially disliked the implications of cruelty in the nunnery. Thus, Vizzard was compelled to leave Belgium and travel to France, where he found a totally different atmosphere. Because there was considerable rivalry between the French and Belgian monastic authorities, there was no objection to using a French convent, the Order of the Sisters of the Oblates d'Assumption at Froyennes, as the stand-in for the Belgian establishment. Indeed, the mother superior agreed to meet with Audrey, and if she were satisfied with her sincerity, she would allow her to take up a brief residence in a guest room, provided that her movements were under strict control and that the studio should make a significant monetary contribution to the convent.

Needless to say, there was no objection on the part of Warner Brothers. Audrey and Mel flew to New York in June and stayed at the Sulgrave, one of the most elegant small hotels in the city, then moved on to Ferrer's father's house at Southampton. Their lawyer Abe Bienstock joined them in Europe, where Mel made *Fräulein*. They returned to Hollywood in the fall, and more serious preparations for *The Nun's Story* began.

Chapter Eight

In September, there was much discussion about the casting of Dr. Fortunati in *The Nun's Story*. At first, Gérard Philippe was offered the role, but did not like Robert Anderson's script and withdrew. The second choice was Yves Montand, who asked for far too much money in view of the fact that his name was not known to the American public. Finally, the Australian actor Peter Finch was offered the part; he, too, was not known in America, but his fee was modest and he was known to be very easy to work with. The problem was that Dr. Fortunati was an Italian, and that a scruffy European type was called for; Finch was all too Australian, and his atmosphere of beer-drinking extroversion was entirely wrong. Nevertheless, Fred Zinnemann and Henry Blanke felt that his skill as an actor would overcome any awkwardnesses of casting, and Audrey was delighted. Though she would have preferred Jack Hawkins, she knew Finch's work and was very pleased about his selection.

Others cast were the great Dame Peggy Ashcroft as Mother Matilda and, when Katharine Cornell had failed to get the part after much negotiation, Dame Edith Evans was cast as the formidable Mother Emmanuel, Sister Luke's mother general in Belgium. The remarkable cast also included Mildred Dunnock as Sister Margharita, Beatrice Straight as Mother Christophe, Barbara O'Neil as Mother Katherine, and Patricia Bosworth (later the well-known author of biographies of

Montgomery Clift and Diane Arbus) as Simone. Audrey knew of every one of these actresses, and, like all sensible stars, knew she would shine more brightly with a strong supporting cast. She was pleased that the costumes would be designed by Marjorie Best, working in close consultation with Marie-Louise Habets, and she sent the sketches to Givenchy in Paris, who was greatly impressed. At her suggestion, set design was entrusted to Alexandre Trauner, who made detailed sketches of the interiors of convents in France.

In early November, Zinnemann and Blanke were in Rome. They were fretting because Audrey was putting them under excessive pressure to know the finishing date — pressure which may or may not have emanated originally from Mel Ferrer. In a telegram dated November 6, 1957, sent from Rome, studio publicist Carl Combs advised Steve Trilling, studio chief, that Audrey was deeply disturbing Zinnemann with her annoying messages and that a firm stand must be taken with her. Indeed, she must not be brought to Rome until the last minute before she was due to leave for Africa, so that her nervousness over the finishing date would not get the better of her. Zinnemann cabled Trilling on the day, saying, "Believe we are courting disaster if Audrey left unaware finishing date much longer. Will decline all responsibility for picture unless Audrey fully aware of true situation. Find myself increasingly unable to cope with endless uncertainty."

Audrey was also worried about the possible effect that the Belgian Congo might have on her health, and the studio had to guarantee that the best doctor there would be available for any kind of emergency and would possess the proper drugs if needed. Her fears for her delicate constitution were again getting the better of her, and Mel too worried about the effect of the equatorial heat.

Audrey also insisted upon having a bidet airmailed to her in Rome, because they were then unknown in the Italian capital, or so she claimed; and it was also to accompany her to Africa. As for her Yorkshire terrier Famous, the Belgians were strict about importing animals, and at that time the Congo was a Belgian protectorate.

Audrey became very edgy and fretful when she was told that although the Italian quarantine rules could be shifted a little to admit the dog, Congolese restrictions probably could not. Lawyers were consulted, government officials approached, and memoranda flew in every direction from Hollywood to Europe and back again over the dog. At last, through God knows what strategy, the star got her wish and everything was cleared for Famous to head for the equator provided he was given the necessary inoculations against rabies and distemper and a certificate was issued confirming the fact.

Very jittery, Audrey went to the airport in Los Angeles, accompanied by Mel, Famous, and Steve Trilling. She flew to Paris, where she checked into the convent at Froyennes. Just before she left, she obsessively composed Ferrer's menus for every single day of her absence, including brunch on Sundays — as though she would in fact be with him every moment.

She told Trilling with her usual firmness that she would agree to a press reception at the airport or at the hotel in Rome, but not both. An airport press conference was decided upon. She traveled with her measurements in case the nun's habits should be lost in the notorious Italian customs sheds: five-foot-six-and-three-quarter inches tall, at twenty-eight she had a thirty-two-and-a-half-inch bust, a twenty-one-inch waist, and thirty-five-inch hips.

Although she was raised an Episcopalian, Audrey was quite at home in the convent and behaved perfectly, never intruding herself too much. Her temperament, however, was more delicate than ever. She still nagged everyone over the finishing date, and, because she had insisted on spending Christmas with Mel, her schedule was now impossibly tight: she would have just nine days' preparation in Rome at Cinecittà before leaving for the Congo on January 16.

Audrey was accompanied by her secretary, and near namesake as Mrs. Ferrer, Helene Ferrero. They arrived at the Hassler Hotel on the Spanish Steps on January 5, their suite, it is painful to report, only twelve dollars a night. Audrey had butterflies in her stomach; everyone echoed Steve Trilling's sentiments in a telegram to Henry Blanke that "Once [Audrey] is fully merged in the production, *Green Mansions* will become dim in her mind, if that's possible." She did some tests at Cinecittà for her costumes and met with her beloved Franz Planer, who had been hired as the cinematographer. His color shots of her were marvelous, and she was deeply grateful, though worried as always about her looks.

Just before leaving for Stanleyville, Belgian Congo, by Sabena Airlines charter plane, Audrey cabled Trilling on January 23 thanking him and Jack Warner for their "wonderful message" and adding, "We are all very happy and excited and most grateful . . ."

Now that the trip was actually on, Audrey was excited, and she, Dame Peggy Ashcroft, Peter Finch, Dorothy Alison, Zinnemann, and the others flew to Stanleyville in a good humor.

The chartered plane had an uneventful flight, but on arrival at Stanleyville Audrey noticed with alarm that the airport was completely blanketed in fog. With the jungle all around, there was no place else to land and, to her great dismay, the plane kept circling round and round until it could finally land. Since Stanleyville was close to the equator, the heat was intense and the sun stood directly overhead in a cloudless sky. The drive into Stanleyville drenched everyone in perspiration. Audrey and most of the cast were driven through the treelined streets, past white houses with corrugated-iron roofs, to the modest but comfortable Sabena Guest House — not exactly the Ritz, but designed to provide as much coolness as possible under the severe tropical conditions. The rooms into which Audrey was ushered by the manager were pleasantly furnished with bamboo chairs and tables, but someone had installed a humidifier instead of an air conditioner, and she felt she was walking into a fever swamp. The manager removed the humidifier with apologies and replaced it with the air conditioner, which made a rattling noise and sat awkwardly under the windowsill. Famous buzzed around chasing imaginary or actual lizards and spiders on the matted floor.

Meanwhile, as Audrey settled in, film equipment began

arriving after a forty-five-day journey by truck, ship, and rail. Urgent equipment had already been flown in by special plane. Water was in short supply, and Famous suffered from the humidity, which was so intense and clinging that it seemed to be raining indoors. Audrey was saved in part by her thinness: lack of subcutaneous fat made the heat far more tolerable than it would have been for most people. Her diet helped too. As she had for some years, she ate only two boiled eggs and a piece of brown toast for breakfast and drank three cups of coffee; cottage cheese and fruit salad for lunch; and thin slices of meat and two vegetables for dinner. This extremely light diet of not much more than a thousand calories a day got her through the suffocating conditions of the next few weeks.

Dame Peggy Ashcroft remembers that it was an inspiration to see Audrey at work: her dedication and ability to concentrate under very arduous conditions were remarkable. She never spared herself, and her charm and courtesy to everyone never failed. Her ability as a linguist was a great asset, since the cast was working with Flemish monks and nuns. After one day of rest, Audrey arrived for work on location at a local railway station. Since the station was bathed in brilliant sunshine and everyone had to leave by noon, when the train would chug by, they had to rise at 5 A.M. and start working at six. They moved after lunch on the twenty-ninth to a small native village and then shot a sequence that involved crossing a river, in which Audrey and Dame Peggy, with the servant played by Orlando Martins, made their way across by canoe. The coifs were tight around their faces and very uncomfortable, and the perspiration ran down, making the headdresses sticky and clinging and the hair hang limply on their heads.

The next day, already exhausted but determined not to show it, Audrey woke in her rooms at the Sabena Guest House to the monotonous rain of the equatorial region. There were rumblings of thunder and odd flashes of lightning, almost like St. Elmo's fire. A scene scheduled for the Black Hospital (white and black were segregated in those regions) had to be canceled and instead a scene was shot at a house next to the White

Hospital between Father Vermeuhlen, played by Niall MacGinnis, and Audrey's Sister Luke. Despite the downpour, Zinnemann felt that the rain was insufficient to achieve the right effect on film and it had to be augmented with a rain machine. The rain machine broke down when the generator gave out, and everyone was upset. When the pump also broke, the cast was in despair. But Audrey never complained: by now she was identifying completely with her saintly role.

Dame Peggy did not quite have Audrey's steely strength, and the heat tormented her. After days on the Lindi River in the terrible rain and humidity, Audrey and Peggy set out on February 4 in a dugout for another river scene and Dame Peggy began to feel faint. While shooting a sequence at the Black Hospital at three-forty that afternoon, she succumbed to the heat and was taken in a state of collapse to the Sabena Guest House. She was laid up for two days with heatstroke. Audrey did everything she possibly could for her.

At last Dame Peggy, displaying a British stiff upper lip, rallied and on Sunday morning Audrey persuaded her to join a group headed by the producer, director, and Peter Finch which would make its way by ferry to prepare a sequence at the famous leper colony at Yalisombo, forty miles up the Congo. Audrey was very excited. Now she would meet Dr. Stanley Browne, the celebrated Baptist medical missionary who had established the colony twenty-two years earlier.

The journey upriver to Yalisombo was one of the most memorable occasions of Audrey's life. She wished only that Mel could have been with her — she had been writing to him every night since she arrived, and now she was mentally forming the words about what she was seeing so that she could convey them to him. The well-equipped ferry was manned by handsome black sailors in white bell-bottomed uniforms and black berets with red pom-poms, and the captain was dazzling in gold braid. The journey took place very early in the morning through ground fog and, for some mysterious reason, it was actually chilly. Animals and birds delivered a barrage of shrieks and cries from the emerald-green jungle, punctuated by the crows of roosters and the lusty yells of children seeking their mother's breasts.

The steady chug-chug of the ferry, the hoot of its whistle, the puffs of smoke emitted from its funnel, the velvet sheen of the chocolate-brown water parted by its prow, and the scent of rust, tar, and ropes were never to be forgotten. As small villages emerged at bends in the river, the local people ran out and waved, and Audrey and the others waved back. The ferry was an exciting moment in the existence of these friendly people. The Belgian Congo was only a step away from independence, and everyone was in a celebratory mood.

Suddenly the captain announced through the public address system, like a guide at Disneyland, "And now we're going to see the island of the hippopotami!" The ferry completely circled the island as everyone got his cameras ready, but the huge fabled creatures were somewhere under the brown water. Then Audrey, sharp-eyed as ever, noticed a massive form looming in the rippling waves caused by the ferry. A male beast raised its great head and began spouting. A cheer went up from everybody on board. Obediently, a female beast emerged and started to wallow. Audrey was as enchanted as a child. She clapped her hands, laughed, and jumped in the air.

A few moments later, the group arrived at the leper colony. They were greeted by Dr. and Mrs. Browne, who bustled cheerfully — he in a dog collar and straw hat, she in a print dress — conducting them to the leper colony as though to a village fete in England. Dr. Browne explained that from the moment a patient was admitted, he had to be relieved of his inferiority complex and made not to feel a pariah of society. It was explained to each patient that leprosy was not a sin, nor was it in a normal sense contagious. The disease could be arrested as long as necessary precautions were observed. These precautions had been determined as a result of experiments on armadillos, the only creature apart from man who was known to suffer from leprosy. The prognosis was excellent for most patients, and the problems of hideous deformities or loss of limbs or digits had now been overcome. Nevertheless, many natives did suffer from severe psychological problems because they were banished from their villages with the dreaded stigma of a leper, and were given the bells and sticks ignorantly associated with the disease.

Always fascinated by medicine, Audrey was deeply impressed. She was even more impressed when she arrived for the Sunday service in the little wooden chapel with its bamboo framework and altar and creeping plants festooning the nave. The lepers, some of them maimed, sat quietly in their Sunday best, listening attentively to the service. They knelt, some of them with great difficulty, on the traditionally hard cushions of a Church of England place of worship and joined in the hymns. It was like a Tower of Babel, because everybody sang in a different language, representing the many linguistic groups of the Dark Continent. At the end of the service, the stars, director, and supporting players received cards along with the leper congregation and sang from them the words of Beethoven's "Ode to Joy." Audrey was moved to tears.

After the service, the visitors were taken to a hall where some twenty leper patients were given their papers of release after their complete cure. The gratitude in their faces was very moving. Returning to Stanleyville, Audrey was very grateful for all that had happened.

Shooting recommenced on Monday. Once again, everyone was up at 5:30 A.M., shooting in the native hospital, the mission schoolyard, and the orphanage. Rain alternated with sunshine, and there were many delays. Steve Trilling bombarded Zinnemann with cables demanding an accelerated schedule, but the director fielded them all, pressing on, inspiring everyone. Audrey was very impressed with his discipline and dedication, and she herself worked into the night, barely able to summon up enough energy when she returned to her room to write to Mel or play with Famous. Rumors flew that she was having an affair with Peter Finch, but these can probably be attributed to his bragging in the local bars. He was drinking heavily (a lifetime habit, learned in the Australian pubs from an early age), and in fact he was having a fling with a Sabena air hostess who would arrive every few nights from Europe. Audrey and he had little in common.

When the work ended in Africa, everyone, from Audrey and Fred Zinnemann to the entire cast, felt a wave of disappointment. Audrey had originally wanted to avoid Africa, but had fallen in love with it from the first day she arrived. She had gotten used to her simply furnished rooms at the Sabena Guest House, the perfumed evenings when Famous would sniff around for insects and she would write her long, complicated letters to Mel when he was in Hollywood and could be reached. She would never forget Stanleyville.

The company flew to Rome at the beginning of March. No sooner had Audrey arrived at the Hotel Hassler than she began to have unpleasant symptoms. She experienced pain in her back and groin, which was made worse by the slightest movement. She vomited and suffered from severe urine obstruction. At 2:30 A.M. on March 22, she awoke feeling miserable, and at noon on the following day she had to leave the set during a scene in the convent in Belgium and visit a local doctor, who took tests to see whether she was suffering from a kidney infection. That night she was still struggling through work, and she finally had to give up at around eight o'clock. The pain was so excruciating that she had to rest all day Sunday, the twenty-third, and in the early hours of the twenty-fourth she woke with such severe pain that she literally fell, twisted in sweat-soaked sheets and blankets, to the floor of her suite. She didn't want to waken the Zinnemanns but instead phoned the hotel doctor, who noticed that she was eliminating gravel and gave her a shot of morphine. The next morning, she went to a clinic for a cystoscopy and the doctor told her that she had kidney stones, which were causing severe colic, and that she must have complete rest, under sedation, followed by an operation if the medication did not break up the gravel.

She returned to her bed for several days, exhausted and miserable because she felt she was letting the company down and also because it would be very inconvenient for Mel to postpone *Green Mansions* any further. He had just returned from a journey as exotic as Audrey's own. He had flown to Venezuela, Colombia, and British Guiana looking for appropriate locations. He found the same fog and rainforests as described in Hudson's novel, although he soon learned that Hudson had re-created them in his own imagination as "benevolent." They were not; he observed that the trees were packed in so close together and the underbrush was so thick that not enough light could filter through to make a good exposure.

At one stage, he was standing in the almost inaccessible heart of one of the few remaining primary fog forests in Rancho Grande, Venezuela, and, as he told Helen Gould of the New York *Times,* "I stood in those same *Green Mansions,* saw the aerial plants, the braided vines, the last mists being filtered away by the few penetrating beams of sun and in the distance the occasional and subtle calls of birds, cicadas, and tree toads."

Mel flew to Rome to be with Audrey during her sickness — an act of devotion, since every moment counted in preparing *Green Mansions* and the strain of the work was considerable. He told her that he had had to abandon all ideas of shooting the film in South America and that it would have to be made, except for some exterior footage, entirely at the MGM studios. No doubt the decision was also influenced by the problem of Audrey's health; it would have been unduly strenuous for her, after twelve-hour days and six-day weeks on *The Nun's Story,* to make her way through the jungles of Venezuela and Colombia, with conditions even more grueling than those in the Congo and only the most primitive accommodations available.

Steve Trilling in Hollywood became intolerably irritating to Zinnemann over Audrey's illness, and he and Jack Warner bombarded the director with inconsiderate and ruthless demands for work to continue. Audrey was aware of the pressure, and when Mel returned to Hollywood, she forced herself to recommence it. The baroness, meantime, had arrived from London to help take care of her, and insisted she should not return to work, but with her usual remarkable determination she did. By early April, she was firmly back on the set.

A pleasant diversion occurred when her half-brother, Jan Quarles van Ufford, flew from Amsterdam to appear as Sister Luke's brother for a photograph that would appear in the nun's room. Jan was working for a soap company headquartered in The Hague; his wife and baby daughter accompanied him.

Robert F. Hawkins of the New York *Times* Rome bureau, who visited the set, was impressed by the closeness and dedication of director and crew. He was struck by the painstaking authenticity and intimacy of the atmosphere on the set; witnessing the director rehearsing, he said, was a rare and worthwhile privilege. He noted that Zinnemann, Franz Planer, Audrey, and Peter Finch were given the opportunity to discuss each sequence with the director before they acted it, and contributed adroit and useful observations toward building a desired final effect. Hawkins noted how Audrey went about improvising action between her lines, suggesting, giving, taking advice, "with a brilliant grasp of the end result wanted. What seemed nearly effortless was doubtlessly the product of much private thought, and of hard work."

Audrey paused to comment to Hawkins on the absolute silence of the crew, and the general discipline that was so rare on an Italian sound stage. "Fred really does everything possible to help his actors, to create a mood, in ideal working conditions," she said. "There's no difference between working under the Congo sun or these blazing studio lights. There's no visual difference in the way we move or act — or should act — in both situations."

The shooting continued in Rome for several weeks. One major sequence called for Audrey to struggle for her life with a mentally ill patient. At first, particularly since she was so weakened by her illness, it was felt that she should use a double, a stunt woman who would be strong enough to fight with the bit player concerned without suffering any injury. But Audrey insisted upon playing the scene herself. No one could talk her out of it, and she took instruction from the stunt double to learn how to struggle without tearing a ligament. Fortunately, she still had the muscles of a dancer, and her wiriness once again helped her. She got through the scene with amazing expertise, and the crew broke tradition to applaude her.

Eventually the time came to move the shooting to Belgium, where exteriors would be shot, since the local authorities were still adamantly opposed to using interiors of actual convents. Audrey was able to visit her birthplace in Brussels, which she found a fascinating and moving experience, and she saw the house where she was born. However, because of the Brussels World Fair, the company of eighty-two had to be quartered in Ostend on the seacoast and moved laboriously to the capital, Bruges, Antwerp, and Ghent. The summer weather was gorgeous, and everyone had a marvelous time. By now, there wasn't a soul in the unit who didn't believe the picture would be an enormous critical and commercial success. Audrey was quite over her kidney colic, and an operation had not been necessary. She flew to an eagerly awaiting Mel in Hollywood in late June.

Mel showed Audrey the background shots for *Green Mansions* as soon as she was settled at their beach house. She was fascinated by the footage of river scenes and jungle, and the sounds of jungle creatures and birds. On the studio back lot Audrey saw the masterful art director Preston Ames's model of a complete Indian village, while at the same time packing cases in the prop department were being broken open to disclose tree-bark canoes, harpoons, trees, grasses, blowguns, and even river snakes.

A crucial element in *Green Mansions* was the fawn which accompanied the jungle girl Rima everywhere. It was difficult to train a fawn, because they were nervous, high-strung, and temperamental, and would eat everything — including celluloid — if they could. The producer, Edmund Grainger, conferred with Clarence Brown, director of *The Yearling*, on the matter of dealing with these creatures, and Brown referred Grainger to an animal trainer. The trainer explained to Ferrer that the only way to handle the fawn would be for Audrey to adopt one in its second or third week of life. She should raise it like a baby, feeding it and tending it, and after a few weeks of disassociation it would accept her completely. Weaning it away from its mother, the doe, would be a slow process and must not be done abruptly. Soon the fawn would believe Audrey to be its mother.

The studio arranged to buy a fawn from Jungleland, a children's outdoor zoo near Los Angeles and a big tourist attraction at that time. When the little creature with its big liquid eyes, supple form, and skinny legs arrived, everyone laughed because it looked just like Audrey. Uneasy at first because she didn't like the idea of taking an animal from its parents, Audrey soon became quite happily a surrogate mother to the creature, all of her frustrated maternal instincts emerging as she housed the fawn with Famous. They got along well together, and their predatory eating habits united them. Ip, as Audrey called the fawn, would eat the laces of Mel's shoes while Famous would eat the leather. Ip would eat the electric-light cords, which had to be disconnected or he might have been electrocuted; Famous often obliged by worrying loose the wall jack. Ip would nibble the cigarette stubs while Famous would upset the ashtrays on the side tables.

Ip would attack furniture, carpets, and bedcovers, and Audrey had to fight gently to keep him from destroying the house, which was rented. Audrey bottle-fed Ip every two hours with warm goat's milk and gave him a bowl of Pablum, which he devoured while they had dinner in the dining room; his bed was set up in the bathroom each night. Once Ip was found to have escaped, and was discovered lying under a tree. After that, Audrey and Mel had to close all the windows downstairs so that there was no way that Ip could get out of the house.

Then, an unsettling incident took place. Just as rehearsals were beginning, Audrey had forced herself after many years of hesitations to learn to drive. The cost of chauffeurs was beginning to grate on her, so she took driving lessons — always an ordeal for foreigners in Hollywood, where no public transportation worthy of the name was available. So she had to endure numerous lessons and, with considerable difficulty, gained a license. She rented a car before making up her mind to buy one, and took off on a trial run through Beverly Hills. Suddenly, another car approached her and seemed to be coming directly at her, on the wrong side of the road. It was later, perhaps unfairly, suggested that she was driving on the left side, as was the British habit. She panicked and swerved, crashing headlong into a parked automobile. At that moment, a pretty young actress, Joan Lora, who was beginning to make some headway as a dancer, was sitting in the car waiting for someone to come out of the building. Lora later claimed that the impact caused such severe injury that she could no longer continue her career, although this was contested in court, since it was claimed that the speed at which Audrey was driving would not have caused such severe injury. However, Audrey was to lose the case some years later, and subsequently had to pay substantial damages. She never drove a car again.

Audrey was very badly shaken by this mishap. Indeed, she was in tears and trembling severely when the police arrived, torn between shock at what she had done and at studio pressure, which not only tried to bury the incident but to minimize the effect on a young performer's career. This studio cover-up was typical, and for many years Audrey simply could not bring herself to discuss this episode at all.

The shooting of *Green Mansions* was delayed by this unfortunate episode and by the fact that the photographic tests made Audrey's face look awkwardly square in the new CinemaScope wide-screen techniques that were mandatory in Hollywood. Robert Gottschalk, creator of Panavision, devised a special lens that settled Audrey's nerves — she had been horrified by the tests. At a special screening, Audrey, who had been afraid to look at the screen, burst into applause and laughter at the marvelous device which left her face looking perfectly normal.

The question of costumes was once again a pressing one. The talented Dorothy Jeakins designed clothes which had the delicate filminess of spiderwebs, their color blending with the jungle foliage. Miss Jeakins took her key from the protective coloring of forest creatures, whose natural coats changed with the seasons to protect them from beasts of prey.

Although there was much talk of quarrels between Mel Ferrer and the crew, who reportedly found him somewhat high-handed, Henry Silva, the gifted actor who played an Indian in the story, insists that it was a very happy company. Audrey was fascinated by the legendary Sessue Hayakawa, a great star of the silent screen who had brilliantly re-emerged in *The Bridge on the River Kwai* and in *Green Mansions* played a venerable Indian; she also much admired the young and gifted Anthony Perkins, who played Hudson's hero Abel, rewritten for a youth. Perkins's aquiline face, flat, wide shoulders and chest, and high-strung manner made a powerful impression on everyone. He and Audrey made a striking and original co-starring team. And once again Mel Ferrer showed a remarkable concern for every nuance of Audrey's screen personality; the photography by Joseph Ruttenberg was consistently handsome and striking. Audrey, who had never worked with him before, was deeply impressed by this man.

But beautiful though it was to look at, *Green Mansions* suffered from some almost imperceptible flaw from the very day the shooting began. As in his own performances, Ferrer's odd remoteness, his very intelligence and sensibility, kept the audience at a distance, and the movie, though faithful to the spirit and much of the letter of Hudson's minor masterpiece, did not have the drive or passion which would have overcome its literary quality and made it appeal to the general public. When the film was released late that fall, the reviews were not encouraging, and the public stayed away.

By contrast, *The Nun's Story* moved ahead to its inevitable triumph. Bosley Crowther remained devoted. He wrote: "Through the radiant-eyed Miss Hepburn, [the picture] firmly details and reveals the effects of this rigorous education on one sensitive young body and soul . . . In the role of the nun, Miss Hepburn is fluid and luminous. From her eyes and her eloquent expressions emerge a character that is warm and involved."

The public responded as warmly to *The Nun's Story* as the critics. Its very theme symbolized the public needs and aspirations of the squeaky-clean 1950s. It was a movie of great intelligence, sobriety, and measured skill.

A few weeks after the premiere of *The Nun's Story*, Audrey was nominated for an Academy Award for the third time. She lost to Simone Signoret, who created a sensation as an aging woman in love with the young Laurence Harvey in *Room at the Top*. But Audrey did receive the New York Film Critics' Award for 1959.

Audrey and Mel (who was licking his wounds following the failure of *Green Mansions*) traveled back to the Burgenstock, where Audrey received a script by Ben Maddow, adapter of the classic thriller *The Asphalt Jungle*, for a movie entitled *The Unforgiven*, to be directed by John Huston. Audrey had always wanted to do a Western, since she had tried most other modes, and she was intrigued by the part of Rachel Zachary, a Kiowa Indian girl and sister of a chief, living with a family in the Texas panhandle in the late 1860s. Audrey was uneasy about one sequence, which called for her to ride a horse; she had been thrown from a frisky pony as a child and had broken her collarbone, and reading the sequence had certainly provoked the unhappy memory. But she decided she would take riding lessons. Also, she was taken by the news that Lillian Gish was cast as her mother, the matriarch of the clan, and that her brothers would be played by Burt Lancaster and by Audie Murphy, America's most-decorated war hero.

About the time she signed the contract, Audrey was cheered by the news from the Burgenstock doctors that, once again, she was pregnant. Perhaps now at last, after the miscarriage that had darkened her life at the time of *War and Peace*, her great dream would be fulfilled.

She told Henry Gris, "If it's a boy, I'm sentimental about my half-brother's name, Jan" (Jan was now with Shell Oil in Southeast Asia), "and if it's a girl, I'll give her my own middle name, Kathleen." Later, she and Mel changed their minds and decided that if it was a boy they would call him Sean. She and Mel celebrated; but tragedy again lay ahead.

Chapter Nine

The decision was made to shoot *The Unforgiven* entirely in Mexico, as it was difficult to deal with the Texas locations, which were too built up. The Durango region of Mexico was still primitive, and it had the dusty look of the Panhandle. The decision was made to build the pioneer sod hut on the spot, upon an artificially built hill. As with *Green Mansions,* the picture was shot in sequence to suit Audrey, since she had become fretful at the lack of sequence in *The Nun's Story.* In addition, overhead was substantially increased because it was impossible to shoot all of an actor's scenes at once, and the performers had to be present during the entire length of the production. After Huston and his assistant director, Thomas F. Shaw, had selected the location, and after Emilio Fernandez was hired as second assistant director, the company arrived in Durango and put up at the Casablanca Hotel.

Audrey was very impressed with John Huston. Tall and gangly, he was a formidable presence, with a driving energy thinly hidden behind an informal, seemingly self-effacing charm. His carefully calculated drawl, shrewd crocodile smile, and lazy throwaway humor made up the image of a fabulous *monstre sacré* of the Hollywood screen. He made Audrey relax, and for the first time (of course, she was excited about the baby) she didn't feel tense to the point of sickness before the shooting began. She said later, "[John] makes the artist take a lot of responsibility and that is like a challenge. You automatically give more of yourself just to prove the director is right."

165

But for some of the technicians, the slack and casual approach was unsettling; and the fact of the matter was that Huston was not at all happy with the script. He had undertaken it because he liked the cast and because it gave him the chance to be close to his family in Cuernavaca, where he had been vacationing, rather than because of any conviction in the property. Of Audrey, he said in his typical growl, "She's as good as the other Hepburn." He had directed "the other Hepburn" in *The African Queen,* and he was fascinated to learn from Audrey the changes that had taken place in Africa in the years since he had been there.

The winds were severe during the shooting of *The Unforgiven,* causing the cast some distress, but Huston characteristically used them, shooting sequences with Audrey's beloved Franz Planer that took place in actual winds — even when dust flecked the camera lenses. Audrey had to put up with dirt in her hair and fretted at her grimy appearance, but this, of course, added to the realism. One problem was that Lillian Gish intensely disliked Audie Murphy. She claimed he was trigger happy, that he would shoot any animal that moved, or would plug a beer can thrown across a bar or a fly-specked light bulb if he was in the mood. She refused to ride with Murphy in the car to and from location. Murphy himself was in trouble at the time, although the facts were carefully kept from the press and there was no mention of them in the memoirs of John Huston. In fact, as his business manager, Morgan Maree's son Andrew told me, Murphy was involved in cattle rustling on large scale and, had it not been for Hollywood influence, Murphy would undoubtedly have gone to prison for it.

A major scene called for Audrey's dreaded experience of riding the horse. She told John Huston she was very frightened and fibbed that she had never been on a horse before. He promised her every possible protection but explained that, although a stunt double would be used for almost the entire sequence, she really would have to ride for about fifty yards. He gave her an extremely experienced teacher and lifted her into the saddle very slowly. But the horse was a mettlesome beast and hard to control, perhaps because, like most horses, it sensed the nervousness of its rider. The horse, aptly called Diablo (and formerly owned by President Batista of Cuba), seemed so restive that Audrey, riding sidesaddle in a long skirt, tried to canter it over to a particular spot by a riverbank. Unfortunately, the combination of the camera lights used to augment the daylight and the sudden movements of the crew caused the horse to buck. One of the crew members made the very serious mistake of throwing up his arms to stop it. Such a movement is anathema to a spirited horse, and the stallion threw Audrey. Huston yelled abuse at the crew member and ran to Audrey with the crew doctor. Mel was in Durango that day and was not present. Audrey lay on the ground in agony, on her back, trying not to scream. She begged Huston not to tell Mel what had happened as she was placed on a stretcher. She told Huston she was sure she had broken her back.

Audrey was flown by ambulance plane to the hospital in Durango, where Mel, very overwrought, hastened to her side. Needless to say, the unit publicist broadcast the story widely. Audrey tossed and turned in agony, worried far more about her baby and about Mel's emotions than her own condition. The X rays showed several broken vertebrae; her doctor, Howard Mendelson, arrived with none other than Marie-Louise Habets, who lived up to her real-life role as a nursing sister and took personal care of Audrey — to Audrey's amazement and delight — accompanying her, as soon as she could be moved, on the ambulance plane to Hollywood. There, Audrey's recovery was agonizingly slow and painful. The picture had to be stopped for three weeks. It was an ill-fated production. Audie Murphy was on a duck shoot near Durango when his boat capsized and he drifted away — an old war wound in one hip prevented him from swimming to safety. He and a friend were just rescued from drowning by a woman photographer who was shooting them from the shore.

In order to be able to return to the picture, Audrey had to wear a very uncomfortable, orthopedic brace, and flying to Durango was an ordeal. She couldn't sit in the studio station wagon that bumped its dusty way to the location, but had to lie on a mattress with Mel at her side. Mel was opposed to her going on with the movie at all, feeling it should have been canceled, and he made his feelings known, much to the director's annoyance. Incredibly, Audrey had to mount the same horse again instead of another horse because the producers insisted on reshooting the same footage as they had to incorporate some of the previous shooting as well. The sequence was done on the very last hour of the last day, with Audrey, clad in her uncomfortable brace, fighting her nerves and Mel's annoyance. It was not one of her favorite moments in pictures.

Audrey was assured that the baby had a good chance of survival and, of course, there could be no question of an abortion. Still, Audrey was very distressed at the thought that the child might be injured. Through the spring of 1959, she was quite ill and worried. Her chief distraction was receiving a screenplay based on a novel called *No Bail for the Judge* by British justice Henry Cecil Leon, who wrote under the pen name Henry Cecil. Alfred Hitchcock personally called Audrey, to her great excitement and pleasure, telling her that Samuel Taylor, who had authored the script, had reworked the part of the heroine with her in mind. He said that Laurence Harvey, whom Audrey admired, had accepted the leading male role.

No Bail for the Judge was excellently written. Audrey would play the part of a young barrister in London, whose father, to be played by John Williams, was an Old Bailey criminal court judge. One evening the judge tries to stop a taxi driver from hitting a dog and falls, causing an injury to his head. A prostitute finds him lying in the street and takes him to her flat; in a deliberate echo of Hitchcock's earlier movie, *The Thirty-nine Steps,* the prostitute dies during the night with a knife in her back, and the judge is accused of murder. His own daughter defends him; she engages the services of a professional thief to save her father from the gallows by exposing the prostitute's true killer. Hitchcock told Audrey he loved this typically British paradox in the dramatic construction of the story.

Audrey told him she was looking forward to reading the script but, in fact, did not do so for some time because she was undergoing medical tests concerning her unborn child, and she was very distracted with fear about the baby's condition after her fall. She told Hitchcock she would do anything he wanted based on the story he had told her, and contracts were drawn up and her casting announced. Then disaster struck: she miscarried. All of her worst fears had been realized. The death of her child was heartbreaking, and Mel blamed John Huston for forcing her on a horse. She suddenly had a feeling that she never wanted to make another picture.

Recovering slowly and in great anguish, Audrey desultorily picked up the script for *No Bail for the Judge*. She began reading it with interest, but then she came to a scene which called for what seemed to be great physical exertion as well as emotional strain. She had asked Mel to ensure that she had another child right away, and she would certainly never do anything again that could possibly endanger her baby. The scene called for her to be dragged into a park and violently raped.

It was typical of Hitchcock to have wanted the quintessential pure lady of fifties films to be so humiliated. It was an element in his personal psychology that he wanted to show impeccable ladies, whom the public associated with fairy-tale innocence and purity, horribly ill-treated on the screen. Later, he was to show Tippi Hedren attacked by birds and violated by Sean Connery in *The Birds and Marnie,* respectively. He even tried to seduce Miss Hedren herself, with disastrous results. His blind rage when she refused has been widely reported. In other movies, he showed various cool blondes humiliated. He also wanted to dye Audrey's hair blond for the movie, since all his life, he had entertained a frustrated desire for a former secretary and scriptwriter, a cool and well-tailored English blond, and he vicariously made love to her in pictures, working out his fantasy through leading men with the charms that he so sadly lacked.

Audrey could have known nothing of this but, apart from

the strenuousness of the scene, she knew it could do great harm to her image. In fact, she was so sensitive about violence that she had refused to watch the execution scene in which Susan Hayward dies in the gas chamber in *I Want to Live,* and she fainted at the premiere of *A Farewell to Arms* during the scene in which Jennifer Jones dies in childbirth.

Back in Switzerland, wanting to become pregnant again, she called Kurt Frings and told him she could not go ahead with the picture. Frings in turn had the unpleasant task of telling Hitchcock that he could not get his way. Hitchcock was furious. Lacking in understanding, he had previously become exasperated by Vera Miles when she had become pregnant and he had had to recast *Vertigo* with Kim Novak. Audrey's defection was the last straw. He couldn't understand how she could allow herself to let her feelings overcome her judgment. To add insult to injury, his new picture, *North by Northwest,* would be held up by *The Nun's Story* at the Radio City Music Hall in New York, and later Hitchcock was humiliated by losing the prize at the San Sebastian Film Festival to the Hepburn picture. Hitchcock took a loss of two hundred thousand dollars and canceled *No Bail for the Judge* permanently. He hated Audrey for the rest of his life for letting him down, and nobody could make him forgive her.

To pick up her spirits, Audrey appeared in a *Harper's Bazaar* fashion spread prepared by Richard Avedon, with Mel, Zsa Zsa Gabor, and Buster Keaton. The gag was that she would wear the costumes of every major designer *except* Givenchy. She looked wonderful, considering her suffering in creations by Balmain, Cardin, and Dior — some of which required even Audrey to diet.

Mel gave her a further gift. After a long rest that fall of 1958, she found she was pregnant yet again. Her emotional condition improved enormously. She was happy again. This time she would not make a picture during her pregnancy, nor would she even risk tension or strain by accompanying Mel to Rome, where he was to film a grisly horror story. *Blood and Roses* was largely based on the supernatural story *Carmilla,* by Sheridan

Le Fanu. This was to be followed by another shocker, *The Hands of Orlac*, the story of a pianist whose hands are smashed in an accident and replaced with those of an executed murderer. These unpleasant chestnuts were certainly not what Audrey needed now that she was with child again.

She spent the winter of 1959 in the Burgenstock. Apart from the Freys, she had little company, and once again the winter was very severe. The three hotels were closed, though busy with carpenters, painters, and bricklayers making repairs. Mel and Audrey were not together again until March, when they took long morning walks through the snow, watching the ice glittering on the branches of the trees and the pallid sun shining on the white paths and the grass. The doctor had ordered Audrey to walk as much as possible to strengthen her muscles, because the child was believed to be very large. Sometimes she and Mel would even wade through slush. She enjoyed it all, but nervously kept her fingers crossed that another tragic miscarriage would not take place.

The baby was due at last, and Audrey checked into the maternity ward of the Lucerne Hospital, the same hospital, ironically, where the scene was shot of Jennifer Jones dying in childbirth. Audrey had superb care there, and she welcomed the dramatic circumstances of the birth. But labor was agonizingly painful for Audrey, with her unnaturally boyish body and small pelvis, and the baby weighed nine-and-a-half pounds. A thunderstorm accompanied the baby's delivery, which, despite her agony, Audrey felt was a good omen. Fortunately, the Swiss surgeons and nurses brought her through the ordeal and, once her son Sean was born, she was in ecstasy. She told friends she felt that this moment was far more important to her than anything in her entire professional career; and indeed her whole life had led up to this moment when, at the age of thirty, she had delivered a son. One might almost say that her marriage, much as she loved Mel, was partly designed for this purpose: for all her sophistication, she was still a Dutch bourgeois at heart.

She said later, "Like all mothers, I couldn't believe at first that Sean was really for me, and I could really keep him. I'm still filled with the wonder of his being, to be able to go out and come back and find that he's still there!"

She and Mel celebrated with customary simplicity, by simply sending wine and baskets of delicacies to their neighbors: a Swiss tradition. They joined in the Burgenstock celebration, and Audrey was swamped with letters and telegrams of congratulation. She moved from the Lucerne Maternity Clinic back to her chalet, and a christening ceremony was held in the small chapel where Audrey had been married. Sean yelled and screamed robustly as the minister scattered holy water on the baby's forehead, and the baroness remarked at that precise moment, for all to hear, "A good cry at the christening lets the devil out!" Everyone looked at everyone else and said nothing.

Henry Taylor, Jr., the ambassador to Switzerland, gave the boy an American passport and an American flag, which, of course, he was quite unable to hold and dropped in his mother's lap. In order to avoid being mobbed by reporters, Audrey consented to a press conference, which she conducted with all the regality of Princess Anne in *Roman Holiday*. She said, "I would like to mix Sean with all kinds of people in all countries, so that he will learn what the world is all about. If he's the right kind of person, he should take his own small part in making the world a better place." Such noble sentiments were well received, and the press bustled off to write a glowing account of the young mother. In far-off Hollywood, Alfred Hitchcock observed icily, "Every word she said was pregnant with meaning!"

During her lying-in period, Audrey read a screenplay by George Axelrod based upon Truman Capote's celebrated novella *Breakfast at Tiffany's*. At first, she was a little nervous about playing it. Although disguised in an antic, somewhat arch mode of humor, the story had various unsavory aspects. The central figure, Holly Golightly, was married, with stepchildren, and had fled her husband to take up a promiscuous life in New York City, where she had turned herself into a kooky character and eliminated her hick-town origins by assuming an air of sophistication and carefree abandon. She read mostly tabloids, travel folders, and astrological charts; she smoked Picayune cigarettes; she lived on cottage cheese and melba toast; her blondish hair was dyed; she kept a cat coyly called Cat and strummed a guitar. In those days, at the end of the 1950s, the book and script seemed daring, and Audrey was concerned with Holly's cheerful predatoriness where men were concerned, her lack of conventional moral principles, and her habit of visiting her keeper, a gangster named Sally, in Sing Sing. The character of Holly's lover as developed by Axelrod was exceptionally risqué, and more than a touch tasteless. He was an attractive writer, being kept by an older woman with lesbian tendencies. His affair with Holly was peculiar, to say the least, because when they first went to bed nothing happened. What with Holly earning fifty dollars powder-room money from her "escorts," setting her cap for a South American millionaire, and teasing a repulsively fat and shapeless Nazi sympathizer named Rusty Trawler, the coyness and archness were suffocating. But Audrey clearly saw an opportunity to break the mold of her screen purity and to play someone not entirely unlike her earlier self in London — poor, struggling, and given to eccentric behavior. There, of course, the resemblance ended; but Audrey, like most actresses, needed to force an identification if a truly authentic one was not possible. Blake Edwards, then young and on his way up before his great fame as director of the *Pink Panther* series and the husband of Julie Andrews, was chosen by Paramount to direct the movie. Audrey rationalized her playing the part by telling reporters that Holly was really a frightened mouse who never delivered, even if she grabbed the fifty-dollar bills.

She spoke to Henry Gris of Holly's personality: "Her wardrobe consisted chiefly of a single black dress which she called her working outfit, and a day dress. Had she really been a *femme légère,* she could have gotten all those minks half-promised her, and there would have been no point in her sidewalk breakfast outside Tiffany's . . ." She was referring to the sequence in which Holly stood outside Tiffany's, the celebrated Fifth Avenue jewelers in New York City, in an evening gown, nibbling a Danish. She added: "Many girls have lived like her and not in America only. I myself lived in circumstances very much like Holly. I didn't have to look far to understand and re-create the character. Just look back to my own days, back in London, as I was starting out . . . Of course, I was much luckier than Holly. She was caught off base. Lost. But she was pretending just as conscientiously as we all did, and she had her identity, which was a total lack of identity. I was luckier. I had a purpose . . . I earned a bit on the side posing for pictures advertising soap and such things. I had met the photographer at one of the parties we girls went to, not always invited but always interested in the food that would be served around. If you pass by the man with the canapés more often than usual, you may get yourself a kind of meal. On the go."

It was, of course, a great source of anxiety to Audrey that she would have to take Sean to New York at the early age of only a few weeks, and she vacillated about accepting the part, despite her fascination with it. This introvert — edgy, nervous, and withdrawn — had to play one of the most extroverted characters in fiction, a jumping bean of high-level energy, pushiness, and pizzazz. But when Blake Edwards visited her in Switzerland, his extraordinary energy and conviction persuaded her that she would be perfect for the role. Of course, he knew that her name on the marquee would ensure the picture's international success. Apart from the ill-fated *Green Mansions,* she had not yet had an unsuccessful picture, and she was one of the five biggest box-office stars of 1960.

Shooting was to begin in the early summer, and in the meantime Audrey remained in Switzerland, devoting herself to Sean. According to Henry Gris, almost from the moment Sean was born she ceased to have a sexual relationship with Mel, and her marriage changed into one of affectionate companionship. But Mel, Gris says, was a man of virile appetite and inevitably, despite his decent nature, gravitated toward other women. Inevitably, too, the seal of doom was set upon the marriage at the very moment that Sean's birth would seem to have cemented it securely.

In those first weeks of Sean's life, Audrey was already undermined in her happiness by nervous fears. There was a kidnapping scare in Europe at the time, and she urged the Freys to increase the security at the Burgenstock entrance. She also fretted about the effect the baby would have upon Mr. Famous. He was so much a part of her that he was like an older child, and she feared he might resent the intrusion on his territory. She told Henry Gris, "I knew that Famous would be bewildered, and he was, by Sean wailing in the nursery upstairs and obviously now the center of gravity in the household. Everybody was fussing over Sean. This may sound silly, but I took special pains to soften the blow to Famous's self-esteem." She invited Famous to sleep at the foot of her bed — an unusual privilege, since he had previously been confined to a tiny wooden chalet-style doghouse. She talked to him and petted him to excess. At last he stopped growling at the baby, and at her, and accepted Sean as his "brother."

A few weeks after Sean was born, a tremendous storm exploded violently over the mountains, and Famous went berserk. He rushed madly in and out of the rooms, up and down the stairs, barking wildly, then suddenly shrank into a corner, whimpering with terror as a particularly loud thunderclap erupted. Then he disappeared. Audrey thought he must have slipped through his little door, but surely he wouldn't be able to face the rain and lightning. She told Henry Gris, "A huge thunderbolt crashed into the forest. I was seized by an irrational fear that Sean might be in danger. I abandoned the search for Famous and went upstairs to my son's room. There I saw a wonderful sight. He was sleeping peacefully in his cot, with Famous keeping vigil beside him."

Audrey engaged an Italian nurse, whose name, Gina, was kept from the press. Gina spoke only her native language, but Mel could speak Italian, Audrey had a smattering of the tongue, and she taught her some English. At first Audrey, with

her strange streak of childishness, was concerned about leaving
Sean for a minute, but soon she learned to trust Gina, a superb
nanny who proved to be totally reliable. Through the latter
months of 1960, Audrey learned to love Gina and to accept her
as a member of the family.

Audrey moved to New York City with Mel, and the shooting
of *Breakfast at Tiffany's* began. With great difficulty, the movie
was shot as much as possible in sequence, to accommodate
Audrey's concern about character building. Her co-star was
the young and handsome George Peppard, whose only
problem in playing the role was a tendency, even at that stage,
to be heavy around the middle. In a bedroom scene, he looked
on the very edge of being plump.

Franz Planer was once more the indispensable cameraman
who could help Audrey with all her many photogenic problems. Givenchy designed her very simple wardrobe and
incidental designer gowns, and the score was composed by a
new friend, Henry Mancini, who wrote a song for her, "Moon
River," which was to become a popular classic. One serious
error (more obvious today than at the time) was the casting of
Mickey Rooney as the Japanese neighbor Mr. Yunioshi, with
a mass of false teeth, a permanent grin, and a *yukata* garment.
He performed with a ghastly false emphasis and an ill-advised
press release was sent out in which an attempt was made to pass
him off as a Japanese. Another mistake was casting the
beautiful Patricia Neal as a woman reduced to keeping a man
for sexual purposes; she was far too cool and self-possessed to
suggest the emotional insecurity that would lead a woman of a
certain age to such desperate measures.

During the shooting, Audrey was still worried about kidnappers, and had bars put on the windows of her New York
house; she was jittery about leaving Sean for a day of shooting,
and quite guilty because she had transported him across the
world.

The opening day of filming was an event. A very large crowd
gathered outside Tiffany's on Fifth Avenue to watch the crew

shooting in the early hours of a Sunday morning. Seeing the mob, many people thought there had been a jewel robbery and the crowd swelled still further. They saw something much more memorable than thieves being dragged off to prison. They saw Audrey, in a beehive hairdo and elegant Givenchy gown, sipping from a plastic coffee cup and munching the Danish in her evening-gloved hand.

What the public didn't see, as Audrey wandered past the windows looking lighthearted and skittish, acting with great assurance, was that she was almost petrified with fear. Hating to be watched while she worked, she was now more ill at ease than ever. And she hated Danish pastries as much as she hated garlic: she could hardly bring herself to nibble this one, and had a strong desire to spit it out. She had asked Blake Edwards if instead she could lick an ice cream cone from Schrafft's, but he had told her that that was inappropriate to the scene. So nervous was she about being watched, and about the hated Danish, that Audrey flubbed take after take, and even the devoted Franz Planer became flustered. He suddenly touched a faulty cable and received a 220-volt shock which flung him, yelling with pain, to the street. Audrey rushed to his side, and shooting was temporarily suspended.

Audrey was very fond of the cat in the film, which was named Rhubarb. Much to her relief, Rhubarb got on with Famous. There was no way that Famous would be kept from watching the shooting; Mel and Sean came whenever possible. Audrey desperately needed the total security of her "family," and even though she was protected by her cameraman, she was uneasy without her inner circle.

One difficult sequence combined studio with location. It was shot entirely in heavy rain, and included a virtuoso matching of dozens of disparate shots and areas in a cohesive and striking whole. It was the scene in which Holly argues with her lover and throws her cat out of the taxi. In the novella, she does not find the cat, but in the picture she recaptures it. She, Peppard, and Rhubarb got soaked hour after hour in the scene, which was as harrowing as any she had done in Africa for *The Nun's Story*. Both she and Mel were concerned that she would catch cold, or worse, but miraculously she did not.

Audrey's performance made the film just tolerable. Although she was essentially miscast (it was impossible to accept so European and aristocratic a creature as the wife of a small-town horse doctor), she created an authentic Bohemian type, not unlike that which she had portrayed in the Left Bank sequences of *Funny Face*. As Holly whistles down cabs, calls everyone darling, sets fire to a woman's hat, sports the world's longest cigarette holder, stores her shoes in a fruit bowl, steals a comic mask from the five-and-dime, and takes off on expeditions with her cat, Audrey created a rounded and convincing personality, at once daring, childish, and vulnerable. Her style and discipline saved the day and ensured the movie's enormous international success.

Within days of completing the picture, Audrey received an invitation from Hollywood to make a movie which would cast her in an even more questionable role than that of Holly Golightly. She was to play a school-teacher faced with charges of lesbianism disseminated by a vicious schoolgirl in *The Children's Hour*, a new version of the famous Lillian Hellman play which had originally been directed by William Wyler in Hollywood in 1937. Merle Oberon had originally played her part; and Shirley MacLaine, who was then up and coming, was to play Miriam Hopkins's part. Miss Hopkins herself was cast in this new version as the busybody aunt, and Fay Bainter as the imperious grandmother of the wicked spying child.

Audrey was extremely uneasy about appearing in the picture because, although her character was not actually a lesbian, there was an implication that she might have been; and the entire subject, cleaned up in the original movie script, was extremely controversial and against her image. However, she was influenced by the fact that William Wyler would return to the job of directing the story for a second time, and also by the strength of her fellow players. She could also relate to the theme implicit in the script: the necessity for privacy, the danger of gossip, and the love that can transcend sexuality.

Audrey arrived in Hollywood with her son, who was just learning to toddle, and with Gina and Mel. She took a house with a swimming pool in Coldwater Canyon. As usual, she gave very few interviews. She didn't like Hollywood or Los Angeles, and felt totally alienated there. She also had very few friends there. Each person who came to talk to her for a newspaper had to be fielded through a battery of press representatives; her very rare meetings with reporters were held at the Goldwyn Studios at lunch over a hamburger (most of which was eaten by Famous), two scoops of cottage cheese, and a sliced tomato on lettuce.

Sean, who had just learned to walk, often came to the studio so Audrey could show him off. She set up his playpen in her trailer living room and brought everyone from Goldwyn to Wyler to ooh and aah at the baby. She had a great rapport with Shirley MacLaine, whose kooky behavior — constant joking and fooling around before and after sequences — greatly irritated Wyler but kept everyone else relaxed during the nerve-wrecking shooting. Unfortunately, Wyler was no longer the brilliant and concentrated master craftsman that he had been at the time of *Roman Holiday.* Years before, the failure of his excellent *Carrie,* a powerful version of Theodore Dreiser's *Sister Carrie,* had disillusioned him, and now he seemed insecure and overemphatic in his direction. Audrey was more fretful than ever, and went to the edge of being unprofessional in having both her son and her dog with her throughout the shooting. Indeed, on one particular occasion she exhibited a remarkable childishness.

There was a crucial scene to be played between her and Shirley MacLaine, when the evil child eavesdrops on them. It was important that Audrey concentrate exclusively on learning her lines and her emotional responses. She was in her dressing room when she discovered that Famous had escaped into the studio streets. Almost hysterical, she called the studio police, and all of them had to go and look for the missing dog. Wyler barely contained his temper. The important scene was delayed, and when she finally came on the set she begged Wyler to forgive her because she couldn't remember her lines; she asked him to let her rest for a moment; and then she started to cry. It is clear that her dependency on her dog had reached the edge of neurosis. Wyler had to take himself in hand not to bawl her out. Instead, he canceled the scene for the rest of the day and sent her to her dressing room. She sat there in agony until a call came: "We found Famous!"

Ecstatic, she ran out only to see something that upset her even more. One of the crew was pointing to a very high wall of the back lot that was reached by scaffolding. Famous was standing on the very top of the wall, trembling, not knowing whether to go forward or back. Audrey dared not call him or have anyone else do so, and told everyone to keep absolutely quiet. Then she climbed up, overcoming her fear of heights, and, very pale, brought him down.

She was unsettled by the incident to an almost unnatural extent, and her extreme maternalism toward the dog and toward her son proved increasingly distracting during the shooting. The picture didn't work out well, and was in many ways a complete flop, both commercially and critically, and the audience could not accept the suicide of Shirley MacLaine following her confession of unnatural love. Surprisingly, the picture received Academy Award nominations in five categories, but won none of them. The picture suffered from James Garner's hopeless performance as Audrey's lover, and *Time* magazine dared to attack Audrey, the unassailable, on the grounds that she had given "her standard, frail, indomitable characterization, which is to say that her eyes watered constantly (frailty) and her chin is forever cantilevered forward (indomitability)." Only Franz Planer's photography gives a hint of quality in the final product.

Audrey could take consolation from the fact that at the time she was still one of the five biggest stars in the world, along with Doris Day, Elizabeth Taylor, Marilyn Monroe, and Shirley MacLaine.

Briefly in Hollywood at the time, Audrey lived opposite Billy and Audrey Wilder on Wilshire Boulevard. One day she noticed to her horror that Famous had disappeared through the tiny door prepared for him. When she ran into the street, there was a traffic jam and people started yelling and screaming. She saw the blinding vision of Famous lying mangled in the street; he had been run over during a collision of two automobiles. Audrey was completely shattered and inconsolable, and she soon returned to Europe. There, in Paris, Mel did the only thing possible to comfort her: he gave her a new Yorkie with the imposing name of Assam of Assam. Gradually, Audrey came to accept him as a reincarnation of Famous.

When Audrey returned to Switzerland, she had a visit from the talented director Richard Quine, who wanted to discuss another script by George Axelrod, *Paris When It Sizzles*. This light comedy, the production package put together by the agent Irving (Swifty) Lazar, was based on Julien Duvivier's movie *La Fête Henriette,* made in 1952. Audrey would play the secretary of a screenwriter who lives out his fantasies in real life.

When Quine arrived in Switzerland, Ferrer was in Italy shooting a movie. This was the couple's first separation of any duration in some time. Quine was the first tenant of the new guesthouse Fritz Frey had built on the grounds of the chalet. Quine remembers being enchanted by Audrey and her house, and walking through the woods with her to discuss the script. He said he had a strange sensation that she was Rima and he was the hero of *Green Mansions*. On this occasion, Audrey was "sprightly, elfin . . . with a big grin, always delightful, always the epitome of politeness, the perfect hostess."

Audrey was excited, although a little uneasy when she heard that William Holden had been cast as the writer. He was still in love with Audrey, having never gotten over his feelings for her. He was drinking more than ever, and when he heard she was to play opposite him he got very drunk indeed.

Shot in Paris, the film was marked by disaster from the beginning. No sooner had Audrey started work than she received shocking news from Fritz Frey: thieves had broken into her house and set fire to part of it. Among the stolen articles was her Academy Award for *Roman Holiday*. Always overreacting to trifles, Audrey was completely calm at this upsetting news. This was typical of her.

She was much more upset by the first shots taken by cameraman Claude Renoir. Quine says, "Audrey's strong, very strong, and she was not happy with the way she looked. Claude had been photographing gorgeous films, absolutely beautiful things, but he wasn't used to doing anything except 'set' shots, or tableau effects. He made gorgeous paintings on the screen, but *Paris When It Sizzles* called for a lot of movement and use of key lights, and as a result he got unsettled and photographed Audrey very roughly."

She panicked. Indeed, her constant hatred of the way she looked got the better of her, and she flatly stated that Claude Renoir had to go. This was unbearably difficult for Quine. The name Renoir was supreme in France, and the idea of dismissing a member of that illustrious family was unthinkable. Indeed, when Renoir was dismissed there was very nearly a strike. Franz Planer was busy on another movie, so Audrey insisted on Charles Lang. With magnificent unselfishness, Renoir held a crew meeting and announced to all concerned that they should cooperate with Charles Lang, who was a superb cameraman and far more experienced juggling key lights in sequences that moved rapidly from one setup to an another.

William Holden was a problem from the very beginning; it was a mistake to have cast him in a picture with Audrey. From the day he arrived in Paris, he was tormented by the thought of being with her again. He was still in love with her, and he was tortured by the thought that because he was sterile and suffered from recurring sexual impotence, he could never become her husband. Now, the very existence of her son reminded him of his inadequacy — of the grim contrast between the real William Holden and the debonair, secure, and unequivocally virile presence on the screen.

Holden drank heavily because of his internal tensions, thus exacerbating his potency problem. He insisted on dragging

Jack Lemmon, who was filming *Irma la Douce* in Paris, to various nightspots, trying to drown his agony over Audrey and not exactly helping Lemmon, who was about to marry Felicia Farr. So soused was Holden that he swayed on his feet and talked like a punch-drunk fighter. Often, he would arrive on the set in no condition to proceed. Audrey maintained her usual stoicism, but shooting opposite Holden caused her considerable suffering. Very often she had to cover for him, and she did everything in her power to make him feel comfortable. Her sweetness to him further intensified his pain. Holden even developed a syndrome that causes the drinker to lose control after only two drinks but not know it. In other words, he would play a scene thinking that it was absolutely all right and then everyone would look at each other until somebody told him that the scene was wrong and would have to be done again.

Quine rented the house next door to Holden's on the Avenue Foch; he went to the extraordinary length of climbing into a tree outside Holden's bedroom to make sure the actor was getting some rest at night. As the not particularly athletic director crawled along a branch, he heard Holden call him from below, where he was seated next to an ornamental pond decorated in Chinese style, with floating candles — a custom he had picked up in Hong Kong. Holden called up to Quine, "You'd better go back to bed and get some rest. It's going to be a hard day tomorrow."

According to George Axelrod, one evening Holden began climbing the wall that led up to Audrey's dressing-room window at the studio. Quine and Axelrod screamed at him to desist, but he refused. Audrey, like Rapunzel in the old fairy tale, came to the window and leaned out to look at her highly improbable knight-errant. Holden kissed her, then slipped and plunged from the tree, landing with a brutal thwack on top of a parked automobile. His wife Ardis arrived in a bad temper and began to denigrate him. Audrey Wilder says that Ardis Holden was bitter and frustrated, and constantly turned on her husband. Holden developed an unpleasant habit of hanging from his iron gate by one hand and howling as though he were a monkey. Quine once screamed at him that he was behaving like a monster, torturing his family and everyone who loved him. He asked him why he did it; Holden replied that he couldn't help himself. In the middle of the filming Holden had to go to a clinic for a drying-out treatment.

In Paris Holden bought a new Ferrari — a make of car that sometimes brought out the worst in its drivers, since it enabled them to speed. Holden decided to relieve the pressure of working with Audrey by going to Switzerland for the Bastille Day holiday weekend. Quine said to him, "You're going to run into something sure as hell. For God's sake, don't go." Holden went just the same, and ended up driving into a stone wall. He returned with his leg in a brace, looking sheepish. This incident delayed the unhappy picture even further.

During all this drama, Audrey became extremely afraid of kidnappers and decided to move to a heavily guarded château owned by the Bourbons, near Paris. As usual, Mel was very strong in their home. His career was now seriously on the decline, and he was asserting his masculinity more than ever as a means of compensation. Quine says, "The fact that Mel was so dominant with Audrey disturbed me more than it should have, because I was so nuts about her. As far as we were concerned, she should have been dealt with with velvet gloves. And Mel doesn't wear velvet gloves. I found her to be very circumspect with him."

There were pleasant interludes during the overall ordeal of making *Paris When It Sizzles*. Audrey's stolen Oscar was discovered in the woods near the Burgenstock; clearly, the thieves had no way of melting it down or handling it in any other manner. Also, Marlene Dietrich, who was a new friend and a great fan of Audrey's (as Audrey was of hers), agreed to make a cameo appearance outside the Dior salon. Quine arranged for Dietrich to be dressed in a special Dior suit, and she was presented with a white Rolls-Royce from which she could elegantly alight. Dietrich also had one further request: although she lived only a few doors from the Dior salon, she insisted upon dressing in a hotel suite next door, rather than making the short journey from her home. She was enough of a superstar at the time for these demands to be met.

Mel himself appeared in the movie. There was a costume party, presided over by Noël Coward, in which all of the party guests were dressed as characters from Hollywood movies. Quine asked Mel to play Dr. Jekyll and Mr. Hyde with masks on the front and back of his face.

Somehow Audrey got through the picture. Yet again, one of her fixations about her appearance became obsessive. This time, it was not so much her nostrils as another old bugbear — a crooked tooth. She talked endlessly about having it fixed, even at this late stage in her career. Apparently she had noticed it in some of the shots taken by Claude Renoir — another reason Renoir had had to be removed. Holden and Quine threatened, Quine says, "to absolutely maim her if she changed that tooth." He felt the tooth was one of the oddities that made her special. "Charm is the word for Audrey. She was the charmer of the world. Of all the people I've worked with in my life, Audrey and Jack Lemmon were my favorites. They don't have a false bone in their bodies, absolutely not a flaw, professional, kind, gentle, considerate, no temperament at all."

Unfortunately, because of the constant delays on *Paris When It Sizzles,* Audrey had to rush into her next picture, *Charade,* without a break of more than a few days in Switzerland.

The screenplay for *Charade* by Peter Stone was an expertly whipped-up trifle in the Hitchcock mode — cool and cleverly sustained. It began with an unnamed man being thrown off a train in France; minutes later, the audience is transferred to Switzerland, where Audrey, with enormous sunglasses and a Givenchy ski suit, is enjoying the sun on the terrace of a fashionable hotel. There she meets Cary Grant, smooth and immaculately tailored. Back in Paris, she discovers that her apartment has been stripped and all traces of her husband have disappeared. Grant helps her to unravel the mystery of his death in a story which lacks in plausibility what it gains in pleasant, if superficial, diversion. As Regina Lambert, Audrey was the exact opposite of her true personality. Confronted by violence and sudden death, this supercool, erstwhile translator never turns a hair, even when she has to identify her husband's corpse; and her impeccable hair, makeup, and Givenchy clothes never suffer a setback during the entire course of the action. Like most performers, Audrey was drawn to the idea of playing a person who was the exact opposite of herself, and she accepted the part with much enthusiasm. She enjoyed the witty dialogue and was pleased that the movie would be shot in Paris. Also, she had never worked with Cary Grant before, and was very excited at the prospect.

With Sean and Gina in tow, Audrey and Mel moved into the Hotel Raphael in the winter of 1961-62 — the coldest winter since 1883. The streets were ice, yet the movie had to be shot almost entirely outdoors.

Audrey met with Herb Sterne, who again, as in *Love in the Afternoon,* was in charge of publicity. He explained that Audrey would be able to approve all of her stills as before, but he warned her that the paparazzi problem had grown enormously worse since she was last in Paris. She was upset and refused to understand. Cary Grant, by contrast, told Sterne that he understood completely. But Stanley Donen, who had an investment in the production, was very niggardly about money and, Sterne says, "couldn't see why the contact sheets couldn't be just a single sheet to show Audrey and Cary."

Sterne continues, "This didn't work because Cary wasn't so particular about how he looked in a still, but he didn't want Audrey to look as good as he did. Audrey didn't want Cary to look as good as she did. So I said, 'Let us have two sheets, so each star can kill a still and the other will not know which still they have killed.' This went great until my secretary, who was busy kissing Audrey's ass, sneaked out a print which Cary had killed and made sure it was published. Cary came in, very gentlemanly, showed me the newspaper picture, and asked me how did it get out? I said, 'I haven't the fuckingest idea.' 'Well,' Cary asked, 'how are we going to stop this happening again?' I told him that each negative would go to him and to Audrey, and both would be given a punch to kill what they didn't like. We couldn't find a punch in Paris so somebody went down and paid all kinds of money and bought punches from the people in the Métro, the Paris subway."

Other problems arose during the production. Audrey was feeling the strain of making two pictures in a row and, Herb Sterne says, "She would keep going for two or three weeks and then she would begin to shatter, not intentionally — just nerve strain."

Matters reached a head when they were working on a closed set in a theater, on a chase scene involving Audrey, Cary Grant, and Walter Matthau. Audrey was absolutely adamant, and so was Grant, that no reporter get onto the set. But without warning, Hollis Alpert, film critic of *Saturday Review,* turned up. He was powerful at the time, and Sterne begged the stars to give him the V.I.P. treatment, which they with a supreme effort did. Both were furious.

Audrey was especially nervous during the difficult scene, shot among the pillars of the building of the Comédie Française, in which she had to decide whether Cary Grant or a villainous Walter Matthau was telling her the truth. The writing was rather weak, and the nocturnal confrontation as improbable as anything in pictures. With her dancer's instinct she worked out a series of movements with the director from one part of the square to the other.

Audrey returned from the Château Crespierre to the greater security of the Burgenstock. She concentrated on spending a good deal of time with Sean, as if to compensate him for her long absences during the making of two movies in a row. She coaxed him to speak English now that he was three but, at the same time, decided not to force him to abandon Gina's language in favor of his parent's native tongue. After all, Gina was, at this stage in his development, as important to Sean as they were.

Chapter Ten

Audrey was at home in the Burgenstock chalet when Kurt Frings called her in a state of excitement. "Are you sitting down?" he asked her on the long-distance phone from Hollywood. "Because if not, you'd better!" She sank into a chair and listened carefully. He said, "You've got *My Fair Lady*!"

As early as *Breakfast at Tiffany's,* she had told a reporter that her greatest desire was to play the role of Eliza Doolittle, the Cockney girl from Covent Garden who emerges from chrysalis to butterfly under the guidance of Professor Higgins. (On the stage, the part of Eliza was played by Julie Andrews). Audrey had told a reporter at the time, "I haven't found Lerner and Loewe [Alan Jay Lerner and Frederick Loewe, respectively lyricist and composer] ready to do the movie yet. I ought to campaign for it, I suppose. I loved the show so much. There's no other role I'm dying to do. I *must* be Eliza."

First conceived in 1954, *My Fair Lady* was based on George Bernard Shaw's play *Pygmalion* and on that 1938 film, which starred Leslie Howard and Wendy Hiller in memorable appearances. The composer and lyricist set about creating the musical by trial and error, writing and discarding songs, sharpening the character of Professor Higgins, with his passion for the English language and his intense dislike of women.

There was a struggle to acquire the rights from the Shaw estate, followed by the challenge of casting. Alan Jay Lerner selected Rex Harrison for Higgins. Harrison was perfect for the part. Underneath his seemingly disdainful hauteur lurked the virile nature which earned him the nickname "Sexy Rexy." Audiences the world over would love the sight of Higgins gradually cracking before Eliza's charm.

Mary Martin was eager to play Eliza, but it was clear that she would not be suitable. Not because the creators felt that she was miscast but because, almost incredibly, she disliked the lyrics and score. Instead, Lerner and Loewe turned to Julie Andrews, then successfully playing the leading role in *The Boy Friend*. She had a perfect light soprano voice, exquisite diction and, at eighteen, an ideal face and figure. They went to see her, and their auditions of her were very encouraging.

My Fair Lady was a vivid success on Broadway, and offered the further delights of Stanley Holloway's irresistible Doolittle and Robert Coote's charming Pickering. The music and lyrics conquered everyone. Moss Hart's direction was nothing short of inspired; he decided to have Rex Harrison half-sing, half-speak the songs because he felt that Higgins should always be harsh, and a singing voice would soften the desired acidity (another reason, of course, was that Rex Harrison couldn't sing). The slightly unusual situation of having Julie Andrews sing perfectly and Rex Harrison merely utter his songs was overcome by the discipline and control of Hart's direction.

Called by Brooks Atkinson "One of the best musicals of the century," *My Fair Lady* won the Tony, the New York Drama Critics Circle, and the Outer Circle awards as the best musical of 1956. In New York and London it enjoyed the longest run of any Broadway musical up to that time. It was produced in twenty-one countries in eleven translations, and the original cast album sold more than five million copies. Warners paid five-and-a-half-million dollars, plus a percentage of the screen rights, to Herman Levin and the composer-writer team for the screen rights.

It was agreed from the beginning that Rex Harrison would repeat his theatrical triumph in the picture, but Jack Warner was nervous about the fact that Julie Andrews was not known to the general public. When he heard that Audrey wanted to play the part, he looked up the grosses on her last few pictures and decided that her name alone could ensure the success of almost any movie. He decided to call Kurt Frings and offer Audrey the role.

Frings was a tough customer. By the time Jack Warner, the stingiest executive in the business, had gotten up off the floor, he had agreed to pay Audrey a million dollars, in ten-year annual increments for tax purposes, with a percentage of the gross. This was not as common then as it became later and, indeed, the salary made history, since Audrey was one of the first million-dollar stars. And she was worth it. Despite the devastating shock to Julie Andrews when she heard the news, Jack Warner was undoubtedly right. The age of musicals had passed by 1963, and the mass public needed the stimulus of one of its idols in order to rush to the theaters in sufficient numbers to justify Warner's colossal expenditure on the rights. Warner further secured his investment by hiring George Cukor—the most famous director of women in the business—to handle Audrey and to bring out the best in her.

When she heard the news from Kurt Frings, Audrey ran from the room. She had to share the magnificent news with someone close to her. She told Henry Gris, "Mel was away. At Cannes. But mother was upstairs, taking a shower. I banged on the bathroom door and screamed something unintelligible about the movie I was to star in, and mother came out soaking wet, wrapped in a towel, thinking the house was on fire or something. And then I dashed back to the telephone to get to Mel."

The 1962 Cannes Film Festival was under way, and Ferrer had gone there to discuss a new movie project. There was an interminable wait as Audrey hung on the line until Mel could be found and brought to the telephone. By the time he arrived, after over half an hour, she was in tears. He asked her what the problem was. She told him her news. He was overjoyed and asked her why on earth she was crying. She responded, "Because it's such an important day and we are hundreds of miles apart."

The degree of her dependence on him, and her childlike

nature, was never more clearly illustrated. Nor was the extent of his extraordinary devotion, because he immediately abandoned a meeting which was crucially important to his disastrously slipping career and flew at once to Zurich, changing plans to be with Audrey at this big moment. He also said he would accompany her to Hollywood to be with her during the long weeks of preparation.

On May 16, Audrey few with Mel, Gina, and Sean to Los Angeles, checking into the Beverly Hills Hotel with a mountain of luggage and her usual number of prized personal possessions. She then moved immediately into a large white rented house. On Sunday, May 18, Cukor, Alan Jay Lerner, and fabled set and costume designer Cecil Beaton (a dandy who affected Edwardian suits, enormous broad-brimmed panamas, and floppy fin-de-siècle hats) came to see Audrey and Mel for afternoon tea. While Audrey cuddled Sean, two maids served English breakfast tea and Audrey's specialty: a large apricot jam roll sliced thinly for each guest.

Audrey came to the point at once. "Are you going to use my voice for the songs?" This was of great concern to her. She had of course sung "How Long Has This Been Going On?" in *Funny Face* and "Moon River" in *Breakfast at Tiffany's*. However, it was decided that in *My Fair Lady* her voice would be matched with another voice in the high notes. (This was to lead to unnerving consequences later. Marni Nixon had already been secretly engaged to double.) Audrey enchanted her guests, but slightly overdid it when she delivered a pretty speech that sounded almost rehearsed, saying, with her careful diction, "The picture is one we must all remember. Wonderful talents, everyone right, everyone happy. It's the high spot for all our lives, let's enjoy it!" Suddenly she resembled a British sports mistress, and Alan Jay Lerner, for one, was very upset. He had been shattered by the decision not to use Julie Andrews, and he was not happy about the fact that Audrey would be singing the songs, albeit augmented by Ms. Nixon. From that moment on, his visits to the cast, and even later to the set, were minimal. He hated the picture from beginning to end.

In the next two weeks of May, Audrey attacked the job in

hand with her usual intensity, and with perhaps an extra edge of concentration and concern. She worked very closely with a New York voice coach, determined to sing the songs from beginning to end when she could. She was adamant about mastering Cockney. Not only did she have a special coach for that London patois, but she also listened very carefully to Limey Plews, a prop man at Warner Brothers who had served in the trenches as a Tommy, or rank-and-file British soldier, in World War I. She was fascinated by him, and she took careful note of his dropped participles and aitches.

During rehearsals for the picture, various tensions emerged. For the first time in their marriage, Audrey and Mel were, according to the ubiquitous Herb Sterne, seriously at logger-heads. In fact, when crew members reported hearing the sounds of quarrels from Audrey's dressing room, it took all of the practiced skill of Audrey's personal press agent, Henry Rogers, to keep the facts from the press.

There were many conflicts between George Cukor and Cecil Beaton. Both men were highly opinionated and imperious, and both enjoyed the self-indulgence of temper tantrums. Their spats were more than a touch effeminate, and caused much unfavourable comment from the crew. Audrey strove to learn as much as possible from both of these remarkable men. She was enchanted by Beaton's sketches of her costumes and wrote to Givenchy, urging him to share her enthusiasm, which he did. She would sit with Mel, in their happier moods, exclaiming lines like, "Oh, it's more than I thought it possibly could be. It's too much!" as she opened Beaton's portfolios in her dressing room.

Audrey invaded the wardrobe department, crying out, "I don't want to play Eliza! She doesn't have enough pretty clothes! I want to parade in all these!" She put on many of the costumes for the picture, and others from off the rack, whether they fitted or not and, like a little child, darted about in Romney hats with broad brims as well as dresses of black velvet and lace, muslin, or satin. Then she was brought by Beaton, holding her hand, to see a mannequin of herself wearing Eliza's pathetic green coat, shabby skirt, and black straw boater. She almost cried at the sight; she was so taken by the costume's authenticity that she immediately put it on and Beaton had to hold back the tears.

On June 4, 1962, Audrey had the unpleasant experience of attending a press luncheon, held on Sound Stage Twelve, to announce the movie's commencement. A platform was set up at one end of the stage, with food of indifferent quality supplied by Chasen's and plastic flowers from the same source. A photographer screamed at Cukor when he accidentally moved in front of Rex Harrison, and Cukor, who hated the press, screamed back. Beaton cringed, only to be told by the grand old actress Gladys Cooper, "Don't sink into the mud with them." Audrey barely tolerated the whole occasion, realizing that worse would come when she finished the movie and had to go through this ordeal again on a national tour.

Audrey was very impressed with the makeup department and set designers at Warners. The makeup people, led by the Westmore brothers, did a fine job de-glamorizing Audrey, with Beaton's cooperation. Her hair had to be filled with an unpleasant substance known as Fuller's earth — which was quite toxic — and she had to wear a special kind of kohl makeup and a drab foundation to make her look sallow and underfed. For the tests she also had to undergo the blackening of her fingernails and the backs of her hands, and her clothes were deliberately made large so that her frail figure would disappear in them.

There was a very uncomfortable moment when she sang part of the score to the assembled company — a mistake whose responsibility has never been clearly established. Certainly, no one who heard it would ever forget it, and Audrey, seeing the brave smiles on everyone's face, had the feeling she was drowning.

Harrison was very odd. First, he was indifferent and cold, and he was greatly aggravated by the squabbles of Beaton and Cukor. He had been quite disagreeable toward Julie Andrews during the stage production (according to Alan Jay Lerner's erstwhile assistant, theater historian Miles Krueger); and although he was on his best behavior with Audrey, and even strove to be charming to her, it was hard for him to relate to her. She melted him finally by mentioning that she had known his late wife, Kay Kendall, at the Marie Rambert Ballet School and by giving him a red bicycle to ride around on with a special basket for his script.

Harrison often forgot his lines, despite the innumerable times he had uttered them, and thus rehearsals were severely handicapped. But Audrey was letter-perfect from the beginning. Tired though she was for much of the time, she stood up to Beaton's rigorous scrutiny. Every scene had to be tested in costume again and again because the essence of the movie lay in the gradual transition of Audrey from goose to swan. Beaton stood over her like a Svengali, ordering, in his own words, "Strands of her hair to be placed in this direction or that, suggesting more or less eyelash, selecting a brooch or a trinket." Every hairstyle had to be argued over and decided upon. Finally, Audrey and Beaton jointly settled on Edwardian bangs like those worn by the famous British music hall star Gertie Millar. Audrey risked having her face look even more square than usual because she wanted total period authenticity, and deeply respected Beaton's taste and expertise.

The picture's preparation benefited from Audrey's testing with no makeup, with a pale foundation, and then with strong makeup. After an entire morning of makeup people pulling her hair this way and that, trying various kinds of paint on her, she would then give up her lunch to work with her singing coach for an hour. She also had to walk up and down so that she would lose her natural grace, then restore it in later tests. She had particular fun choosing the right hat for the Ascot scene. She and Beaton finally chose one that was replete with cloth poppies and antic bows and would tremble when she jumped up to see the horses.

There were minor and major ordeals. Audrey had to sing some numbers in a sealed cubicle while André Previn conducted the orchestra outside. Rex Harrison had already prerecorded everything. No one was prepared to say that her voice simply wasn't up to it — even in the lower register — but instead of admitting defeat, Audrey continued to record for well over another month although it was quite obviously a waste of time. Her poor girl's coat had to be dyed seven times and rubbed to look old, and she got very tired of this. When her hat fell apart, Beaton and her dresser were quite distraught. All efforts to have the right coiffure prepared for a ballroom scene were disastrous and, Beaton said, after a particularly long day, "By some mischance I saw my face reflected in Audrey's triple mirror: it was drawn, and the color of Gorgonzola cheese. Audrey was patient and polite, but behind her expression one could tell that she was tense." Several days later, the Ascot hairdo, as well as the one for the ball, still looked like a bird's nest. Weeks dragged on until at last shooting began in the suffocating August of 1963.

Audrey insisted that a white picket fence completely surround her dressing room as though it were a country cottage, with a sign saying "Positively do not disturb" on the gate. Herb Sterne recalls, "Mel was not very much in evidence. He would come in, the door would be closed, and he'd come out looking like a storm." Audrey, as so often before, decided that the entire company and crew had to keep out of her line of sight. She even went to the extent of having black screens put up around the set, and as soon as Cukor ordered the scene to begin with the instructions "Roll 'em," everybody ducked. Sterne says, "Some of the scenes were quite long, and you get cramps working on the floor seated or kneeling. The crew resented it terribly."

Even during the actual production, Audrey was still recording songs. As late as August, she was doing poorly in the famous "Wouldn't It Be Loverly?" One particular afternoon she was feeling terrible — her head was aching and her hairdresser was massaging her neck. She was so upset and irritable that she refused to allow still photographers to remain on the set. When they protested, she said sharply, "The movie camera doesn't bother me, but your lenses do. I'm sorry." Bob

Willoughby and Mel Travel fled: it was the worst experience they had ever had. If they wanted to sneak in the smallest still, they had to wear pitch black and hide behind the flats so Audrey would not see them.

The fights over costumes, wigs, and music continued. The "Rain in Spain" number was particularly exhausting. Rex Harrison was at his snippiest, and especially disliked feeding Audrey lines. He actually refused to allow Beaton to take portrait photographs of him, and Audrey followed suit. Frustrated, Beaton developed laryngitis and walked around with a sign on his neck reading "I am unable to speak." A crew member was heard to say, "Why doesn't he just say he's dumb?"

Somehow, everyone struggled on. Then, there was a major row between Beaton and Cukor. Cukor forbade Beaton to take photographs of Audrey off the set, and Audrey had to tell Beaton, "I can't be in the middle of this, but try not to be too upset." All attempts to referee the fight proved disastrous.

At last Cukor relented and during some lunch hours Audrey sat for a portrait by Beaton, meanwhile nibbling on salads. She somehow managed to sustain this extra work despite a whole series of catastrophes. Sean had developed a fever of 103, and she was frantic with worry. Her canary flew out of its cage at feeding time, and there was now no noble Burgenstock expert to retrieve it. Despite all the security of her dressing room, her wedding ring was stolen. Rising at 5:30 A.M. and going to bed at 9:30 P.M. day after day became monotonous and, at last, Audrey gave out and the picture closed down at vast expense for a long weekend so that she could sleep uninterruptedly for days. Audrey became more and more fretful. At last audio music director Ray Heindorf prevailed and it was made known to her that all her weeks of careful singing practice — the gruelling sessions of dubbing and matching to Rex Harrison — were wasted. All of her songs, every note, would have to be dubbed. Not even a visit from Givenchy could console her. When she was given the news by some unfortunate minion (since Jack Warner characteristically ducked the task), she responded sharply and immediately walked off the set. When she returned the next day, she apologized to everyone. She had had a horrible evening and night in between.

Audrey delivered outbursts of temperament unprecedented in her career. There was no question that these had much to do with the increasing rifts in her marriage to Ferrer. During one number, Audrey was dancing on rubber cabbage leaves when she, to Cukor's great consternation, did the unthinkable. Without waiting for him to order a retake, she simply stopped the scene twice, announced to the hidden crew or anyone else who was listening that she hated her performance and thought herself a lousy Cockney, stamping her feet in frustration and bursting into tears.

In spite of everything, though, she still had good friends at the studio. She adored Roy Moore, a prop man who kept her supplied with filtered cigarettes, which she couldn't bear to be without. Young men in the production office who handled the call sheets or daily schedules always watched her when they could and, in homage to her, put a special "Miss" in front of her name as a grace note. She invited the entire crew to a screening of *Charade*, and presented her hairdresser Frank McCoy with a Yorkshire puppy named Henry Higgins. She delighted everyone by riding the bicycle — renamed Eliza — given her by Billy Wilder years before and by refusing the use of a studio limousine. These things made up for the closed set (only her friend Doris Brynner [wife of Yul], Mel, and Givenchy were exceptions to the rule).

Audrey was accompanied everywhere by the ill-fated Famous's successor, Assam of Assam, who barked and jumped constantly behind the picket fence surrounding Audrey's dressing room and responded only to French.

On November 22, 1963, one of the scenes in Covent Garden was being shot when a studio carpenter who had been listening to the radio came in with the shocking news that President John F. Kennedy had been assassinated. At first, Cukor didn't believe it. He asked an assistant to check the story. The man called Washington and received confirmation. Cukor said he couldn't bring himself to make an announcement; the words would stick in his throat. Everyone realized that something ghastly had happened when they saw Cukor's face, and they saw that he was in no condition to continue with the scene. He did manage to tell Audrey. He told her, "I can't tell them." Audrey replied, "I'll do it."

In tears she took a microphone and ascended a small platform. She said with great courage, fighting back the tears, "The President of the United States is dead. All that we know is he has been shot in Dallas. I think we should have two minutes of silence to pray or do whatever you feel is appropriate. May he rest in peace."

There were exclamations of horror, and several women began to cry. Jack Warner insisted work continue, but everyone walked off. Audrey called Mel, who was shooting the picture *Sex and the Single Girl*, and that night was one of the blackest in their lives. The tragedy brought them closer, but in the final weeks of production Mel grew more chilly, and there were reports that he was rude to some of the cast. It was generally known by now, despite a published statement that Mel would star Audrey in a picture called *Isabella of Spain*, that their marriage was heading rapidly for the rocks.

Audrey finished *My Fair Lady* a few days before Christmas. She was exhausted, summoning just enough energy to play with three-year-old Sean and with Assam of Assam. The next months constituted a nerve-wracking schedule designed futilely by Audrey to hold the floundering marriage together. Instead of the rest she needed, she made sixteen trips in eight months through every part of Europe so as never to leave Mel alone. There was no necessity for her to go on any of these journeys, but she was clearly afraid of losing Mel and her romantic daydream of a show-business marriage.

She couldn't bear to let him out of her sight, and no doubt the many rumors of his interest in other women were getting to her. Ferrer made a series of mediocre movies, the most notable of which was *El Greco*, in which he played the title role, and which created barely a ripple and was not released in the

United States. They went to Spain for a period, then to Lausanne, Switzerland, then to Paris, then to Rome, and back again. The packing and unpacking was endless, and Audrey still insisted on traveling with trunks crammed with her favorite possessions.

One one of the sixteen trips, Mel was producing and appearing in an obscure movie in Spain. It was entirely shot on location and on a miserably tight budget. Mel had to lead a small motorcade on dusty, bumpy roads through flood, storm, and burning heat via a number of extremely primitive small towns and villages with no proper hotels, shabby and depressing inns, and very little food worth eating. Coming from the luxury of the house in which she had lived during the filming of *My Fair Lady,* and the kid-glove treatment she had received at Warner Brothers, she now was living in conditions of extreme discomfort, forced to occupy accommodations suitable for paupers, and feeling, as the badly sprung auto bumped over potholes, as though every bone in her body had been broken.

She told Henry Gris, "I knew it would be very hard on Mel, this whole trip, because he is so demanding of himself. I was rather worried about that, and I thought if at least I went along I could somehow help." This great star, this idol of millions, found herself making beds, inspecting them for fleas, disinfecting the baths, and preparing food herself, often to the fury of the cooks at the inns.

Not for the first time in her life, she had to rise at dawn and stand under a broiling sun all day long with food or production notes like any script girl, and at night she was so tired she often fell into bed without dinner. She seemed to be acting out a program of her own making, and the effort was considerably exhausting.

In Spain, Audrey heard the disappointing news that she had not even been nominated for an Oscar for *My Fair Lady.* A possible reason is that Marni Nixon, who had dubbed her voice in all the songs, had rashly announced the fact; according to Nixon she was blacklisted as a result of this and didn't work for years afterward. The Academy voters were very annoyed at what they took to be a deception to which Audrey was privy — they simply didn't know the facts. Moreover, many people in the industry were disturbed that the enormously popular Julie Andrews had been pushed aside; this may have been the reason that they rubbed salt in Audrey's wound by nominating Andrews for her performance in *Mary Poppins*. To add insult to further injury, Rex Harrison was also nominated, for his performance as Professor Higgins.

Although Audrey was shocked by the news, she felt there was justice in the decision. She wasn't happy with her performance in the first half of the picture, feeling, perhaps with some reason, that she didn't get "into" the Cockney guttersnipe sufficiently. However, she was marvelous in the second half, admirably suggesting the pain and anger caused by Higgins's ill-treatment of her, and looking stunning when the butterfly emerges from her cocoon at Ascot.

It shows how extraordinarily sporting Audrey was, when she actually went to Hollywood to present the Oscar for best actor to Harrison, and when she was among the first to congratulate Julie Andrews on her triumph. What her thoughts were at exactly that moment can only be conjectured, but, brave and bold though she was, she must have felt at least a twinge.

This humiliating defeat, following an exceptionally tiring period of travel, strained Audrey's temper to the limit. She had, in fact, been showing some edginess and frayed nerves for quite some time. Shortly before the Oscar nominations, she had fired her devoted publicist Henry Rogers, today one of the best-known press agents in Hollywood, for a peculiar reason. He had criticized Givenchy — as Mel, to Audrey's annoyance, persistently did — for not giving her free perfume and clothes in return for her worldwide advertising of his scents and clothes. Givenchy had brought out a line called Audrey, and she had not claimed any money for the use of her name. Also, Rogers had irritated Audrey by attacking Favre Le Bret's running of the Cannes Film Festival and by insisting that only certain changes would make it worth Audrey's while to go

there. Audrey severely resented Roger's seeming high-handed-
ness in these matters, and dismissed him on the spot. But
typically, she softened the blow by saying that she hoped they
would always remain friends. It was the steel hand in the velvet
glove, without a doubt.

In Spain, Audrey was once again caught up in one of Mel's
projects and, on this occasion, she took a very definite hand in
it. They were in Madrid when the celebrated Duchess of Alba,
one of the great beauties and social leaders of Europe, invited
them to a party at her magnificent home in the most luxurious
part of the city. She had never met Audrey, although she knew
Mel, and promised them a special treat: she would perform
a flamenco — her specialty — accompanied by a band from
Granada.

Despite being worn out from a day of work on Mel's picture,
Mel and Audrey went to the party. There they met a remarkable girl named Marisol. She was the toast of Spain. Sixteen
years old, with huge glittering eyes and voluptuous breasts,
filled with fire and joie de vivre, she thrilled the elegant gathering with her high, vibrant voice and her powerfully evocative
guitar playing. She danced, clapping her hands, and she was
superb. Audrey was amazed by her talent. When the duchess
danced the flamenco, it took all of her skill and daring to begin
to complete with the electrifying Marisol.

That night, as Audrey and Mel left the mansion in the small
hours and walked to their car in the darkness, they decided they
must build a whole movie around the girl. They talked about it
until four o'clock that morning, then fell into a restless sleep for
two hours until it was time to drive to the studio. On the way,
Mel saw in the semidarkness the carts of the *traperos*, the
famous ragpickers of Madrid who scavenged the streets at
night. The *traperos* were picking up their loads left for them
outside the houses and leaving Madrid for the miserable shanty
town on the city's outskirts where they scratched out a meager
subsistence. The carts moved slowly — a strange and silent
procession as the dawn broke.

Mel noticed a figure behind one cart which could have been

either a boy or a girl, wearing overlong culottes, baggy coat, and broad-brimmed felt hat with a hole in it. Suddenly, Mel thought, this would be the perfect character for Marisol. She could be a ragpicker who became a great performer of some kind. She would dream of glory . . . what would the glory be? He decided she would become a *reconeador*, or *caballero*, a bullfighter on horseback, whose horse would carry her into the ring to face Spain's most savage bull.

Back in the apartment that night, he spun Audrey the story, which he called *Cabriola*. Audrey helped him with the screenplay, and together they persuaded Marisol to star with the celebrated Angel Peralta. Audrey personally took Marisol to Alexandre, the well-known hairdresser, and he himself styled Marisol's hair under Audrey's supervision. They spent a wonderful time together in Paris, and back in Madrid they again worked closely together as Mel directed the picture. Audrey was on the set constantly, collaborating in the direction with countless suggestions. She also helped greatly in the climactic scene, in which the great Peralta and Marisol ride into the arena, he on his stallion, she on her pathetic pony Cabriola. It was a marvelous scene, and Audrey overcame her intense distaste for the bullring and the *corrida* by being present at the filming, which was done, at her request, without bloodshed.

Sean was growing stronger and taller every day. At one point, he traveled with his nurse Gina to Marbella, an unspoiled coastal town with broad, sandy beaches on the Costa del Sol, in southwestern Spain. Audrey and Mel found a house there, in an olive grove overlooking the ocean, with a slope leading up to a mountain and a striking view of the Rock of Gibraltar. They bought the house and then made another decision, quite major considering Audrey's need to have a permanent base in the Burgenstock. They decided to leave the Burgenstock and buy a home in another part of Switzerland since, if they had stayed on at the Burgenstock, Sean would have had to attend a German school. Audrey could not tolerate that idea, and she wanted to get Sean out of German Switzerland entirely. She also wanted to secure a home for him, and the property in the Burgenstock was still not for sale. Her gypsy existence would no doubt be harmful to the boy, now that he was past the age of four. He had been in hotels in most of the major cities of Europe for the past few years and his education, such as it was, had been scattered, including a Madrid kindergarten and a Los Angeles infant school. Sean spoke Italian like a native because of Gina, and he had picked up Spanish; Audrey spoke to him in Italian and Mel in Spanish and Italian. Sean spoke very little English at the time.

He had an exceptional vocabulary for his age, and was articulate and intelligent as well as physically active and strong. Audrey's adoration of him amounted almost to an obsession. She now wanted the perfect place for him, so she began house-hunting.

Mel spent several months looking, and so did Audrey. At last they found the perfect place. It was a very beautiful sixteenth-century farmhouse in the small village of Tolochenaz, about half an hour's drive from Lausanne, overlooking Lake Geneva and with a fine view of the Alps. The two-story farmhouse was built of pink-beige local stone, with a slate roof. It was utterly simple but had a sense of strength and permanence, severity and coolness ideally suited to Audrey's character. For centuries, the farmers who owned it through several generations had kept their cows in one half of the house and lived in the other half. There was a fine orchard, which surrounded the building, and a small but pretty garden, overgrown with weeds and totally informal — unlike most gardens in Switzerland. Certainly, there was nothing about the house to suggest it was the appropriate residence for a movie star. Audrey, with her simple tastes and tight purse, did not want anything in the least opulent, extravagant, or ostentatious. As she redecorated the farmhouse, she designed it as the kind of home a settled European aristocrat would enjoy, comfortable rather than showy, immaculately maintained but seemingly casual.

At last, from all over the world, she brought all of her

countless possessions, which had been stored in basements, storehouses, hotels, and with friends. Finally, after weeks of exhausting work, bringing valuable things down the winding road through the mountains of the Burgenstock, conducting packing cases and trunks off freight and passenger planes, greeting various moving vans that trundled along from Lausanne, she had around her an incredible array of her favorite objects. It was like a family reunion, or a gathering of old friends.

There was a noise problem from the newly constructed Geneva-Lausanne autostrada, which was muffled to some extent by the trees and the walls around the orchard that flanked the house, but otherwise Tolochenaz was pleasantly quiet and secluded. It had only one main street, the Route de Biere, with just two shops — a hardware store and a grocery. There were no bistros, and the nearest restaurant was at the town of Morges. There were only about four hundred fifty people living in Tolochenaz, and most of them were farmers who tended the orchards and vineyards covering the fertile slopes leading to Lake Geneva. There were three cattle farmers and some Spanish and Italian workers who assisted the Swiss in tilling the soil. Sean attended school in a tiny schoolhouse with Swiss, Spanish, and Italian children with whom he happily conversed. He also quickly picked up French, with a charming Vaudois accent. Audrey would bring him daily to the lovely two-room cantonal school, which had two bright young teachers. It was a thrill for her when the teachers reported that Sean was well ahead of his class.

Audrey traveled to Paris in July to make *How to Steal a Million*, opposite Peter O'Toole, for her old friend William Wyler. She played the daughter of an art forger, played by the wonderful old British character actor Hugh Griffith, who had made a great hit in the movie *Tom Jones*. In *How to Steal a Million*, Griffith forges a statue of Venus so expertly that it is exhibited in Paris as a Cellini. The daughter is so upset over this that she arranges with a society burglar (O'Toole) to steal the statue from the museum. The shooting took place in

August, when Paris was virtually deserted by its residents, and once again she ran into severe heat. During the production, thieves broke into the studio and stole two very costly swan-necked vases, antiques obtained for the picture by art director Alexandre Trauner, and one morning a group of men in masks seized the studio concierge, tied him hand and foot, and cracked the safe, making off with the payroll for cast and crew.

The movie was a superficial concoction, not worthy of Audrey's or Wyler's talents, but Audrey liked O'Toole, whose zany antics appealed to her. He had been very nervous about appearing with her, as he had heard she was stern and formidable, but he revealed later that in one sequence, in which the two were locked together in a closet, it was all he could do not to let himself go with her. In fact, he became very attracted to her as the work began.

Rumors flew that O'Toole and Audrey were having an affair, and indeed several people still insist upon it. Audrey, who was very wrapped up in her child and trying to hang on to her marriage, probably wouldn't have risked destroying her domestic situation.

Back in Switzerland, Audrey kept a very close eye on the redecoration of her house and on Sean's education. She knew that if she wanted to continue her career, sooner or later she would have to leave him, despite the fact that she was very nervous about kidnappers. All through the shooting of the picture, she flew by Caravel to Geneva on Fridays and returned to Paris on Sundays so she could spend some time with him, and even if she had to work on a Saturday she would fly home and spend Sunday with him. She didn't want him to be separated from his friends. The garden of the house was filled with children all the time; a typical scene had them clamoring at his window to wake Sean from his afternoon nap, summoning him to come and play. These were village children, and Audrey loved the sound of their laughter and chasing about.

Audrey refused to have Sean photographed by anyone because a newspaper picture might possibly aid potential kidnappers. Actually, this was a futile precaution, since paparazzi had taken many photographs of Sean and Gina during one unguarded afternoon walk at Tolochenaz. Audrey would have offered any amount of money to retrieve those pictures, but it was impossible. The Swiss police kept the house under surveillance, and when in Paris Audrey hired special guards. A bodyguard always accompanied Sean when he went to school. But despite these precautions, Audrey often had nightmares as the reports of kidnapping grew more and more extreme, leading to the celebrated kidnapping of the Citroën heir and that of the Getty boy years later.

Sean needed a guard dog, and dogs, of course, were the heart of the household. There was not just Assam of Assam but also Mouchie, a German shepherd who was trained as a guard dog from the time he was a puppy. He looked after Sean diligently, but he was so overprotective that he began snapping at the children who surrounded the boy, and some parents began to fear he would bite. Eventually, despite loud complaints from Sean followed by tears, Audrey had to give Mouchie away. A couple took him temporarily and then fell in love with him, so the parting was final. In his place Audrey brought an Australian sheepdog, rather like a collie, that was very sweet and didn't snap at the schoolchildren. Everyone was relieved.

Audrey worked constantly in the garden, pulling out every red flower or plant because she hated the color. There was nothing she disliked more than a blaze of red blossoms. Instead, she cultivated white flowers; her brothers sent her bulbs for white Dutch tulips. She loved white flowers more than anything else. The garden shone with white, giving the impression of being saturated with moonlight.

Audrey was never happier than when she was covered in soil, digging with gloves on, a scarf around her head, and watching living things grow. She was also thrilled because she again became pregnant, and no doubt she hoped that this new child might save her marriage. She may also have hoped that Sean would be happier with a little brother or sister. Like many mothers, she didn't feel it was a good idea for her son to be an only child. But once again she suffered a miscarriage, and she was devastated.

There were some compensations. The greatest of them was the Sunday before Christmas at Tolochenaz, which was the children's night, when the young boys and girls performed in Christmas plays. Later, Sean would appear memorably in one of them. Audrey was offered the leading role opposite Cary Grant in a musical version of the film *Goodbye, Mr. Chips,* but arrangements fell through and Petula Clark was cast opposite Peter O'Toole. For a time, Richard Burton was mentioned as Audrey's prospective co-star. Her greatest disappointment was when Mel was kept from fulfilling a long-cherished dream of making *Peter Pan* with her. She would have been marvelous as Peter — even at the age of thirty-seven — but Walt Disney, whose 1953 cartoon version was still being shown, secured an injunction and stopped the project. In the wake of this disappointment, Audrey was offered two fascinating scripts. The first was *Two for the Road*, by the gifted novelist Frederick Raphael; the second was *Wait Until Dark*, based by Robert and Jane-Howard Carrington on the play by Frederick Knott.

Two for the Road was a departure for Audrey, and her most daring and sophisticated role to date. She would play the relaxed, sexy and outgoing, but very independent wife of an absentminded but physically attractive man, reliving in the present the events of years before, when she first met her husband. A running gag has him losing such items as a passport or a wallet, which she has lovingly retrieved. Both characters were shamelessly adulterous; and the marriage, like Audrey's in real life, was already doomed. Beneath the cool texture of the dialogue, behind the insistent rhythms of Henry Mancini's score, the picture was to achieve an extraordinary level of emotional intensity, all the more remarkable because it was hidden in humor. Audrey's portrayal of a range of emotions as the seemingly lighthearted Joanna Wallace betokened a striking advance for her as an actress, and this was perhaps her finest performance on the screen. In one sequence in the south of France, as she ran tearfully through a garden to a swimming pool followed by Albert Finney's Mark Wallace, she was astonishingly open in her expression of personal pain.

Once again, Audrey was working with director Stanley Donen and was headquartered in Paris. Donen and Raphael had to reassure her over the script, because it was such a departure from the sort of material to which she had become accustomed. Once she agreed, however, she committed herself with her usual passion, only to face a truly serious problem. Donen was adamant that she must not be dressed by Givenchy, either as the young student who meets the addle-brained architect or as the mature woman whose husband has become an obsessive careerist. Not only was it thought that Givenchy would be beyond the budget of an architect's wife, but also that the styles would have clashed with the informal, mod look that the writer (who had also created Julie Christie's sensational *Darling*) and director wanted. Audrey was very uneasy: she always felt so much more comfortable when Givenchy protected her figure and made her feel more certain of herself. Moreover, the director wanted her to appear nude in a love scene and not wear a flesh-colored swimsuit as she proposed, and to eschew a body double in a scene at the beach. She was very uneasy about appearing in a swimsuit, with her skinny upper body and tendency to look awkward. And her body had changed; her hips had broadened since childbirth.

Donen overcame her doubts and fears with extreme firmness and confidence. He went shopping with her in Paris and London while Mel and Sean stayed in Switzerland; for the first time in years, she shook off Mel's absolute control and severity and became her own woman in the Swinging Sixties. After all, she was still quite young, and more attractive than ever, and much as she adored her son, it is clear that something rebellious in her was coming to life after years of repression in her marriage. No longer was she trying to become exactly what Mel wanted; without a love interest, free and released from responsibilities, she was ready for a lighthearted romance.

Ken Scott, the well-known designer, was brought in as fashion coordinator and, among other designers, Audrey accepted Mary Quant. Scott was impressed, he says, by the fact that Audrey was extremely rigid, even in dealing with her informal clothes. Although she might be more relaxed in her style of living, she could never be where work was concerned. The color red was forbidden, of course, along with almost all primary colors. "Busy" dresses with heavy patterns were eliminated. Swimsuits had to be carefully padded and cut very tight around the hips, with straight lines to disguise them. Scott grew tired of struggling with Audrey over every tiny detail and was replaced by Lady Claire Rendlesham, a London specialist whom Audrey adored. Lady Rendlesham worked very hard on the sweaters, blouses, and shirts with falsies that were to fill out Audrey's upper body, and on the stockings and boots that emphasized her calves. Certainly, dressing Audrey off the rack was a grueling task.

Audrey had not met her co-star Albert Finney before. There is no question that his effect on her when they met in Paris was great. Finney was at the height of his attractiveness in 1966. Stocky, with a powerful, muscular body and a keen intelligence, he was supremely masculine and authoritative. Although devoted to his career, and a serious actor who had already earned the admiration of such great figures as Laurence Olivier and Charles Laughton, Finney rejoiced in his youth, and had a great sense of humor and a boyish love of fun. Finney was equally impressive as a devastatingly attractive young architectural student and as a manically successful architect.

Albert Finney said later, "Audrey and I met in a seductive ambience in . . . a *very* sensual time in the Mediterranean. We got on immediately. After the first day's rehearsals, I could tell that the relationship would work out wonderfully. Either the chemistry is there, or it isn't. I find I can have very good rapport with an actress I am working with, but occasionally there's an absolute attraction. That happened with Audrey. Doing a scene with her, my mind knew I was acting but my heart didn't, and my body certainly didn't! Performing with Audrey was quite disturbing, actually. Playing a love scene with a woman as sexy as Audrey, you sometimes get to the edge where make-believe and reality are blurred. All that staring into each other's eyes — you pick up vibes that are decidedly not fantasy. The subject and the situation [of Audrey] are very tender . . . Working together was like a well-organized tennis game. I'd throw up a ball and she'd throw up a ball to match. People are always asking me when I'm going to marry her. Well, you tell me . . . I won't discuss it more because of the degree of intimacy involved. The time spent with Audrey is one of the closest I've ever had."

Finney was as far removed from the stern and austere Mel Ferrer as it was possible to be. As the shooting went on in the stifling summer heat, from Paris to the south of France via the Loire, the romance developed rapidly.

William Daniels, who played the bespectacled American tourist who accompanies the quarreling couple on their motor tour with his wife and obnoxious child, says that he wouldn't deny (though he didn't actually know) that Audrey and Albert were lovers. He says that Audrey was constantly laughing, relaxed, and joyous, and that she and Finney would take off to very humble boîtes and bistros to enjoy themselves drinking and dancing. It was a relief to Audrey to become a kid again, carefree and seemingly indifferent to gossip. The age had passed at which it was necessary for stars to hide even the slightest hint of adultery and, dressed in Michele Rosier, Paco Rabanne, or Mary Quant creations, Audrey literally blossomed on camera, freed not only from Mel but from Givenchy as well. Her friendship with Finney unquestionably gave a sparkle to Audrey's acting that had never been seen before.

It became a very delicate matter when a bedroom scene had to be shot between Audrey and Albert, with both in the nude. First, the scene called for shooting at night in an apartment building, but due to a shift in schedule this proved impossible and it had to be shot in the daytime. Cameraman Christopher Challis recalls that the windows had to be blacked out completely to suggest total darkness, and the heat in the room was insufferable. The entire crew had to be crammed into the tiny space, with Audrey and Albert very self-conscious in bed. In the morning the weather was cool and rainy, but as the day went on it became stickier and stickier.

There was another problem. In those days, cameras could not shoot cars in motion from the inside — and most of the movie took place in cars. Challis remembers, "We had to rig up all the cables and lights inside the car, with the generator in the trunk, and Albert had to press all the buttons and start the whole thing moving. He and Audrey laughed so much it ruined take after take. And Albert was so mischievous he would put on the soundtrack words like, 'I wonder what Stanley Donen is getting paid for, when Audrey and I are doing the directing!' As a result, the soundtrack had to be done over."

It was tough for Audrey, though at last she seemed a little freer of her dislike of her own body, when she had to swim with Finney in a secluded cove not far away. She was jittery about the whole thing, and told Donen she wasn't sure she could go ahead with it. It was all right for Albert, who had an athlete's physique, to run in and out of the water unself-consciously, but Audrey, with her awkward proportions and painful thinness, would be physically exposed for the first time to her millions of fans as she really was. Donen appealed to her professionalism by reassuring her that her body was the envy of most women of her age. She came through like a trouper and played with extraordinary simulated relaxation.

Whenever she could, she would snatch days to fly to Switzerland to see Sean, but no doubt newspaper reports of the Finney "romance" caused Mel much concern. His consolation was that he would be producing *Wait Until Dark* by arrangement with Warner Brothers — a partial compensation for the now-complete lapse of his career. At least, Mel and Audrey found a common ground in Sean. In the Christmas of 1966, there was a wonderful event at the children's night at Tolochenaz. In the church a Christmas tree was lit with red wax candles that rose up into the apse. The children were reciting poems; Sean, aged six, delivered a Christmas verse in French. Audrey had worked with him very closely on it. With butterflies in their stomachs, she and Mel watched the little boy playing a sheep in a white costume with paper ears and cotton on his head. After the Nativity play, he was chosen to recite first and on his own because he was the youngest there. Audrey said later, "Our little boy stood up straight as a die, opened his mouth, and in a loud French voice recited this little French poem, hands by his side. And he spoke good and loud as I'd asked him to. And he did fine. And we were absolute wrecks because to the very last line we were afraid he would forget, or lose his confidence. But he didn't. He did us proud. It was a big thrill."

Against this scene could be set Audrey's concern at rumors that Mel was having an affair with Marisol, whose name was kept out of the papers. When she left for the United States in the beginning of 1967, to make *Wait Until Dark*, she was once again very tense. Albert Finney, of course, was out of Audrey's life by now.

Before she left, she studied very carefully with Professor Streiff, a physician who specialized in teaching the blind at his clinic in Lausanne. She had to understand what it meant to be blind because she had to play a blind girl menaced by gangsters in a Greenwich Village apartment.

Audrey had been determined from the beginning to have the British director Terence Young helm *Wait Until Dark*. A very quick, able young man, he had known Audrey for quite a long time. In fact, early in her career he had tested her for a picture called *Valley of the Eagles*, and had been enchanted by the grace with which she received rejection: the central female role called for a buxom, strapping young woman. Audrey had never forgotten Young's charm and kindess to her at the time.

Negotiations for *Wait Until Dark* had begun in June 1965, when Jack Warner decided she should play the part of the blind girl; he had been concerned that she would not be covered by insurance because of her fragile health, and had to be reassured on the subject, Ferrer wanted Sean Connery to play a sympathetic role in the movie, but this was overruled. Walter MacEwen was put in general charge of the production, with Mel as producer. Terence Young wanted George C. Scott to play the villian, the drug-seeker who imprisons Audrey, but Alan Arkin got the part. There were several delays because Terence Young was held up by the shooting of *Triple Cross*, the story of the famous British agent Eddie Chapman. While Audrey waited in Spain at the Marbella Club as her new home was being completed. Ferrer had several meetings with Young at Young's house at Cap d'Antibes. In the fall of 1966 there was much discussion about possibly making the picture in Europe, and Audrey would have preferred this, but it was out of the question; Walter MacEwen and Jack Warner were adamant that it be made in Hollywood. Letters and telegrams flew back and forth, and finally MacEwen stood firm. He told Ferrer over the phone and later by telegram that there could be no question of any such foolishness and, in a very stiff cable to Kurt Frings, MacEwen made clear that California it was and California it would be. He also threatened that "Any failure on the part of Miss Hepburn or either of your other two clients [Ferrer and Young] to comply with their contractual obligations will result in legal action for damages being brought against all concerned, including you and your agency. In this connection, we wish to remind you that *Wait Until Dark* is a very costly and important theatrical property and if we are deprived of services of a star of magnitude of Miss Hepburn and forced to make picture with lesser artist, damages could amount to a very large sum . . . This is a public corporation and we cannot do business for personal convenience of stars and others to whom we pay such tremendous sums" (August 30, 1966).

Even before the completion of *Two for the Road*, at the end of August 1966, Audrey had to go through makeup and hair tests done by her friends Alberto and Gracia Di Rossi, who had been with her since *War and Peace*. She was still fretting about making the picture in Hollywood, but by September 5 she at last agreed, and MacEwen cabled Jack Warner from Hollywood to New York: "Audrey will be good girl and do picture here as always planned." She went to Paris (when she was overruled in the matter of using Givenchy) to shop with Lady Rendlesham, and bought clothes off the rack in smart little Parisian boutiques.

Audrey then proceeded to New York City, while Young

was delayed on the island of Elba, near Italy, by a heavy storm. The delay continued, and Jack Warner told Walter MacEwen, who repeated the story to me, that Young was "holding everyone up for money." In fact, the Italian papers show that Elba was swept by severe gales amounting almost to hurricane conditions, and Young cabled Ferrer, begging him not to drop him as director or he would be "heartbroken." He was prepared to waive salary for the two weeks he didn't work. Jack Warner approached Sir Carol Reed to take over, but Audrey flatly refused to even consider Reed; her loyalty to Young was typical of her. She fought Jack Warner over it, and despite furious communications between MacEwen and Frings, in which MacEwen proposed other possible directors, Audrey stood firm.

Indeed, she worked hard in New York to try to understand what it would mean to be blind. When Young at last freed himself of the crushing problems of budget and weather on *Triple Cross*, he joined her in her most rigorous study for any part. She managed to obtain the cooperation of the well-known school, the Lighthouse for the Blind. Audrey and Young wore specially made blinder masks used on patients who were losing their sight. Bit by bit, she learned to touch properly, to feel surfaces of different textures with the tips of her fingers. She also learned to sit absolutely still and listen to different levels of sound, so that she could judge how far or near someone or something was to her.

She learned to walk with a stick, and could tell by the sound of the tapping whether she was walking on tiles, hardwood floors, rubber surfaces, or stone. Sometimes, she was given very difficult tests. A typewriter would be used in a doorway, and she would have to know whether or not it was inside the room. She was told how to use a blind person's telephone, which operated on a special digit system, and she had at least a passing brush with Braille. She learned how to make a cup of tea by feeling her way to the canister with the teabags, measuring the distance to the stove with her hand, and then taking the pan and heating the water before she poured the water into a teacup. She had to pick up the teacup without rattling it or spilling any tea.

She learned how to make her face up without smearing the lipstick or mascara, and how to comb her hair. It was a very unsettling experience for anyone as sensitive as Audrey. Suddenly, she realized what it meant to live without seeing colors, movements, human expressions, mirrors, the way a room looked at different times of day, the sunlight and the moonlight. It was very moving to her, and in a way almost shocking, when she removed the mask and suddenly the reality of the world assailed her, with all its beauty and ugliness, almost as though she had died and been brought back from the grave.

Terence Young had to struggle to cope with being temporarily "blinded," but Audrey sailed through the experience with astonishing expertise. She worked very closely with a young college girl named Karen Goldstein, who had been blind since the age of six. Karen lived at college and participated in college life as much as she could. She was extremely bright and perceptive, and Audrey spent a good deal of time with her, fascinated by the fact that Karen was studying English and psychology. Another blind girl would work with Audrey in Hollywood, so that Karen would not have to interrupt her studies.

Above all, Audrey relied upon her cane, now standard for blind people, which was made of delicate, vibrant bamboo, since wood was an unresponsive substance and could not pick up sounds and touches nearly as well. She began shooting in New York. That January of 1967 was very cold. Indeed, before they joined Audrey for the location shooting in Greenwich Village, Ferrer and Young had endured temperatures of twenty degrees below zero while filming a preliminary sequence in Montreal, Canada. The weather in New York was not much of an improvement.

It took Mayor John Lindsay's personal intercession to block off the traffic in the Village for several blocks, which created frenzied traffic jams filled with yelling and horn-honking drivers. Every inch of the barricades was jammed with people wanting to see Audrey. But unfortunately, for all her careful training, Audrey ran into trouble from the first moment that the rushes were shown to Walter MacEwen in Hollywood after having been flown by special plane from Manhattan. Audrey's eyes were so brilliant and expressive that MacEwen felt they simply did not suggest blindness. He had complained of this in earlier tests, but Audrey had insisted that she could simulate blankness in her eyes when shooting actually began.

MacEwen says he was very shocked and demanded that Audrey yield to his original suggestion and wear contact lenses. She hated the idea. She detested putting them in and taking them out, since they irritated her eyes but at last she agreed and shooting recommenced. Audrey had to endure the constant itching and watering they induced without every touching her eyelids or even scratching in the region of her eyes. She and Mel were quite annoyed with MacEwen over this.

At the same time there was a more definite row over Lady Rendlesham, who was fighting with the studio over her travel expenses and the cost of trips to Paris and London and back again in order to pick up Audrey's wardrobe. The matter was so delicate that, in the middle of a tight shooting schedule, the much-harassed Ferrer had to write to Lady Rendlesham in London to insist on knowing how many days she had worked for Audrey and to tell her that she could not be paid one cent more than agreed. To make matters worse, seven pairs of the wrong-size shoes arrived from her office in London, and they had to be returned at once. Lady Rendlesham responded that she had not overcharged and apologized about the shoes (which had been too large on *Two for the Road*) without explaining why she hadn't bothered to check the measurements, and Audrey finally settled her unpaid fees.

When shooting began in Hollywood, another row developed. Ferrer and MacEwen were locked in a struggle over Ferrer's expenses; some of these were challenged, and there was considerable discussion of approximately twenty-five hundred dollars that had not been paid. Certainly, neither Ferrer nor

Audrey lived up to their reputation of thriftiness bordering on stinginess at the time. Although their marriage was definitely on the rocks, they still moved into an extremely lavish bungalow together at the Beverly Hills Hotel, along with their complete staff of cook and maids. However, much to Audrey's annoyance, Sean was not with them. She had had to leave him at school at this stage in his education; she consoled herself by filling her dressing room with pictures of him — for her then, he was the truest love of her life. Comments by friends were very bitter. Henry Gris talked to Yul Brynner, whose wife Doris, from whom he had recently separated, was a close friend of Audrey's. Brynner said, "I don't know how Audrey could put up with it for so long . . . but then, I suppose, she was so desperate to make it work and she is so sweet, loyal, and human. I'm sure that, above everything, Mel was jealous of her success, and he could not reconcile himself to the cold facts of life. She was much better than he in every way, so he was taking it out on her. Finally, she couldn't take it any longer. God knows, she did everything a woman could do to save her marriage."

The picture grew more and more troublesome, not only because Audrey was under a strain simulating blindness in scene after scene with the dreaded contact lenses and trying to match the movements of a blind girl hired as technical adviser, but also because of the tortuous separation from Sean and the anguish of her marriage falling apart. Walter MacEwen remembers that so complete was the personal rift between husband and wife, Ferrer was very busy "auditioning" one model after another for a scene in which a pretty girl is found hanged behind a door.

Audrey tried to relieve the tension as best she could. She called Tolochenaz on Sundays, so as not to interfere with Sean's schooling; she had to rise at two o'clock in the morning to call him before ten, so that she wouldn't interrupt his life too much and he could go out for his daily walks. She spent Sundays rummaging through Hollywood book and stationery stores to send him picture cards, Valentine cards, standup cards, and cards that folded out into railway trains. In Switzerland, Sean used to race the servants to the door every time the mailman rang the bell, and added a new item to the collection from Mama that hung from a string across the length of his room.

The cast found ways to relieve the tension on the set. There was a tradition in Hollywood of somebody, usually an assistant director, issuing a signal, often a whistle, to announce that a scene was about to begin. Actress Greer Garson always had her scenes announced by a tiny, sterling-silver dinner bell. This time, to amuse everyone, the assistant director got a bicycle horn and honked it. The actors decided to respond in kind. Alan Arkin pumped away vigorously at an ancient bullhorn taken from a turn-of-the-century automobile. Audrey matched him with an even more squeaky, grunting piglike horn. Jack Weston used a fire bell. Richard Crenna was not to be outdone. He obtained a foghorn from an old liner and rigged it up and blasted it off until Audrey and the others thought they would go deaf at any minute.

Audrey insisted on breaking every afternoon for tea. She hadn't been able to persuade either George Cukor, who was very edgy and impatient, or Jack Warner to allow this British custom during the shooting of *My Fair Lady*, but this time she got her way. The fact that Terence Young was British made all the difference: perhaps there was more than admiration for his talents that made Audrey want him for the picture. The tea ritual was very elaborate. The Ferrers had their own cook and maid (as well as their limousine with uniformed chauffeur), so everything was perfect. Ferrer had even managed to force stingy Warner's into allowing the construction of a complete British tea garden by the art department right next to the Greenwich Village apartment set of the movie.

At the exact stroke of four, a bell rang, the picture stopped, and everyone sauntered into the "garden" under the artificial trees and trellises to enjoy watercress wafer sandwiches, sponge cakes, and ladyfingers, with tea brewed in the pot. Audrey adhered to the iron rule of one spoonful of tea for the pot, one for each guest, and a waiting period of ten minutes for the tea to settle and brew. The pot was in a tea cosy, of course, and the crockery bought in Switzerland was of the finest English quality. Jack Warner was exasperated by this habit. Indeed, he tried hard to stop it without success. He hated the fact that the picture was made during French hours — that is, it was shot from twelve noon to eight at night. After considerable complaint, and threats of resignation from the entire cast, the hours were changed with great reluctance to eleven-thirty to seven-thirty.

Another pleasant aspect of the picture was that Richard Crenna and Jack Weston would pull gags constantly, making Audrey break up with laughter. She was convulsed when these overgrown kids borrowed suits of armor from the neighboring *Camelot* set, put on Viking mustaches, and then descended on Audrey and Alan Arkin behind the scenes with screams and yells.

At long last, Sean came for a visit during his Easter vacation, and Audrey was in a state of rapture. She spoiled him outrageously during the length of his stay, his first in Hollywood. He was already tall for his age, and by fifteen he would shoot up to six-foot-three. He took after Mel in his height and striking good looks. She adored taking him off to Marineland, Disneyland, and Knott's Berry Farm. Surprisingly few people recognized her as she mingled with the crowds like an ordinary tourist.

Audrey gave a surprising number of interviews at the time, bravely reasserting a series of fibs that her marriage was gloriously happy, that Mel was the only man in the world for her, and that after almost fourteen years they were still one. But nobody really believed her. The columnists were in full cry about a rift, and when Audrey returned to Switzerland on the day shooting finished on *Wait Until Dark,* she went into complete seclusion. The reviews turned out to be excellent, and Kathleen Caroll of the New York *Daily News* summed up popular opinion with, "Miss Hepburn does very well by the role with her special way of being femininely fragile, yet independent. More important, she never lets one feel sorry for the character." Like *Two for the Road*, which also garnered Audrey excellent reviews, the picture was a huge success, pulling in seven million, eight hundred thousand dollars in domestic rentals. It had even been brought in under budget and schedule, in spite of the French hours and the tea breaks.

Despite the good word on the picture, however, Audrey was going through a difficult time that summer of 1967. Mel came to see her from Paris, where he was staying temporarily, and they were seen lounging around on the patio of the Swiss house and walking in the garden as Audrey picked the full-bloomed roses. But in Paris the rumors grew stronger every day that Ferrer was infuriating Audrey. First, he was embarking on yet another version of *Mayerling* — this time without her. It was said that she was very displeased about this, and that insult was added to injury when he cast the exquisite Catherine Deneuve as Maria Vetsera opposite Omar Sharif's Prince Rudolf.

By the time Ferrer began shooting *Mayerling*, with none other than Audrey's favorite director, Terence Young, it was clear that the marriage was finally over. Another miscarriage set the final seal of doom upon it.

Audrey told Henry Gris, "When my marriage to Mel broke up, it was terrible; more than that, it was a keen disappointment. I thought a marriage between two good, loving people had to last until one of them died. I can't tell you how disillusioned I was. I'd tried and tried. I knew how difficult it had to be to be married to a world celebrity, recognized everywhere, usually second-billed on the screen and in real life. How Mel suffered! But believe me, I put my career second."

Audrey had had a wretched winter, but she finally took Sean to Marbella to get away from the cold and damp, and there she met the handsome and celebrated Prince Alfonso de Bourbon-Dampierre, a pretender to the throne of Spain. They were seen everywhere together — dancing close in nightclubs, holding hands on the banquettes of fashionable restaurants, and, it was believed, sharing a suite in a Madrid hotel. Mel was naturally inflamed by these reports. He was also greatly aggravated when he went to meet Sean at Kennedy Airport for a visit under the unofficial terms of the separation and Sean was not on the plane. Mel exploded. Airline officials coolly handed him a message from Audrey informing him that Sean would not be coming to visit after all. This was quite against their arrangements; Ferrer had even gone to the expense of renting a home in Beverly Hills for the boy. It was only much later that Audrey allowed Mel to have brief custody of the child.

In the summer of 1968, Audrey decided she desperately needed a rest. She left Sean with her staff at Tolochenaz and accepted an invitation from two friends — millionaire gasoline king Paul Weiller and his wife, the glamorous Princess Olympia Torlonia — to join them on a cruise of the legendary islands of Greece. It was a golden season, and the sail from Piraeus on the shimmering, azure Aegean Sea was magical. The yacht was filled with fascinating, immensely rich people, large amounts of champagne, and superb food prepared by a master chef. One of the passengers intrigued Audrey. He was the tall, blond, strikingly handsome thirty-year-old Italian psychiatrist, Dr. Andrea Mario Dotti. Although psychiatry and neurology were his avocations, Dotti's family was enormously wealthy in their own right, and he lived in great splendor in Rome while working as an assistant to the distinguished Professor Leoncarlo Reda of Rome University.

The attraction between Audrey and the handsome young doctor was instantaneous. Dotti, an extremely virile man of vigorous appetite, was an enchanting companion — witty, effortlessly charming, and above all very youthful and very much alive. His legendary temper was not visible in the relaxed atmosphere of the cruise, and as he and Audrey soaked up the sun on the yacht's deck, enjoying good conversations and good wine, the inevitable happened. The combination of the two was dynamite. Although mindful of her son and terrified of any scandal, Audrey could not help herself: apart from the arguable romantic fling with Finney and the more likely one with Prince Alfonso de Bourbon-Dampierre, she had been bottled up as a woman for years, repressed by Ferrer into acting as his virtual puppet, imprisoned by his coldness, his ambition, and his inescapable severity. He was one kind of Latin: the rather harsh, Spanish kind. Dotti was a wealthy Italian sensualist another breed of animal altogether.

Audrey's relationship with Dotti grew on the cruise. The host and hostess, the Weillers, say that they could see their love blooming right in front of them. Audrey threw caution to the winds for once, and was in heaven. But she had just made the most serious mistake of her life.

Chapter Eleven

At the beginning of their relationship, Dotti told Audrey a charming romantic tale. As a boy of fourteen he had seen her in *Roman Holiday*, and had rushed home to tell his mother that he was going to marry the beautiful lady who played the princess in the movie. He had fallen in love with her at that impressionable age of puberty, and she had recurred in his sexual dreams many times over the subsequent years. He had run into her at a party in the 1960s and had expressed his interest in her very clearly through his eyes and gestures, but she had not responded. Indeed, when he brought up the matter of this previous encounter, Audrey could not remember it.

Audrey was very uneasy because of the age difference between them and because she felt that she was influenced by the fact that she was on the rebound. It would be foolish to describe this new relationship as truly romantic in Audrey's sense of the word, given her intensely romantic and perhaps somewhat naive nature. She entered into the relationship without completely understanding what it might imply. This was characteristic of the intense self-absorption of most actors, who, in concentrating so utterly on themselves (and, in Audrey's case, on her mother and son as well), could not always see deeply into others.

It is incumbent upon stars, as it is upon their press agents, to create an illusion of blissful happiness and roseate self-confidence for the public. In those first weeks of her relationship with Dr. Dotti, Audrey gave interviews and issued statements expressing her joy in the new relationship and in her psychological condition as a whole at the time. Yet, from the beginning, she was gravely troubled. First of all, for anyone like herself, who had carefully created an insulated existence in which every detail was meticulously organized, it was horrendous to have to face meetings with lawyers concerning the details of her divorce from Ferrer. Millions were at stake, since both husband and wife were extremely wealthy, and there was an ongoing battle between the lawyers for the two of them over who would get the Tolochenaz house and how the many stocks, bonds, and real estate holdings would be split up.

At the same time, Audrey had to face the fact that, in Italy, the Catholic Church and families ruled by the Church objected most gravely to the idea of a favored son or daughter marrying a divorced person; in fact, special dispensation would have to be obtained from the Vatican to permit marriage to Dotti. Although Audrey was Episcopalian, Mel Ferrer was Catholic, and despite the fact that Audrey was married to him in the Protestant faith at the Burgenstock chapel, that fact could not be ignored. Furthermore, Audrey was faced with other torments. She realized that her position as a motion-picture actress might preclude her from certain areas of Italian society. This was not important to her, with her reclusive nature, but it was important to Dotti as a prominent physician. It might be difficult for him both at the hospital and in his private psychiatric practice, as well as in the austere and rigid medical and ecclesiastical circles that ruled Rome. Again, Audrey knew that many would comment unfavorably upon the difference in their ages.

Audrey also had to bear in mind that Dotti, as a Catholic husband whose virility would be constantly surveyed by his entire family, would want to have children both as proof of his masculinity and to sustain the family line. Audrey was already on the edge of her menopause and could certainly not bear more than one child at that stage. Even then, pregnancy could be risky for her because of her uterine problems and her continuing frailty. Some women grow stronger in middle age; Audrey emphatically did not. For all her extraordinary fame, wealth, and position, she still felt as insecure and threatened as she had when she was struggling at the barre in Marie Rambert's ballet classes.

Dotti tried to persuade his family that marrying Audrey was not a mistake. After all, as far as they were concerned, he had the world at his feet. He was thirty, he was reaching the first peak of a brilliant medical and social career, and he could easily have married a woman of the Italian aristocracy and become the father of a healthy brood destined for wealth, good looks, and all the pleasures that money can obtain. A middle-aged actress, no matter how prominent, was scarcely the ticket.

First, his trump card: his mother, Signora Roberti, adored Audrey from the moment they met. She could see that Audrey and her son were very strongly attracted to each other, that they respected each other, and that they both loved music, painting, and literature. Moreover, Signora Roberti was pleased with Dotti's desire to protect Audrey from publicity. He had made a home movie of the Weillers' yacht voyage but had deliberately not filmed Audrey because he knew how much she hated photographs in which her face and figure were unprotected by the skillful lighting of the Hollywood studios. He also knew that Italian film laboratories would often sell footage of stars to newsreel makers and others for considerable sums of cash. This, too, he wished to avoid.

Signora Roberti was also impressed by the fact that, when he came to Rome to meet his prospective stepfather, Sean, so carefully trained by Audrey in good manners, so healthy in body and spirit due to her intense dedication to his physical and psychological welfare, did not, as many children might have, seem to resent Dr. Dotti at all. Thus, a major objection to the marriage was overruled. Then, most importantly, Audrey captivated everyone in the Dotti household. She was so unpretentious, so shy and anxious to please and full of humor, that the entire family fell in love with her at once. Signora Roberti's husband, of the newspaper *Corriere Della Sera,* and

Dotti's three brothers — an electrical engineer, a banker, and a sociologist — and their wives all gathered round, inspected the fabulous creature who had arrived in their midst, and murmured approval. It was a considerable strain on Audrey to undergo this ritual of inspection, but she rose to the occasion with her usual skill. It helped, of course, that she was already friendly with a number of distinguished figures in Italian society, among them the celebrated Count and Countess Crespi; Count Dino Pecci-Blunt; the Duchess Marina Lante della Rovere; and, above all, the brilliant and charming Countess Gaetani, at whose exquisite home on the Islo Giglio Audrey and her new lover most happily stayed.

For appearance's sake — her son's as well as her own — Audrey spent the final weeks before her divorce from Ferrer at Tolochenaz. With great discretion, and at some neglect to his patients, Dr. Dotti flew often to Switzerland to see Audrey. Henry Rogers, who was again her press agent, kept the reporters at bay; and the Swiss inhabitants of Tolochenaz behaved with much-appreciated indifference to the liaison. The divorce was handled with extraordinary discretion, the kind of discretion that immense wealth can secure.

Sometimes Audrey would fly to Rome for the weekend, sometimes Dotti would fly to Geneva. After the divorce was final, they spent Christmas with the Dotti family in Rome, and all the conflicts with the Vatican were solved. To celebrate both the season and the engagement — which was now possible — Dotti gave Audrey a magnificent Bulgari solitaire diamond, and a small reception was held to announce the engagement.

In those weeks Audrey and Dotti were with Audrey's two closest friends (Doris Brynner and Capucine) and with Dotti's (Queen Frederika of Greece and Christina Ford, then wife of Henry Ford II). They decided to get married in Switzerland, in part because it was Audrey's place of residence and in part because of the dreaded paparazzi, who would have turned a wedding in Rome into a circus. The religious problem was neatly overturned by the decision to have a civil marriage ceremony in a Protestant country. The ceremony took place on

January 18, 1969, at the town hall of Morges, the town that neighbored Tolochenaz, and was presided over by Madame Denise Rattaz, the registrar. Bridesmaids included Doris Brynner and Capucine; the groom's witnesses were Paul Weiller and the distinguished painter Renato Guttoso. Audrey wore a Givenchy pink jersey suit and held in her hands a small posy of flowers. She looked pale but beautiful.

The honeymoon never took place; the couple merely moved into Tolochenaz. It was probably a wise decision: the paparazzi would almost certainly have ruined the experience as they had ruined her honeymoon with Ferrer. Luckily, Sean still accepted Dotti. There was no tension between them, or no more than would be considered normal when any three people were living together in a place that had usually accommodated two. Audrey expertly fielded any problems that arose. And of course, Doris Brynner and Capucine were always around to help.

Audrey became pregnant in April. She was naturally overjoyed, but she had to consider her health. At the time she learned that she was going to have another baby, the couple had moved to Rome, although retaining the Swiss residence. For a time they lived in the Dotti family villa, then managed to locate an appropriate apartment overlooking the Tiber, with a spectacular view of the city. It had many rooms, in the Italian mode, and rather resembled a labyrinth. The place was high-ceilinged, spacious, cool in summer, and drafty in winter, and had a delicious scandal connected with it — it had been the home of the secret mistress of a high papal dignitary. The apartment was on the top floor of the building. The building staff provided dubious security but operatic entertainment at all times. Sean loved the building, racing about in it as any healthy, robust nine-year-old boy would.

Audrey, with no film envisaged, became exceptionally extroverted for the first time in her life. She actually did the unthinkable and listed her own and her husband's telephone number in the phone book. Although she gave few interviews, she was warm and welcoming to the press. She strolled around the streets with her husband on weekends, hand in hand, seemingly indifferent to the paparazzi. She told Henry Gris, "I'm in love and happy again. I never believed it could happen to me. I'd almost given up. Now Mia Farrow will get my parts. After all, I worked nonstop from when I was twelve until I was thirty-eight. I feel a need to relax, sleep in the morning. Why should I resume work and the life I rejected when I married a man I love, whose life I want to live?"

The couple went to movies and nightclubs and to the gorgeous Gambrino Beach Club, where Sean felt particularly at home. There were visits to the Countess Gaetani at the Islo Giglio, and sometimes the couple would dance up a storm at a lavish party. Yet already there were problems underlying the apparent charm and glamor of this idyllic period. Audrey began to hear rumors that Dr. Dotti was casting his eyes on other women. Audrey was told something which in her strange, almost childish naiveté she surely should have understood from the very beginning: that an Italian male does not consider marriage the end of his free sexual life. Indeed, in certain Italian circles it is considered appropriate for a man to keep a mistress — or mistresses — while supporting a wife. After all, Dotti was thirty, at the height of his youth, physical strength, and sexual virility, and, as Henry Gris says, Audrey lacked eroticism, her sexuality expressing itself in cuddly affection and tenderness rather than in sensual excitement and abandon. An older man might have welcomed the lack of sensual challenge in a relationship, but for a man in the first flush of his youth, such a situation could only lead to trouble.

Audrey, a total romantic, never would understand that a man might not be as devoted to her as she was to him; and this lack of understanding foredoomed her short period of happiness. Perhaps because she wanted her child to be born only in Switzerland, and perhaps because she felt that the rumors already whirling about her head must be kept at one remove, Audrey took off for Tolochenaz for the long lying-in period. She had to rest for months, confined almost entirely to her bedroom. This was difficult for her because she still possessed a restless nature. But with several miscarriages behind her, she realized that she dared not make the slightest mistake. A miscarriage this time would be disastrous because she could have no more children, and it was crucial for her to keep her promise to Dotti. Had he not fathered a child, he would have been disgraced in the eyes of his family.

This lying-in period was marked by a very disagreeable circumstance. Dotti was largely in Rome during those months — of necessity, because of his practice, and he behaved with all the impetuousness of youth. In the evenings, instead of remaining within the family home or the apartment over-looking the Tiber, or devoting himself to work, he was seen nightclubbing with a variety of women, and allowed himself to be photographed publicly with them. Audrey got wind of this (she had only to pick up a newspaper to do so), and her mental state was severely affected in this delicate period. Worse was yet to come, because Dotti was actually photographed with one of the most notorious and glamorous beauties of the city: the model Daniela, who had appeared in virtually every magazine from *Vogue* to *Oggi* and was considered to be one of the most energetic of the members of the international set in Europe. This scandal-ridden beauty became — at least on the surface — the centerpiece of Dotti's social life in Rome. Stories about her were endless: she was said to have once interrupted a Beatles press conference in Milan to insist that the group listen to her sing a wild rock-and-roll song. Allegedly, they had ignored her completely, and she had pursued them to Rome, futilely offering herself as an Italian fifth in a quintet. Abandoning this absurd idea, she had become a regular at the raffish Piper Club in Rome and had become engaged to Antoine, the well-known French singer. Afterward, separating from him, she became engaged to Rolling Stones star Brian Jones, who later died of a drug overdose.

The toast of fashionable Mod society in the wake of one scandal-sheet story after another, Daniela had whirled about London. Now, with Dotti, she was a most glittering figure of the Roman *dolce vita*.

Officially, Dotti was said to be giving Daniela psychiatric treatment (he specialized in drug rehabilitation), but since she always denied she had anything to do with drugs, everyone became totally confused — everyone, that is, except the sophisticated and those in the know. Newspaper columnists had a field day implying that Dotti was having a fling at the same time that his wife was expecting a baby in another country. It is easy to imagine the extreme tension between Dotti and Audrey when he flew to Switzerland to see her on weekends. Yet he seems to have made no effort to discontinue the alleged affair with Daniela, even up to the point of the baby's birth.

It became evident in the final week of Audrey's pregnancy that the baby would have to be delivered by Caesarean section. Professor Willy Merz, the famous Swiss gynecologist, who was the surgeon in charge of her, was quite firm about this decision. The child, delivered at the hospital in Lausanne on February 8, 1970, was a seven-pound, eight-ounce boy. He was to be called Luca, in honor of Dotti's beloved brother. Dotti was overjoyed, but there is no question that Audrey's pleasure — and the family's satisfaction at the birth of a son — was undermined by Dotti's public behavior at the time.

Sean enjoyed his baby half brother, and there seemed to be little if any evidence of sibling rivalry. This was probably because Sean was so good-natured, and also because the children came from different marriages and were many years apart. In fact, Sean became a kind of uncle to baby Luca. With her marriage in trouble and with Daniela still on the scene, Audrey concentrated all of her emotional strength and affection on her son. Eventually Audrey and Dotti returned to Rome to live at the apartment overlooking the Tiber. At last, Dotti began to behave, and he concentrated more on his work. Audrey paid great attention to creating a home for her new child and a nest that would also appeal to Sean. She spent hours arranging flowers, improving the furnishings, hanging new curtains, creating an oasis in a noisy and troublesome city. She prepared her irresistible pasta salads with herbs, tossing them to perfection and never gaining an ounce. She turned down script after script, and told Henry Gris and other visitors that her life had an orderly domesticity she would on no account disrupt. She worked on her marriage to the extent that she took yacht cruises with Dotti, traveled to Switzerland or Spain with him, and always tried to take vacations with him during the intolerable heat of the Roman summer. Asked whether she felt she had made a mistake in retiring from the screen, she said to Gris, "I've never believed in this God-given talent. I adored my work and I did my best. I don't think I'm robbing anybody of anything and I think I would be robbing my family, you know, my husband and two divine children, of the attention they should get. Otherwise, there is no point in having a wife and mother. No? You know I've always thought this way. Nothing has changed it."

Gris protested, saying that she had given joy to so many millions. She responded with the words, "Well, I'll tell you. If one day a movie is going to be made right down the street and I can come home for lunch, I might accept it, but I am not going to go traipsing off to the other end of the world being locked up in a studio all day long and not being here when my husband comes home for a minute or when the baby is being fed or when Sean comes home from school . . . It's no hardship. I mean I love it so and I truly have no desire to work."

Audrey told D. Audrey Judge of *Ladies' Home Journal*, "It is most interesting being married to a psychiatrist." She added that she had known nothing about psychiatry before her marriage to Dotti and didn't know if she had learned anything from it, but hoped so. Audrey felt that everyone was involved in psychiatry whether they liked it or not, and that the processes of the science were all applicable to daily living. She said that a psychiatrist was somebody who understood people better than anyone else; that there was more understanding and compassion and patience in such a person; that it wasn't as important to know everything as it was to understand the workings of someone you love; that no one should be scared to go to a doctor; and that if problems were agonizing, people should get help. She added that she was fascinated by doctors in their constant fight against suffering; she felt that the anguish of so many people sprang from the thought that they had missed so much in life, as well as from the intrinsic anguish that came from being lonely.

Audrey took an intense interest in Dotti's work with his patients. Even before *The Nun's Story* and her fascinating meetings with Marie-Louise Habets, she had been interested in medicine; now she wanted to hear every detail of the psychopathology of her husband's patients. She wanted to know the latest achievements in drug treatments and electric-shock therapy. Sometimes she would visit Dotti at work. His regime was strict: he spent mornings at the university clinic and afternoons at his private practice. He would often come home for lunch to Audrey's aromatic dishes and then take a siesta, not seeing his private patients until after three o'clock. He would return home again at nine at night, and the couple would dine at about ten o'clock. Sean would go to school at the elegant French Lycée of Rome.

In the summer of 1970, the heat in Rome became unbearable. Audrey took the baby Luca to Switzerland because she was afraid the heat would affect him adversely. She and Dotti would fly to Switzerland to see him every weekend, where he was left in the baroness's charge; she had slowly come to accept the idea of this new marriage. In August they actually had a whole month in Switzerland, and many rifts were cemented.

Audrey continued to desert Givenchy somewhat during that period. She just couldn't face flying endlessly to Paris for fittings at his salon. And of course, the seventies brought a glittering flourish of boutiques in Rome, where she spent almost all her time. Often, Audrey went to movies, no longer bound by the tedium of public premieres but able to slip unrecognized with her husband into one of the overdecorated and stuffy Roman movie theaters to see the latest pictures from Hollywood.

Occasionally Audrey was tempted by a professional prospect: *Nicholas and Alexandra* was offered to her, and indeed she would have been fascinating as Queen Victoria's ill-fated granddaughter who married the Czar and ultimately faced a firing squad at Ekaterinburg. But the probability that the movie would have to be made in Russia and Yugoslavia finally put her off, and she yielded the part to Janet Suzman, who eventually took over and made a great success of the role.

However, Audrey did yield to pressure and appeared on a UNICEF television special in 1971. Then, because of her lifelong fascination with Japan, where she remained an idol, she shot four one-minute television commercials in Rome for a Tokyo wig manufacturer. She even thought that she might appear in *Forty Carats* with Edward Albert, son of Eddie Albert and Margo. (This movie was the story of a middle-aged woman who falls in love with a young athlete barely out of college.) But the producers could not agree to shoot the picture in Rome, and Liv Ullmann was cast instead.

Opinions on Audrey's relationship with Dotti were extremely varied. Some friends were struck by Dotti's attentiveness and consideration; others, notably David Niven and Yul Brynner, were most critical. In fact, David Niven told me that "Many people felt she was much too good for him and that he took incredible advantage of her. And that she gamely played the wife of the social Roman and let her career stand still, on purpose, to help him." Audrey Wilder says, "Dotti was not much of an improvement on Ferrer."

In the summer of 1972, when Audrey was staying on the French Riviera with Dotti and Luca, there was a telephone call from California. It was Mel Ferrer, who told her that something horrifying had happened: eleven-year-old Sean had been visiting with him at the Wild Animal Park when a savage lion had reached out of its cage and slashed him with its claws. Audrey was appalled, but the wounds were superficial, and she did not have to go to California after all.

During that period, Audrey grew warmer toward possible movies. Ross Hunter, a producer who specialized in purple-tinted melodramas with aging female stars, planned a film called *The Marble Arch* with her, but by 1972 the mode for romantic, glossy make-believe movies had faded and a new era of sex and violence had erupted, leaving Ross Hunter awash. Terence Young asked her to star in *The Survivors,* based on a novel by Anne Edwards about a girl whose family has been brutally murdered, but this so-called suspense film in the Hitchcock tradition fell through just after Audrey had reached an agreement with the producers to shoot it entirely in Rome. Yet another project, Garson Kanin's novel *A Thousand Summers,* also collapsed. When Audrey came to New York with Dotti in 1973, it was only to attend a medical conference with her husband, who again was surrounded by rumors of extramarital affairs.

Then, after the collapse of yet another project — Terence Young's *Jackpot,* a film about gambling — Audrey seriously considered a script. It was written by the famous playwright James Goldman, author of the hugely successful play and film *The Lion in Winter,* which had starred Katharine Hepburn. Now that Sean was a towering six-foot-two at fourteen and Luca was a strapping five-year-old, she felt more in the mood to risk a comeback, despite the fact that the Goldman script called for extensive shooting on location in Spain. The story was *Robin and Marian.* It dealt with Robin Hood and Maid Marian in middle age, as they reflect upon their earlier adventures, immortalized in *The Adventures of Robin Hood.* Audrey liked the unabashed romanticism of the script and the touching way in which the tale worked against the sex and violence of the 1970s from which, with her delicate sensibility, she felt totally alienated. The story showed the couple, as famous in legend as Romeo and Juliet, feeling the banking of passion's fires, the physical stresses and pains of middle years, and the desire for life beside the domestic hearth.

Audrey identified utterly with the theme of the movie, in which a living legend, Maid Marian, would want to escape the world if only the world would let her achieve absolute privacy. She looked carefully for any sign of violence in the script, but there was none. She loved the fact that it was difficult now for Robin to wield a heavy broadsword; she loved the element of good and evil in the story, when most movies had no moral basis; and she liked the fact that the movie had an autumnal quality and that she could play almost her exact age. She was very taken with James Goldman, who discussed the part with her at some length, overruling any slight objections she might have had. She was respectful of the director, Richard Lester, who for Sean had the inestimable advantage of having directed the Beatles in *A Hard Day's Night*. Of course, there was the ultimate joy for Luca that Audrey's co-star as Robin Hood would be none other than James Bond — Sean Connery. In fact, if Audrey's traditional reluctance had made her hesitate at the last minute, then certainly Luca would have overridden her. How could he miss meeting his hero?

Audrey traveled to Pamplona, Spain, with Luca, her hairdresser, her makeup woman Mrs. Di Rossi, and Luca's nanny Yolanda. Sean and her husband stayed in Switzerland and Rome respectively. No sooner had Audrey arrived in Spain than she already began to have severe qualms. In the seven years since she had made a picture, she had not realized how completely filmmaking had changed. Now there was no afternoon tea break, no retinue, no studio to protect her, none of the spoiling and cosseting that had gone with superstardom. Richard Lester, an able director who worked with tremendous speed, had no time for star sicknesses or displays of nerves. He was in a hurry all the time, and his personality was grating, tough, and totally at odds with both Audrey and the subject matter of the film. She looked aged and worn in the cruelly frank daily rushes, and she was visibly uncomfortable in the rough conditions that she had more cheerfully ignored when making *Cabriola* with Ferrer. She drank beer in order to try to gain weight. Her metabolism was amazingly active, however, and she couldn't put on an ounce. She was diverted by the fact that Luca enjoyed wielding a broadsword and trying to decapitate the daisies. The weather was maddeningly changeable and difficult, and her delicate skin suffered in consequence. But she struggled on, fighting against her own nature to try to give the best performance she could. Finally, though, the Spanish heat got the better of her. She was stricken with dysentery and had to resort to various nostrums to cope with it. She was totally reclusive as always, and never joined the other members of the cast at the crowded Pamplona hotel bar at night. She flew to Rome every weekend, determined to spend as much time as she could with her husband and Sean.

The picture was not what she had dreamed of. It lacked the old-fashioned romantic richness that she had had in mind. It was altogether too roughly hewn, too clumsy, too lacking in the refinement, the delicate craftsmanship that had marked her earlier work. But she still promised to do everything possible to promote the film when the time came.

Back in Rome, a shocking incident took place. For years, as we know, Audrey had lived in terror of kidnapping and she constantly kept a guard on her children. For two years, she had been unable to walk in the street in case she and her children were pulled into a car — something that often happened to tourists. She was compelled to put both Sean and Luca into school in Switzerland and to fly to see them on weekends. It was a very difficult, quite exhausting way to live, and Audrey had nightmares, tossing sleeplessly night after night. Then something terrible happened. A group of men wearing masks jumped from a car and tried to drag Dr. Dotti, who was standing outside his hospital, into the car. He struggled; fortunately the men were not armed and he was able to escape. This incident so appalled Audrey that, had it not been for Dotti's career, she would certainly have left Rome and insisted that he join her. As it was, she lived in terror from that moment on, never certain that Dotti would return to her at night, never sure she would even be able to go anywhere herself.

A blow fell when the *National Enquirer* reported that Dotti was dating numerous women again. Also, Tony Menicucci, one of the most aggressive of all the paparazzi, gave an interview to the *Enquirer* saying that "whereas Dotti was a son of a bitch, but Audrey was a saint." It was alleged that Dotti picked women up in nightclubs, but when Audrey was in town, he behaved like an angel. When photographed with actress

Dalila di Lazzaro and models Matelda Boston and Emanuela Croce, Dotti became furious and tried to run and hide the women in the car. Menicucci also told *The Enquirer* that Dotti was usually drunk when he left nightclubs around 3:15 or 3:30 A.M., where the determined Menicucci would be waiting for him. Dotti would allegedly give photographers a merry chase. There was much talk of a separation, but Dotti's mother refused to entertain any such suggestions. Unfortunately, in the midst of all this, Audrey had another miscarriage.

Audrey was very nervous when she traveled to New York City for the premiere of *Robin and Marian*. Nine years had passed since she had made her last picture: what kind of reception would she have? Before the premiere, she had had to fly quickly to Hollywood to make a speech at William Wyler's elaborate tribute from the American Film Institute, at which he was given the Life Achievement Award. She read a long, complicated doggerel poem of her own composition and was greeted with rapturous applause, which greatly surprised her. Later, she flew to New York for the Radio City Music Hall opening of *Robin and Marian* as scheduled. She was genuinely amazed when some six thousand people cheered her as she arrived and many, apparently not primed, chanted, "We love you, Audrey!" in chorus.

Whether or not this was a publicity stunt, she was quite unprepared for it and was startled into tears by this demonstration of enthusiasm. She then again flew back to Hollywood for the *Robin and Marian* West Coast opening and for the Academy Awards, at which she presented the Best Film of the Year award to *One Flew Over the Cuckoo's Nest*. This was a special delight to the movie's star, Jack Nicholson, who was a great fan of Audrey's. But she was even more nervous than usual as she entered the Dorothy Chandler Pavilion of the Los Angeles Music Center with Dotti, who had joined her for the occasion. She lost her purse backstage and became quite flustered over this, and she refused to attend the traditional press conference.

The reviews for the movie were good, although Audrey

herself did not greatly admire it and complained to Rex Reed
about the shot of rotten fruit at the end, wondering if this was
supposed to be a symbol of herself and Sean Connery. Certainly, despite raves for the photography, she did not look at all
good in the picture, and many of the close-ups were distinctly
unflattering. Although Rex Reed reported in his column that
she looked miraculously youthful, she certainly did not on
screen, and the movie, despite strong praise for the acting,
failed to attract a wide audience. She blamed the casualness of
the direction, the improvisation throughout, and the lack of a
true emotional undercurrent with which audiences could
identify; but she overlooked the fact that a new generation of
movie-goers was already emerging which wanted to identify
with the people on the screen and found it difficult to relate to
middle-aged romantic figures.

Audrey's life assumed a depressing monotony in the late
1970s, devoid of any real pleasure. She continued to turn down
more parts and to suffer from endless reports of Dr. Dotti's
alleged infidelities. She was consoled only by her two sons and
their success at school. Her wealth meant little to her, since she
lived frugally. Perhaps out of sheer boredom, she accepted an
invitation from her old friend Terence Young to make a picture
called *Bloodline*, based on the novel by Sidney Sheldon, about
an heiress who is threatened by a dangerous killer. Young
offered her the part knowing that it was written for a woman
many years her junior, and that it contained a good deal of
explicit violence and sex, which was totally alien to her. But
apparently his powers of persuasion were greater than ever,
and perhaps she felt that she would update her image if she
entered the new world of the movies. She was paid a million
dollars plus a percentage for *Bloodline*; clearly, the producers
felt that her name would ensure the picture's international
success, and there is no question that foreign exhibitor guaran-
tees, essential in obtaining front money, could be stacked up on
the strength of her name. However, a name alone cannot carry
any picture; the script has to be strong, and the material easily

identifiable by the new audience that by 1979 was setting the tone and tenor of almost all successful Hollywood pictures.

Young slowly but surely overcame Audrey's objections to the script, which was toned down to suit her requirements. She was also told that many scenes would be shot in Rome, widespread locations would be matched in, and she would only have to travel to Munich for a brief period — not too far from Luca in Rome and Sean (now nineteen) in Switzerland. There was also some location shooting in New York, but it was short-lived. Audrey saw more press on the picture in Rome than she had for several years. She stayed in a lavish suit at the Grand Hotel, but the place was dreary and drab, for all its luxury, and Audrey didn't particularly care for it. As always, she was on edge about working. She still had the feeling that she was handicapped by her introspection; and she was affected by the contrast in quality with an Ingmar Bergman film which overpowered her at the time, *Autumn Sonata* with Ingrid Bergman and Liv Ullmann. Not only did she feel the painful difference between the quality of the movie she was making and that of Bergman's masterpiece, but she identified painfully with the Liv Ullmann character, who had to repress her emotions because of disciplined training and suffer in silence, her anguish increased by the fact that she could never be vulgar or overtly expressive.

Her extremely introspective self greatly resembled that of a typical Ingmar Bergman figure, "inwardly turned and tortured . . ." as Nicholas Freeling most sensitively reported in a mid-production interview with her in the Sunday Magazine of the London *Daily Telegraph*. There were stories of difficulties on the set. Audrey was exceptionally edgy and problematical — that she was serene only on the surface became obvious to her friends. Even the most skilled arts of her beloved Italian makeup team, the Di Rossis, could not conceal the pain in her eyes, the shadows beneath them, or the strain in her jawline and neck. Every day brought new worries and new arguments. The misery of her marriage had really taken its toll, and she began to make plans for a divorce. When Andrea Dotti panicked at this, they attempted a second honeymoon in Honolulu, but it didn't work. Matters were not helped either by the fact that Audrey had become attracted to Ben Gazzara, one of her fellow actors in *Bloodline*.

Gazzara was an Italian-American as far removed as possible from Andrea Dotti, both socially and in terms of temperament. Whereas Dotti was a product of wealth, sophistication, and social distinction, Gazzara was the son of a poverty-stricken immigrant Sicilian laborer, a street kid who had survived by fists on Manhattan's Lower East Side. He was extremely temperamental — explosive, hardbitten, and ambitious — a man who had a passionate conviction of his own talent. Handsome, muscular, and energetic, Gazzara was a product of the Actors Studio who fought his way to success in *Cat on a Hot Tin Roof*, Tennessee Williams's play about an impotent war veteran in the South, and *A Hatful of Rain*, a powerful melodrama set in Manhattan in which he gave an electrifying performance. His sensational film debut in 1957, as Jocko de Paris, the cruel cadet of the military college in *The Strange One*, made quite an impact. He also made an impression in *Anatomy of a Murder, Husbands*, and the television series *Run for Your Life*. At the time he met Audrey, Gazzara was married to actress Janice Rule, whose sensitive performances in such pictures as *The Chase* and *The Swimmer* exemplified a career that was sadly unacknowledged. By the late 1970s the marriage and disintegrated into bitter fights and recriminations, and Janice Rule had left the screen to become a lay analyst.

The ground was fertile for both Audrey and Gazzara to become romantically involved; and their relationship was the object of very wide attention on both sides of the Atlantic. The fact that Gazzara was cast in a new picture, *They All Laughed*, directed by his friend Peter Bogdanovich, played a crucial role in Audrey's accepting the part in the picture of the wife of a European millionaire looking for a pleasant escapade in Manhattan.

Perhaps to distract public attention from her romance with

Gazzara in New York, publicists invented an affair with Bogdanovich who, much as he admired Audrey, was in fact attracted to younger women. Bogdanovich's career had a classic American quality of early struggle, sudden and spectacular success, and professional ruin before he was forty. Cold, humorless, and driven by ambition, Bogdanovich began as a film scholar and off-Broadway play director, the most public of enthusiasts of John Ford and Orson Welles. His first film, *Targets*, directed in 1968, attracted some attention; in 1971 he emerged as a director of talent with *The Last Picture Show*, the story of a small American town in the 1950s. He enjoyed a big commercial success with the Barbra Streisand-Ryan O'Neal comedy *What's Up, Doc?* and with the more subdued rural comedy *Paper Moon*. He then made the fatal mistake of committing himself out of blind love to a weak performer: Cybill Shepherd, who replaced his very gifted wife, the designer Polly Platt, in his affections. His critical reputation collapsed as he began to receive increasingly bad reviews. His subsequent movies were dire. *They All Laughed* represented a futile attempt at a comeback. His own money (he was a millionaire from *What's Up, Doc?*) was invested in it, and he even took over its distribution.

Fascinated by Italians, Audrey was drawn to Gazzara, but she was greatly distressed by the publicity surrounding him, and was still more so when the columnists blamed Janice Rule's misery and subsequent divorce from Gazzara on Audrey, who was certainly not responsible. These strains made life very difficult indeed, in addition to the fact that Audrey was upset by stories linking her romantically with Bogdanovich. Actually, Bogdanovich was involved with a pretty new actress, Dorothy Stratten, whose tragic history (she was later to be murdered by her former husband, Paul Snider, a hustler from the wrong side of the tracks) was to form the basis of the movie *Star 80*, directed by Bob Fosse. Stratten would watch Audrey working day after day, fascinated by her discipline and technique, and Audrey was gentle and sweet to her, sensing her insecurity and inexperience. She was horrified by the news of the murder.

The relationship with Gazzara was interrupted by Audrey's

separation from Dotti in Rome, a matter of grave distress to his family. Soon after, Gazzara suddenly married again, and there seems to be little doubt that the romance with him made little or no impression on Audrey in the long run. It was nothing more than a sometimes tense, sometimes desirable interlude.

Audrey very much wanted to find another man, and her friends took note of the fact. One of those friends in Hollywood was the spirited Connie Wald, widow of the celebrated and ambitious producer Jerry Wald, upon whose career Budd Schulberg had allegedly based his novel *What Makes Sammy Run?* Connie, a good hostess, usually entertained Audrey when she was in Los Angeles. One of Connie's friends was the handsome actor Robert Wolders, widower of the glamorous and romantic movie star Merle Oberon, who had died on Thanksgiving Day of 1979. Beginning as a struggling player of little or no talent, Wolders had met Merle some ten years before her death and they had married, enjoying a May-December relationship that was misinterpreted by many. In fact, Wolders, a man of great integrity and decency, was devoted to Merle, who programmed herself, after a lifetime of romantic adventure, to become, like so many women of her type, a paragon in her later years. Their relationship was conducted in seclusion, emerging in the public eye only when they embarked on a disastrous picture, *Interval* — an example of vanity filmmaking which probably should never have been made. He and Merle traveled the world, mostly by ship, at times joyously, at others disastrously, particularly when visiting Merle's imaginary birthplace (she was born in India) of Hobart, Tasmania, where she had given a speech at the lord mayor's luncheon discussing a place she had never previously seen. This deception, caused originally by a desire to hide her nationality from her audience, undoubtedly advanced the severe emotional and physical condition which caused Merle's early death.

Wolders was kindness itself to her, tending her like a child with a devotion that her heart surgeons said was unrivaled in their experience. This decent Dutchman was not only a compatriot of Audrey's but would, Connie Wald felt, be an ideal candidate for an affair with her.

In 1980, Wolders was in New York trying to arrange a memorial to Merle on television, presented by such friends as Charlton Heston and Rod Steiger, while he also sorted out the details of Merle's estate. Connie Wald suggested that he approach Audrey, who had known Merle fairly well and would probably want to participate. Audrey was in New York making *They All Laughed,* and Connie gave Wolders her number.

Wolders called Audrey and said there was a project he would like to discuss with her; he asked her if they could possibly meet for lunch or dinner, provided she did not consider it an imposition. She said she would love to see him but that shooting was at night and she had to sleep during the day. She would call him if the schedule improved.

Days went by, and Audrey did not call. She was very busy, but she hadn't forgotten. Wolders recalls that he was about to leave the city and was changing for a dinner party when suddenly Audrey called without warning to say that the night shooting had been canceled and that she had a few hours. Would he like to meet her?

Wolders was totally taken by surprise and stammered, "How silly this is, but tonight I'm invited to this farewell dinner party in my honor. Maybe you would like to join me?" No sooner had he said that than Wolders, always fastidious to a fault and extremely respectful toward stars, felt he had said the wrong thing. But Audrey laughed and replied, "I haven't been out at all in New York on this occasion. So that's fine." Relieved by her response, Wolders asked her if she would have a drink with him before dinner, and she immediately said, "That would be nice." By the time both had dressed, met and had drinks, and got to talking, they were two hours late for the dinner party. The hostess was ready to strangle Wolders.

Audrey and Wolders were attracted to each other at once. Wolders felt guilty about this, since Merle was only recently dead, and being so proper a man he had a sense of discomfort, of a certain impropriety in being drawn to another woman. But he also remembered something Merle had told him, very tenderly, when she knew she was stricken with her heart condition. She told him, in the gallant manner of all great romantic figures, that when she died he must not be alone, that he must find another wife. She added only the condition that the other woman be worthy of him.

Wolders told me in 1981 that Audrey reminded him of Merle both in her exquisite looks, with her slightly slanted eyes and high cheekbones, and in her delicate, sensitive, and introspective nature. Of course, his and Audrey's mutual Dutch nationality was an added attraction, along with their similar temperaments. Although they saw little of each other, both being anxious not to commit too far and Audrey busy on the picture, they spoke frequently on the telephone. Audrey unburdened herself concerning her problems with her husband, speaking of his alleged infidelities and admitting that the marriage was virtually dead. She also told Wolders of her pride and joy in Sean, who was working as an assistant on *They All Laughed*. She spoke of Luca, and her fear that the breakup of her marriage to Dotti might adversely affect him. She seemed to have returned to the tragedy of the Ferrer breakup, and emotionally she was at a low ebb, concealing her torment by being exceptionally antic, spirited, and full of fun during those weeks in New York.

Audrey returned to Rome at the end of production. Wolders was quietly obsessed. He called her at Tolochenaz, said he was coming to Europe, and asked if they could meet. She was uneasy, though attracted, because she sensed that a relationship would lie ahead, and she was a little afraid of it. Wolders, says Henry Gris, "came to Tolochenaz, not to claim a place in her life but to seek one. He could not and would not press her. But he would try to convince her, and it took him some time, that she could still love and be loved."

One of Audrey's fears was that if she became involved with Wolders she would lose Luca to Dotti. She was prepared to sacrifice her own happiness to remain a mother to her child. Wolders said later, "I had to impress upon her that she could be a mother, but not at the price of surrendering her womanhood."

Wolders himself was not free of pain in advancing the relationship. He kept thinking of Merle, but he also remembered Merle's behest. He was concerned that Merle's children, Bruno and Francesca, would like Audrey; and Audrey was concerned that Luca would like Wolders. Also, there was the fact that once before, when Merle Oberon had been married to Bruno Pagliai, Wolders had helped to break up a marriage through no fault of his own and had greatly provoked the powerful Pagliai's wrath. Cuckolding another Italian husband of great power and influence was not something the cautious Robert Wolders took any pleasure in doing.

Nevertheless, strain or no strain, guilt or no guilt, the affair between these two rare and special beings inevitably developed in the peace and serenity of Switzerland.

Audrey's attitude toward Wolders, according to her friends, was one of intense happiness because at last she had found joy in the man she loved. Up to now, her husbands and lovers had been very domineering. Now she had found a gentle spirit, a man who instead of dominating her was like a younger brother to her, and anxious to please her in every possible way, taking care of her many problems, always accepting her decisions, never competing with her. Though not in the least effeminate, Wolders was also not in the least aggressive. Moreover, the nurse and mother in Audrey had found a kind of child in him, since he suffered from poor health, despite his seemingly robust appearance. This seemingly healthy Dutch burgher suffered a variety of ailments, including violent headaches, fainting spells, sudden attacks of weakness and giddiness, and, in general, a malaise that may have come from experiencing hardships similar to Audrey's during the occupation of Holland by the Nazis. He often told me that, because of those deprivations, his teeth, gums, and digestion had been permanently damaged.

Both Wolders and Audrey, for all their wealth (Merle Oberon had left millions to him in her will), were among the walking wounded. Like so many people who suffer from delicacy of health and spirit, they had moved toward each other in tenderness and mutual understanding. Their love for each other was deep, almost like that of two people adrift on a raft on a stormy sea with no certainty of safety at the end of the voyage. They could gaze into each other's eyes and see pain there; they had that, at least, in common. And although Audrey lacked the wide aesthetic sense and knowledge of Merle, she had the essential refinement and feminine understanding of beauty without which Wolders, as finely tuned as an expensive violin, could never have found succor.

In 1981, Wolders took the bold step of actually moving in with Audrey, and living at Tolochenaz without benefit of marriage, before the marriage to Dotti was dissolved. On the surface, everything seemed serene, but friends observed that there were ripples on the pond. Henry Gris, the only journalist to whom either Audrey or Wolders would talk at that time, observed that Luca greatly resented Wolders and did not appreciate the fact that his mother had acquired a foster-father for him. At the age of eleven the boy was not old enough to have achieved an understanding of such sophisticated matters, and obviously his father's anger and irritation at his cockolding greatly influenced the boy. Wolders did everything to overcome the problem, without much success.

During the writing of my book on Merle Oberon, I had many meetings with Wolders. He spoke of Audrey with great affection, and also stood firm on the matter of her privacy. She traveled often in 1982 and 1983, sometimes with Wolders, sometimes without. Japan was always a favorite of hers, and she made a special point of responding to invitations from Tokyo. She appeared in a Japanese television commercial for the fashion house World Company Ltd., whose clothes she much admired, and she flew to Manhattan in May of 1982 to appear at Givenchy's retrospective evening at the Fashion Institute of Technology. She also attended a similar Givenchy tribute in Tokyo. Her mother was suffering from old age, and Audrey had a particularly nerve-wracking forty-eight hours when, after heading for Los Angeles to see Wolders, she had to return at once to Europe where the Baroness van Heemstra was stricken with a serious illness. A familiar sight to visitors at Tolochenaz was Robert Wolders dutifully pushing the aged baroness around the house in a wheelchair.

Whenever Audrey did travel, she attracted enormous attention, particularly in Japan; but as of 1983, she seemed to have made no plans to resume her career. She was offered a new version of Franz Lehár's celebrated operetta *The Merry Widow*, but Wolders says she was dissatisfied with the script and did not feel particularly sanguine about spending several months in Vienna, with Luca in Rome. She also turned down *The Thorn Birds*, for the same reason — a potential separation from Luca in Hollywood, where the mini-series was shot.

She did not entirely close the door on her career however, and 1983 brought the news that at last the way was cleared for the dissolution of her marriage because Dotti wanted to marry the actress Christiana Borghi. But when Audrey was asked if she would marry Wolders, she did not respond; and indeed, according to Henry Gris, Luca stood in the way. Visits to Rome when Dotti had custody or access to Luca were uncomfortable for Wolders, to say the least. At Christmas 1983, she was alone with Luca for the skiing at Gstaad, a fact noticed widely by the international set at the Swiss mountain resort. But in February of 1984 she and Wolders stayed happily with Connie Wald at her home in Beverly Hills.

Whether or not marriage lies ahead, Audrey at fifty-five seems at last to have found a degree of serenity in her troubled life. There are indications that the long period of sexual abandon, of violence and crudity in movies, may be coming to an end and that a new era of romanticism, monogamy, and seriousness in the arts is beginning to emerge. If there is indeed going to be a return to the innocent atmosphere of the Eisenhower era, in which Audrey Hepburn first emerged and had her meteoric career, it is possible that she may move center stage once again. The millions of fans she has never lost, who think of her with a wistful and tender sense of nostalgia, could certainly wish nothing more.

Filmography

One Wild Oat, Young Wives' Tale, Laughter in Paradise, The Lavender Hill Mob, We Go to Monte Carlo, 1951
The Secret People, 1952
Roman Holiday, with Gregory Peck, Eddie Albert, 1953
Sabrina, with Humphrey Bogart, William Holden, 1954
War and Peace, with Henry Fonda, Mel Ferrer, 1956
Funny Face, with Fred Astaire, Kay Thompson, 1957
Love in the Afternoon, with Gary Cooper, Maurice Chevalier, 1957
Green Mansions, with Mel Ferrer, Henry Silva, 1959
The Nun's Story, with Peter Finch, Dame Peggy Ashcroft, 1959
The Unforgiven, with Burt Lancaster, Lillian Gish, 1960
Breakfast at Tiffany's, with George Peppard, Patricia Neal, 1961
The Children's Hour, with Shirley MacLaine, James Garner, 1962
Charade, with Cary Grant, Walter Matthau, 1963
Paris When It Sizzles, with William Holden, Marlene Dietrich, 1964
My Fair Lady, with Rex Harrison, Wilfrid Hyde-White, 1964
How to Steal a Million, with Peter O'Toole, Hugh Griffith, 1966
Two for the Road, with Albert Finny, William Daniels, 1966
Wait Until Dark, with Alan Arkin, Richard Crenna, 1967
Robin and Marian, with Sean Connery, 1976
Bloodline, with Ben Gazzara, James Mason, 1979
They All Laughed, with Ben Gazzara, John Ritter, 1980

Index